CRITICAL ESSAYS
ON
AMERICAN LITERATURE

James Nagel, General Editor
University of Georgia, Athens

Critical Es.

ANNE T

Critical Essays on
ANNE TYLER

edited by

ALICE HALL PETRY

G.K. Hall & Co. / New York
Maxwell Macmillan Canada / Toronto
Maxwell Macmillan International / New York Oxford Singapore Sydney

G.K. Hall & Co.
Macmillan Publishing Company
866 Third Avenue
New York, New York 10022

Maxwell Macmillan Canada, Inc.
1200 Eglinton Avenue East
Suite 200
Don Mills, Ontario M3C 3N1

Macmillan Publishing Company is part of the Maxwell Communication
Group of Companies.

Library of Congress Cataloging-in-Publication Data

Critical essays on Anne Tyler / [edited by] Alice Hall Petry.
    p.   cm. — (Critical essays on American literature)
   Includes bibliographical references and index.
   ISBN 0–8161–7308–7
   1. Tyler, Anne—Criticism and interpretation. I. Petry, Alice
Hall, 1951– . II. Series.
PS3570.Y45Z63   1992
813'.54—dc20   91-37651
                                        CIP

The paper used in this publication meets the minimum requirements of
American National Standard for Information Sciences—Permanence of
Paper for Printed Library Materials. ANSI Z3948-1984. ⊗™

10 9 8 7 6 5 4 3 2 1

Printed in the United States of America

For
Jean and Dave Bruce

Contents

♦

ARTICLES

ORIGINAL ESSAYS

General Editor's Note

◆

The Critical Essays on American Literature series seeks to anthologize the most important criticism on a wide variety of topics and writers in American literature. Our readers will find in various volumes not only a generous selection of reprinted articles and reviews but original essays, bibliographies, manuscript sections, and other materials brought to public attention for the first time. *Critical Essays on Anne Tyler* is one of the first collections of essays ever published on this contemporary American writer, whose work is only beginning to receive the attention it deserves. The volume contains a sizable gathering of reviews and nearly every important article published about Tyler. Among the authors of reprinted articles and reviews are John Updike, Nicholas Delbanco, Mary F. Robertson, Mary Ellis Gibson, Larry McMurtry, and Wallace Stegner. There is also an extensive section of interviews and personal statements by Tyler that adds a valuable biographical dimension to the collection. In addition to a substantial introduction by Alice Hall Petry, which presents an overview of Tyler's career and critical responses to it, there are also three original essays commissioned specifically for publication in this volume—new studies by Sanford E. Marovitz, Grace Farrell, and Elizabeth Evans. We are confident that this book will make a permanent and significant contribution to the study of American literature.

JAMES NAGEL
University of Georgia, Athens

Publisher's Note

♦

Producing a volume that contains both newly commissioned and reprinted material presents the publisher with the challenge of balancing the desire to achieve stylistic consistency with the need to preserve the integrity of works first published elsewhere. In the Critical Essays series, essays commissioned especially for a particular volume are edited to be consistent with G. K. Hall's house style; reprinted essays appear in the style in which they were first published, with only typographical errors corrected. Consequently, shifts in style from one essay to another are the result of our efforts to be faithful to each text as it was originally published.

Introduction

◆

ALICE HALL PETRY

OVERVIEW

In just the past few years, the novels of Anne Tyler have enjoyed an extraordinary increase in serious scholarly attention. Whether Tyler herself is enjoying it is another matter. The common reader has been attracted to her novels in ever-increasing numbers over the past quarter-century, and although this has not translated into an economic boom for "ATM, Inc.," Anne Tyler Modarressi herself has derived personal satisfaction from her readers' warm response to her work: "I see that they in their solitude, and I in mine, have somehow managed to touch without either of us feeling intruded upon. We've spent some time on neutral territory, sharing a life that belongs to neither of us."[1] The downside of this popular acclaim has been the critical interest in her novels, an interest that seems all the more intensive—and uneven—for its unaccountable belatedness. The misinterpretations and inappropriate responses to Tyler's novels have been a source of personal dismay to her, as has been the widespread assumption that her private life can and should be a matter of public comment. Caught in the artist's conundrum of believing that her writings must speak for themselves but knowing their words too often are misheard, the intensely private Anne Tyler has made tentative gestures toward shaping the critical response to her work through the medium of interviews, which now are always conducted by mail. One hopes they will help. Though the more than 25 years since the publication of her first book, *If Morning Ever Comes* (1964), hardly constitute a total dry spell—dozens of reviews, plus a smattering of scholarly essays, were produced during this period—the fact is that the critical response to Anne Tyler, unlike the popular one, has been slow, modest in scope, and too often misguided.

She has deserved better from the academic community. To be sure, scholarly journals had over the years published an occasional study of her writings, and especially so the southern-based periodicals whose regional nepotism had rendered them peculiarly receptive to Baltimore's most famous writer since H. L. Mencken. Indeed, it was her status as a southern writer—a status she personally denies[2]—that had resulted in the earliest commentaries on her work outside of book reviews. The best of these was Bruce Cook's "New Faces in Faulkner Country," which appeared in the *Saturday Review* in 1976. Though Cook had less interest in Tyler herself than in the whole pantheon of contemporary southern novelists, his essay has value in Cook's wise refusal to lump Tyler automatically with other southernists simply because her novels are set in North Carolina and Maryland. It also provided Tyler with the opportunity to deny publicly that she was a student in the school of Faulkner. As a writer with scant interest in race, sex, dialect, broad historical sweeps, the Civil War, or technical experimentation, Tyler would indeed seem to be an unlikely writer to pair with William Faulkner, and yet that is the approach taken by Mary J. Elkins in "*Dinner at the Homesick Restaurant*: Anne Tyler and the Faulkner Connection," in a 1985 issue of *Atlantis*. In an interview we conducted by mail in August 1989, Tyler confirmed that she had never read *As I Lay Dying* (1930), and in fact most of the parallels between the two works can be attributed to the conventions of the "deathbed novel," a venerable form in Western literature. Even less convincing is Laura Miller's "Woman as Hostage: Escape to Freedom or Journey into Bondage?," which strains to detect the influence of Tyler's *Earthly Possessions* (1977) on *Heading West*, a 1981 novel by North Carolina writer Doris Betts.[3]

Studies that tended to focus on Tyler's novels without considering influence fared somewhat better, though often they were modest in reach and, on occasion, rather self-evident. The first of these was Stella Nesanovich's seminal "The Individual in the Family," which appeared in the *Southern Review* in 1978. Nesanovich's thesis that *Searching for Caleb* (1976) and *Earthly Possessions* explore the problematic relationships between individual needs and familial expectations in Tyler's worldview was resurrected and probed more deeply in Frank W. Shelton's "The Necessary Balance," which appeared in the same journal in 1984. Both studies are sensible but limited. A far more ambitious approach to the individual/family paradigm was offered by Mary Ellis Gibson in "Family as Fate," in a 1983 issue of the *Southern Literary Journal*. Working from both Classical and existential thought, Gibson explores the degree to which Tyler regards families as deterministic forces in individual lives. Gibson's study is one of the most important scholarly essays devoted to Tyler to date, as is Mary F. Robertson's lengthy "Medusa Points and Contact Points," which examines patterns of connection and misconnection between individuals in Tyler's novels.[4] The essays by Cook, Nesanovich, Shelton, Gibson, and Robertson are reprinted in this collection.

Beyond these, the record of essays and book chapters devoted to Anne Tyler has tended to be eclectic. Novelist Doris Betts argues in the *Southern Quarterly* that Tyler's first nine books evince a steady accommodation of the methods of the short story to the demands of the novel form. It seems a valid approach, albeit a rather impressionistic one. Paul Binding, in his book-length meditation on southern literature entitled *Separate Country* (1979), offers personal responses and some solid critical insights into Tyler and her real and fictional Baltimore. Margaret Morganroth Gullette, in an essay that first appeared in the *New England Review and Bread Loaf Quarterly* (1985) and then was incorporated into her book on middle age in American fiction, observes that the accumulation and abandonment of "things" are important gauges of maturity in Tyler's novels. Bradley R. Bowers in *Mississippi Quarterly* suggests that the narrator, the reader, and certain family members in Tyler's novels collectively constitute groups of insiders who can respond in concert to her humor and irony. It's a minor study, as is William K. Freiert's "Anne Tyler's Accidental Ulysses" in *Classical and Modern Literature,* which looks at Macon Leary of *The Accidental Tourist* (1985) as a modern-day Odysseus.[5]

Far more than with most contemporary writers, the consistently solid and imaginative responses to Tyler have appeared in sources that are traditionally regarded as minor elements in the scholarly record. In *The Hollins Critic,* a periodical that aims modestly to provide biocritical overviews of individual writers' careers, Anne G. Jones in 1986 offered an astute analysis of Tyler's achievement in her first 10 novels, with special reference to her ambivalence about homes. Equally strong evaluations appeared in standard reference works. In *Fifty Southern Writers after 1900* (1987) and the *Dictionary of Literary Biography* (1980; updated 1983), Anne R. Zahlan, Mary Ellen Brooks, and Sarah English produced balanced, critically sound evaluations that one might have expected to spawn more scholarly work of the caliber of the essays by Gibson and Robertson.[6] Why they did not remains a mystery in an era otherwise notorious for the relentless scholarly analysis of even quite minor writers, although to a certain extent the slack has been taken up by that other poor cousin to the scholarly essay, the book review. Many of the contemporary reviews of Tyler's work have been commendable for their insights and sensitivity. Some, of course, have not. When informed that David Klinghoffer's review of *Breathing Lessons* (1988) claimed that Tyler's "distaste" and "condescension" for "depressing class signifiers" was "palpable" in the novel, Tyler was clearly upset: "I'm very distressed to hear someone thinks I'm mocking my characters. Why would I bother writing about people I look down on?"[7] That Tyler feels an urgency to like personally all the characters she creates is well documented in the revealing 1981 interview with Wendy Lamb that appeared in the *Iowa Journal of Literary Studies.* Both the Klinghoffer review and the Lamb interview are included in this collection, along with a generous sampling of the book reviews that have appeared since 1964. So important are these contemporary evaluations of Tyler's novels that they will be examined at length in the third portion of this introduction.

But special reference must be made to Tyler's single most important reviewer: John Updike. Beginning with "Family Ways," his 1976 evaluation of *Searching for Caleb,* Updike used the pages of the *New Yorker* to introduce Tyler to a much wider audience, while giving the stamp of approval by one of America's most acclaimed novelists to one of America's most neglected.

Though occasionally mannered in their presentation and heavy on plot, Updike's reviews—including "Loosened Roots" (on *Earthly Possessions*), "Imagining Things" (on *Morgan's Passing* [1980]), "On Such a Beautiful Green Little Planet" (on *Dinner at the Homesick Restaurant* [1982]), and "Leaving Home" (on *The Accidental Tourist*)—further confirmed the quality of Tyler's achievement and the need for serious evaluation of her work.[8] Four of the Updike reviews have been reprinted in this volume.

Despite Updike's public support, that serious evaluation did not begin in earnest until Tyler received the ultimate stamp of approval: in March 1989, her novel *Breathing Lessons* was awarded the Pulitzer Prize in fiction. Almost immediately there began, at long last, the march of serious scholarly studies and collections of substantive critical essays from academic presses. Happily, most have been worth the wait. The first to be published was Joseph C. Voelker's *Art and the Accidental in Anne Tyler*.[9] Voelker's thoughtful study is unusual in that it offers a variety of approaches to Tyler's novels: in *If Morning Ever Comes,* for example, he sees Tyler exploring the degree to which she could, or should, write consciously within the tradition of southern literature. Voelker reads *The Accidental Tourist* as a seriocomic burlesque of Freud, while he sees *Breathing Lessons* as a Keatsian meditation on the autumnal nature of middle age. Most elaborate is Voelker's study of time in *Dinner at the Homesick Restaurant*—a subject explored at length by Karin Linton in the other 1989 book devoted to Tyler, *The Temporal Horizon: A Study of the Theme of Time in Anne Tyler's Major Novels.*[10] In 1990 there appeared a collection of essays drawn primarily from the April 1989 Tyler symposium held at Essex Community College in Baltimore. *The Fiction of Anne Tyler,* edited by symposium organizer C. Ralph Stephens, offers 13 essays that take a wide variety of approaches to her work. Three can be singled out. Virginia Schaefer Carroll's "The Nature of Kinship in the Novels of Anne Tyler" draws on the writings of such commentators as Bronislaw Malinowski and Claude Lévi-Strauss to argue persuasively that Tyler's much-discussed families are actually "clans" in the anthropological sense, replete with "totems" (like the Leary family's official vegetable, the baked potato) and imaginatively re-created oral history as a means of nurturing the unit's solidarity (witness Maggie Moran's lies to engineer a reconciliation between her son and daughter-in-law). In another essay, Joseph B. Wagner offers a psychological study of the Tull children in *Dinner at the Homesick Restaurant.* His "Beck Tull: 'The absent presence' " suggests that the different personality types of Ezra, Cody, and Jenny are actually strategies for dealing with what psychoanalysts term "father hunger"—and that Ezra's childhood experiences may well have left him a latent homosexual. And Doris Betts, in "Tyler's Marriage of Opposites," argues that Tyler's seemingly relentless optimism is less a rose-colored view of the world than a reflection of her determination to function despite its dark edge.[11] Finally, my own *Understanding Anne Tyler*[12] offers an overview of her achievement, plus detailed analyses of each of her novels.

ANNE TYLER'S LIFE

As noted, Tyler herself has tended to be peripherally involved in the critical response to her work. Her interviews-by-mail, although awkward for all parties concerned, are her only means of shielding her personal life and family from public scrutiny, but they are also a way of preventing interference with her work—and of controlling what is, or is not, known about it. In the August 1989 interview we conducted by mail as I researched *Understanding Anne Tyler,* for example, she exercised this control by revealing virtually nothing about her twelfth novel (it "centers on a 17-year-old boy" was all she would say) and declining to answer my question as to whether she enjoyed the movie version of *The Accidental Tourist.* But one can hardly blame her for her reticence, given her experiences with face-to-face interviews and public statements. Her earliest interview, conducted by Jorie Lueloff and published in the Baton Rouge, Louisiana, *Morning Advocate* in 1965, paints a portrait of a disarmingly young Anne Tyler, munching on chocolate cookies and waxing eloquent on the wonders of black dialect—an element that, to be frank, rarely appears in her work.[13] Her chattiness in this early interview presumably would embarrass Tyler today; more serious, however, is the insidious problem of jinxing. She had discussed the problems of writing *Morgan's Passing* in the Wendy Lamb interview—and the novel proved to be so weak that most critics lambasted it, while Joseph C. Voelker declined even to discuss it in *Art and the Accidental in Anne Tyler.* Worse, she had described at length a work-in-progress in a 1977 piece in the *New York Times Book Review*—Marguerite Michaels's "Anne Tyler, Writer 8:05 to 3:30"—and the book in question, *Pantaleo,* turned out to be the first novel since her apprentice years to be literally unpublishable. As a deeply superstitious writer—witness her 1976 *Washington Post* account, " 'Because I Want More Than One Life' "—Tyler presumably will not again risk jinxing her career by discussing it.[14] (This account, plus the interviews with Jorie Lueloff and Marguerite Michaels, are included in this collection.)

Tyler's relative silence about her life and work, coupled with her well-known reclusiveness—no media darling à la Mailer, she shuns public appearances of any sort, including those at professional conferences—have limited the amount of information available about her personal life. The bare facts are related quickly. Though routinely classified as a southern writer, Tyler actually was born in Minneapolis, Minnesota, on 25 October 1941. Her parents, Lloyd Parry Tyler (a chemist) and Phyllis Mahon (a journalist and social worker), actively encouraged the creativity of their daughter and sons. As with most writers-to-be, from an early age Tyler invented stories ("So far as I can remember, mostly I wrote first pages of stories about lucky, lucky girls who got to go West in covered wagons") and read extensively: her favorite book was, and continues to be, a children's book, *The Little House,* by Virginia Lee Burton.[15] What sets Tyler apart from most other writers, however, is her peripatetic childhood. She was raised in a series of Quaker communes in accordance with what her father has termed the "Emersonian ideal."[16] As a consequence, Tyler evolved not only the self-reliance needed to thrive in her unsettled life but also the embracing worldview that several of her commentators have found stridently antithetical to the grim realities of life in the final decades of the twentieth century.

By the time Tyler was 11 years old, her family had established itself permanently near Raleigh, North Carolina. She seems to have taken in stride her differences from her classmates—"I had never used a telephone and could strike a match on the soles of my bare feet"—and indeed would draw on the notion of outside perspective, the "setting-apart situation," in many of her novels.[17] Tyler did exceptionally well in the Raleigh school system, while devoting her summers to field labor on area tobacco plantations—an ideal activity for someone absorbing the nuances of local speech. With the intention of someday being a book illustrator, Tyler took a particular interest in her art classes but also studied English under Phyllis Peacock at Broughton High School. Peacock's earlier protégé had been Reynolds Price, soon himself to be a famous novelist. And when Tyler entered Duke University on full scholarship, she coincidentally was enrolled in a freshman writing course taught by Price.

Rather surprisingly, however, in college Tyler did not major in English. Her declared field was Russian, and not long after graduating Phi Beta Kappa from Duke in 1961, she began graduate study in Russian at Columbia University (1961–62). She worked as a Russian bibliographer at Duke from 1962 to 1963 and then married Taghi Mohammad Modarressi, an Iranian medical student and novelist, in May 1963. Modarressi did his residency at Montreal's McGill University, while Tyler worked in the McGill Law Library (1964–65).

At this juncture, Tyler's life was undergoing two major changes. She had decided to begin a family: her two daughters, Tezh and Mitra, were born in 1965 and 1967. And she had begun to write in earnest for the first time since college. Although at Duke she had twice won the Anne Flexner Award for creative writing, after graduating at age 19 in 1961, she felt "no real sense of urgency or commitment" about continuing to write.[18] This period of inactivity may be attributed to her unsettled personal life, but it may also be due to a feeling familiar to many authors: that writing—especially in the early stages of a project—can be an all-absorbing, frustrating, and even psychically painful experience. To this day, Tyler feels a degree of dread over the process of writing (she discusses one of her stalling tactics, the five-mile drive for shoelaces, in the Wendy Lamb interview), and one can well understand her initial preference for that far-less-demanding career option for the bookish, librarianship—a type of work whose quiet pleasures she explores in a heartfelt way in her third novel, *A Slipping-Down Life* (1970). There is, however, that other side to authorship: the urge to write can assert itself overwhelmingly—and a good day's work can be exhilarating. And so Tyler began to create fiction once again, though there were several false starts. She produced one manuscript, still unpublished, before her first novel, *If Morning Ever Comes*. Yet another abandoned novel—*Winter Birds, Winter Apples*— came after her second published novel, *The Tin Can Tree* (1965). Its manuscript is now with Tyler's papers at Duke.

Thereafter Tyler rarely lost her footing. A new novel has been produced approximately every two years, with the only difficult period coming between *Earthly Possessions* and *Morgan's Passing*. During that three-year period in the late 1970s, Tyler had written the aforementioned *Pantaleo*. The loss of a year's effort was further complicated by a series of domestic crises that occurred while she was working on *Morgan's Passing*.[19] But after this juncture she was steadily productive, with her three subsequent novels usually counted among her best: *Dinner at the Homesick Restaurant, The Accidental Tourist,* and *Breathing Lessons.* Currently she is at work on her twelfth novel. With her daughters now grown and her husband well established in his career as a child psychiatrist in Baltimore, Tyler is able to devote more time to her writing, which includes short stories (more than 40 to date), essays, and book reviews in addition to novels. A study by Elizabeth Evans of Tyler's achievement as a book reviewer was written especially for this collection.

The Reviews

It is Tyler's novels, however, that by far have commanded the most attention. And even with the advent of book-length studies of her work, the dozens of contemporary reviews in newspapers, magazines, and scholarly journals continue to constitute the most extensive record of the response to her novels— and the most sensitive indicator of the often wide gap between popular and scholarly responses to her work, for although the common reader often admits to "loving" Tyler's novels (a reaction rarely inspired by, say, the books of John Hawkes), the professional critic and the scholar have not always been so enthusiastic about her. Anne Tyler has suffered more than her share of scorn and condescension, especially in the latter half of her career, when her most successful novels seem only to have thrown into more vivid relief her weaker efforts. Tyler is a tough act for even Tyler to follow.

The earliest commentators, though, were very generous toward her, at least in part because of her age—and, one suspects, her gender. The reviews of her two earliest novels, for example, applauded Tyler's mastery of fictional craft and her depth of thought, but this praise was couched—and thereby qualified somewhat—in terms of her youth. Marilyn Gardner, writing on *The Tin Can Tree* for the *Christian Science Monitor,* noted that "appearances can be deceiving": "On the surface this may appear to be a fairly ordinary novel. . . . But . . . Anne Tyler is no ordinary writer, and her second novel is no ordinary book. If her subject matter is common, her treatment of it is not. With a depth of understanding that belies her 24 years, she has fashioned a quiet but enchanting narrative, at once charmingly simple and deceptively profound."[20] Orville Prescott seemed even more astonished about *If Morning Ever Comes:* "This is an exceedingly good novel, so mature, so gently wise and so brightly amusing that, if it weren't printed right there on the jacket, few readers would suspect that Mrs. [*sic*] Tyler was only 22."[21] Writing about the same novel for *Harper's,* Katherine Gauss Jackson reported that an acquaintance ("a young man, an editor and critic") had said to her, "It scares me. How can a twenty-two-year-old girl know so much about how a man feels?"[22] As we have seen, however, this "twenty-two-year-old girl"— would anyone ever speak of a "twenty-two-year-old boy"?—had had a fairly substantial literary apprenticeship at college, coupled with the kinds of life experiences that were ideal for a career as a novelist. And though Tyler has since disowned both of these early books, indeed avowing that they "should be burned,"[23] they are in fact highly readable, sensitive stories that ushered in a series of fine novels, beginning with *A Slipping-Down Life.*

This third novel garnered rather mixed reviews, perhaps because its setting and subject matter seemed so alien to its mostly middle-aged reviewers. Set in the netherworld of rock music and teen love, *A Slipping-Down Life* features one of the few instances of violence in an Anne Tyler novel: a chubby teen carves the name of a local would-be rock star in her forehead with fingernail scissors. Critics seemed confused by this act, which Tyler drew from an actual incident in Texas involving an Elvis Presley fan,[24] and their confusion was hardly assuaged by its unexpected consequences: self-mutilator Evie Decker actually marries her hero, gets pregnant, leaves him, and embarks on what is evidently destined to be a well-adjusted life as a single parent. Barbara A. Bannon of *Publishers Weekly* spoke for many in noting that "lives of quiet desperation don't necessarily make for the most pleasant reading, but they can be genuinely touching"; even so, "however poignant and complex" these characters may be, "they never progress much further than Grade A soap opera."[25] Martin Levin, writing for the *New York Times Book Review,* seemed more sure of his response. Terming the mutilation an "attention-getter," Levin deemed the novel itself a "wry little fable"—an astute appreciation of Tyler's subtle, ironic humor that too often is lacking in commentaries on her work.[26] Tyler herself reportedly still speaks of *A Slipping-Down Life* "with great tenderness," noting that its creation constituted for her "a certain brave stepping forth."[27] And as a writer who regards as real the "little paper people" she creates, Tyler admits that occasionally she wonders whatever became of Evie Decker's baby.[28]

Even more mixed reviews greeted Tyler's fourth novel, *The Clock Winder* (1972). For example, Barbara A. Bannon found it "beautifully structured," but Martin Levin felt that "the novel pursues a serpentine way, and any bend in the road might just as well be marked finis."[29] Many seemed particularly put off by the novel's central group of characters, the Emerson family of Baltimore, whose wealth and social standing seem only to exacerbate their helplessness and incapacity to communicate. In contrast, most commentators seemed to admire the clock winder herself, handyperson Elizabeth Abbott. Writing for the *Saturday Review,* Elizabeth Easton argued that Abbott's charm resided precisely in her believability: "with her run-down moccasins and dungarees," she "is like a lot of kids today"—a response that may explain how *The Clock Winder* came to be classified as a book for "young adults."[30] Sara Blackburn was particularly impressed by "the strength of [this] delightful heroine," even as she bemoaned the novel's ending: "the result smacks of a group of hurt and inept people propping one another up."[31] In fact Tyler had intended it to be a sad ending, as Elizabeth is absorbed into the enclosed world of the eccentric Emersons, and Tyler cannot understand why so many readers deem it a happy one (see the interview with Wendy Lamb). Tyler no longer feels much affection for her fourth novel, perhaps because she had patterned Elizabeth after herself during an uncharacteristic period of adolescent rebellion—a time "when I seemed determined to do whatever seemed the most contrary thing."[32] (See the 1972 interview with Clifford A. Ridley, included in this volume.)

Much of Tyler herself is also evident in her fifth novel, *Celestial Navigation* (1974), which required two painful years to create. Although Tyler maintains that the character of collage-artist Jeremy Pauling was inspired by an ex-mental patient whom she had known slightly, there are enough parallels between him and Tyler to suggest that she was in large measure writing about her own situation as a creative individual.[33] This identification lent an urgency and authenticity to her depiction of Jeremy to which most critics responded warmly, even if they had difficulty with the idea of the seemingly asexual Jeremy fathering several children.[34] Many especially criticized Tyler for the uncertainty of the novel's ultimate message. Jay L. Halio, writing for the *Southern Review,* felt it was a "defect" in the novel that "we never see the stars [Jeremy] navigates by,"[35] though closer examination would suggest that there is no difficulty with the novel's central trope. As an artist, Jeremy does "navigate" in accordance with guideposts undetectable to the average person. He functions on a higher ("celestial") plane, which neither his common-law wife and his boarders nor, evidently, his critics can appreciate. Hence, most critics steered clear of these choppy waters, preferring to focus instead on the unusual degree of technical experimentation in this novel. Utilizing the points of view of five people over a 13-year period, *Celestial Navigation* showed Tyler manipulating narration to an unprecedented degree. Many disliked the development, chiding her for needing to pin down sections of the book with specific dates; others were delighted, especially those who detected that its collagelike structure mirrored the complexity of Jeremy's own art and life.[36]

Critics had far fewer reservations about Tyler's next novel, *Searching for*

Caleb. The broadest in scope of her novels and the only one to be set (through flashbacks) partially in the nineteenth century, *Searching for Caleb* elicited responses that suggested its critics were dazzled by its nostalgic charms. Victor Howes of the *Christian Science Monitor* deemed it "easy-going" and seemed unconcerned that there "isn't much of a plot" to it, while Lynn Sharon Schwartz of the *Saturday Review,* noting that the novel "rarely gives us heights and depths of emotion or the excitement of discovery," still praised it for having "the very welcome old-fashioned virtues of a patient, thoughtful chronicle."[37] Indeed, Philip Howard of the (London) *Times* spoke for many when he noted, without a hint of irony, that "it is a book about chasing rainbows, and finding happiness by enduring, adapting, accepting what comes along, and liking people."[38] Where most commentators seem to have missed the mark is in their failure to detect the serious questions about fate, freedom, and identity at the book's core. Far from being "wonderfully inconclusive,"[39] the ending delineates the destruction of a once-proud family because of its incapacity to acknowledge and reconcile the two sides of its nature: (a) the serious, business-minded side embodied in Daniel Peck and (b) the creative, musical side embodied in Caleb Peck. *Searching for Caleb* thus offers what Catherine Peters correctly identified as an "existential examination" of the rise and fall of the Pecks, a parable of self-destruction conveyed eloquently in their diamond-shaped family tree.[40] Though to a fair degree *Searching for Caleb* is indeed a sunny and nostalgic book, it also is sobering, even grim.

These same existential issues were raised more insistently in Tyler's next two novels—indeed, perhaps too insistently, as her commentators frequently expressed keen disappointment in *Earthly Possessions* and *Morgan's Passing. Earthly Possessions* was criticized on both technical and thematic grounds. In it, Tyler had broken from the relatively straightforward narration of *Searching for Caleb,* offering alternating chapters of present action (Charlotte Emory's kidnapping by would-be bank robber Jake Simms) and flashback (Charlotte reevaluating her childhood and marriage under the pressure of geographic distance and threat of death). Though the technique actually is quite effective for Tyler's purposes, many commentators disliked it. Doris Betts felt it was "too neat a book," with Tyler's "tinkering" far "too conscious," while Gilberto Perez, writing in the *Hudson Review,* felt Tyler wasn't conscious enough of what she was doing:

> I'm not sure Miss Tyler is aware that the alternating chapters of her novel, though all in the first person, are really in two different voices: the retrospective and the eyewitness first person, one may call them. We accept the convention, in an eyewitness account of ongoing events, that the narrator will come to find out things unexpected at the beginning, as indeed Charlotte does in her experience with the bank robber. But in a retrospective account, a summing up of past events from the perspective of the present, we feel cheated unless we get some sense all along that the narrator knows how things will turn out.[41]

One may counter this, however, with the observation that although Charlotte knows the facts of what happens to her, she does not know their implications until the end of her kidnapping ordeal—and the end of the novel. But beyond the question of technique, critics were dismayed by the implications of the ending of *Earthly Possessions.* When Charlotte walks away from Jake and returns to her minister-husband, Saul, she seems to be surrendering to the life from which she had tried to escape when she was taken hostage. She would appear to be submitting passively to cooking interminable breakfasts for her children and the wayward souls her husband keeps bringing home from his Holy Basis Church, and to dusting endlessly her own furniture, her mother-in-law's furniture, and the doll-size carvings of these furnishings in a house so packed with people, "earthly possessions," and guilt that Charlotte can barely breathe. Although Tyler was trying to draw that fine line between endurance (which she admires)[42] and mindless tolerance (which she does not), most reviewers seemed impatient, even disgusted, with the novel's ending: Anatole Broyard, in the *New York Times Book Review,* for example, argued that Charlotte "merely rolls around until she stops."[43] Largely because of Charlotte's apparent lack of progress, many critics dismissed the book as just another "runaway housewife novel," too trivial to warrant serious discussion.[44] It was perhaps reflective of the respect generally accorded Tyler at this juncture that even those critics who were harshest about *Earthly Possessions* were the most defensive about Tyler herself. Observed Nicholas Delbanco in the *New Republic,* "[A]nyone who wrote the splendid *Celestial Navigation* and *Searching for Caleb* should be allowed to take a breather," though he hoped that with her next novel Tyler would "once more be fully engaged."[45]

The consensus was that she was not, as the response to *Morgan's Passing* was even more negative. To be sure, a few critics liked Morgan Gower, Tyler's Baltimorean imposter who changed his identities as quickly as he changed his outfits, or, more precisely, they were amused by the antics of this latest addition to Tyler's pantheon of eccentrics. Robert Towers, for example, admired her for being willing to resurrect that "comfortable Victorian enjoyment of eccentric characters in fiction," while Thomas M. Disch compared Morgan to John Irving's T. S. Garp for being "plausibly flawed" yet "improbably lovable."[46] More commentators, however, were inclined to agree with Eva Hoffman that roughly halfway through the novel, as its "absurdist complexities are neither clarified nor deepened, [the reader's] curiosity turns into exasperation."[47] The seeming disorderliness of the novel's structure was also called into question repeatedly; Frank W. Shelton, for example, termed it "unruly and untidy."[48] Peter Grier of the *Christian Science Monitor,* however, detected the method behind the madness: as with *Celestial Navigation,* the structure of the novel—which seems "stuck together with baling wire and chewing gum"[49]—is related subtly to the personality and life-style of the protagonist. It is characteristic of Tyler's career that although *Morgan's Pass-*

ing elicited the largest measure of critical contempt, it was also the first Tyler novel to be widely honored. It earned her a nomination for the National Book Critics Circle Award for 1981, as well as the Janet Heidinger Kafka Prize, presented by the University of Rochester for outstanding achievement in fiction by an American woman.

A collective sigh of relief was almost audible with the publication of Tyler's next novel, *Dinner at the Homesick Restaurant.* Not since *Searching for Caleb* had the critical response been so uniformly enthusiastic. True, there were some negative reviews, most notably that of James Wolcott in *Esquire,* who felt the novel "grindingly forced and unfelt." Wolcott's discomfort with the darkness of *Dinner* was compounded by his annoyance at its structure. Deeming the novel "hobbled from page one on by its rickety plot structure," Wolcott chided Tyler for resorting to the venerable mode of the deathbed retrospective, a technique that he felt had "been worked to the nub in fiction" and that Tyler did not improve: "she simply creaks through her characters' pasts."[50] In contrast, most commentators admired Tyler's use of Pearl Tull's deathbed scene and the attendant alternation of multiple points of view in flashback; Updike, for example, observed that the plot "moves its extensive cast agilely along, with flashback and side glance, through ten chapters that are each rounded like a short story."[51] But beyond matters of technique, most reviewers praised the book for its evidences of Tyler's maturity. Noted Benjamin DeMott in his appreciative essay for the *New York Times Book Review, Dinner at the Homesick Restaurant* "edges deep into truth that's simultaneously (and interdependently) psychological, moral and formal— deeper than many living novelists of serious reputation have penetrated, deeper than Miss Tyler herself has gone before. It is a border crossing."[52] Jean Strouse of *Newsweek* spoke for many in deeming the novel "extraordinarily good."[53]

Three years later, Tyler scored another success with *The Accidental Tourist,* her first best-seller and the only one of her novels so far to be made into a motion picture. Even so, the book garnered a surprisingly large number of isolated negative comments. An anonymous commentator in the *Antioch Review* chided Tyler for its "standard soap-opera plot," while even Updike admitted that Muriel Pritchett's effect on Macon Leary was "predictable."[54] Some reviewers, such as Larry McMurtry in the *New York Times Book Review,* felt that the dead son Ethan was "mostly a premise, and not one advanced very confidently by the author," while Edward the Welsh corgi—a character singled out by many reviewers, who found him endearing—was seen as suffering "unaccountable neglect" in the last portion of the novel.[55] Still others were annoyed by the romance of Rose Leary and Julian Edge: "For once, the author's desire for a plot-twist takes precedence over truth to character: Rose has been portrayed with such dry sexlessness that when she mentions Julian's romantic interest in her the reader is cued to diagnose virgin dementia."[56] But despite these reservations, most reviewers responded enthusiastically, if not always eloquently, to the riches of *The Accidental Tourist.* Updike, for example, termed it "a real page-turner," while the *Virginia Quarterly Review* proclaimed that "if any book deserves to be a best seller, this one does"; after all, "there's nothing trashy about it."[57] Less faint was the praise of Jonathan Yardley: "Words fail me: one cannot reasonably expect fiction to be much better than this."[58]

Tyler's eleventh novel, *Breathing Lessons,* elicited a far different response. Not since *Morgan's Passing* eight years earlier had a Tyler novel been so disliked, as commentators were appalled by the antics of Maggie Moran and the seeming transparency and superficiality of Tyler's TV-movie-level study of the onslaught of middle age and the fact of mortality. Robert Towers, in the *New York Review of Books,* observed that "Maggie sometimes seems too broad in relation to the much subtler handling of the other characters—she is too awkward, too silly, to carry the burden that has been assigned to her. The sentimentality in the conception of her character becomes an irritation."[59] Others found *Breathing Lessons* compromised by strained humor and inappropriate slapstick; Marita Golden, for example, bemoaned the "Lucy Ricardo quality" in Maggie.[60] Still others, citing the "slenderness" of the story—a quality usually attributed to the limited (24-hour) time span—pondered how any novelist as gifted as Tyler could so lose control of her material: after the funeral reception for Max Gill, noted Robert McPhillips, Tyler left the reader with a "two-hundred-page denouement."[61] David Klinghoffer stated bluntly what most reviewers seemed to be feeling: one wonders "what kind of contractual obligations the talented Miss Tyler had that convinced her to dig this one out of her manuscript drawer."[62] There were basically two dissenting voices in the din generated by *Breathing Lessons:* (a) that of Wallace Stegner, who felt Maggie's "essential goodness and capacity for affection make us want to comfort rather than kick her,"[63] and (b) that of the Pulitzer Prize committee, which granted this novel the award for fiction in March 1989. Of course, no law requires that a Pulitzer go only to a writer's finest achievement—witness Faulkner's *A Fable* (1955)—and indeed the prize seems usually to be awarded for career-long achievement rather than a particular novel. But Tyler's Pulitzer Prize for what is almost universally regarded as her weakest book in years—some would say her weakest book ever—does lend credence to Susan Gilbert's thesis that Tyler was being rewarded publicly for avoiding touchy political issues, for suggesting conservatively that no individual or group could, or should, try to change our society.[64]

The unevenness of Tyler's achievement, coupled with the belatedness of the scholarly response to her work, leaves one wondering where Tyler—and Tyler scholarship—is headed. As of this writing, she is well into her twelfth novel, but her checkered track record offers no clues as to the nature of that book. All one can surmise is that her decision to write about a teenage boy might suggest she is making a conscious effort to break the pattern of focusing on characters who are approximately her own age—a pattern responsible for the creation of Maggie Moran.

One can surmise far more about the future of Tyler scholarship. Though a few books and a handful of articles are now in print, it seems clear that the field is wide open. The possible influences on her work, for example, have yet to be established, although various contemporary reviewers of her novels have astutely detected Tyler's kinship to the Russian writers she studied in college and to the transcendental authors according to whose precepts she was raised.[65] (This latter element is examined by Sanford E. Marovitz in an essay prepared especially for this collection.) Her Quaker heritage would also be worth exploring, as would her interest in the arts, especially photography, puppetry, music, and collage art. Also valuable would be studies of Tyler's knowledge and utilization of psychology, or her place within the southern existential movement best reflected in the writings of Walker Percy. Likewise revealing would be examinations of Tyler's seeming defiance of traditional literary classification: that she has variously been deemed a feminist, a nonfeminist, a postmodernist, a Victorian, a realist, a naturalist, and a romantic would suggest that a firmer understanding of Anne Tyler's place in contemporary fiction might well lead to a clearer understanding of the nature of literature in this century.

For their assistance in obtaining essays and reviews, I wish to thank the staffs of the John D. Rockefeller Library at Brown University and the Phillips Memorial Library at Providence College, as well as Mr. K. Haybron Adams of the Harold B. Lee Library at Brigham Young University. For their advice and assistance in the preparation of this volume, I am especially grateful to in-house editors Lewis DeSimone and Vida Petronis of G. K. Hall & Co., and to general editor James Nagel of the University of Georgia, Athens. It has been a pleasure to work with them.

Notes

1. The copyright of Tyler's first novel, *If Morning Ever Comes,* was held by "Anne Modarressi"; that of her tenth, *The Accidental Tourist,* by "Anne Tyler Modarressi, et al."; that of her eleventh, *Breathing Lessons,* by "ATM, Inc." The changes presumably reflect the dramatic increase in royalties earned by her novels, although as recently as 1977, she noted that her best year had brought her just $35,000. (See Marguerite Michaels, "Anne Tyler, Writer 8:05 to 3:30," *New York Times Book Review,* 8 May 1977, 43.) The quotation is from Anne Tyler, " 'Because I Want More Than One Life,' " *Washington Post,* 15 August 1976, sec. G, 7.

2. Tyler is not sure why the "Note About the Author" in the Berkley paperback editions of her novels stresses that she "considers herself a Southerner." In an interview we conducted by mail in August 1989, Tyler surmised that "way back when my first novel was published, the publishers stressed Minnesota [her birthplace] in my biographical note and I pointed out

that I was really more from North Carolina; but I can't be sure." Tyler goes on to say that she does not consider herself a southerner, and that she is "most definitely not a Southern *writer,* although I think of that as a very honorable tradition."

3. Bruce Cook, "New Faces in Faulkner Country," *Saturday Review,* 4 September 1976, 39–41; Mary J. Elkins, *"Dinner at the Homesick Restaurant*: Anne Tyler and the Faulkner Connection," *Atlantis* 10 (Spring 1985): 93–105; and Laura Miller, "Woman as Hostage: Escape to Freedom or Journey into Bondage?," in *Proceedings of the Second Annual Conference of EAPSCU* [English Association of the Pennsylvania State Colleges and Universities], Ed. Malcolm Hayward, (1983), 49–52.

4. Stella Nesanovich, "The Individual in the Family: Anne Tyler's *Searching for Caleb* and *Earthly Possessions,*" *Southern Review* 14 (January 1978): 170–76; Frank W. Shelton, "The Necessary Balance: Distance and Sympathy in the Novels of Anne Tyler," *Southern Review* 20 (Autumn 1984): 851–60; Mary Ellis Gibson, "Family as Fate: The Novels of Anne Tyler," *Southern Literary Journal* 16 (Fall 1983): 47–58; and Mary F. Robertson, "Anne Tyler: Medusa Points and Contact Points," in *Contemporary American Women Writers: Narrative Strategies,* Ed. Catherine Rainwater and William J. Scheick (Lexington: University Press of Kentucky, 1985), 119–52.

5. Doris Betts, "The Fiction of Anne Tyler," *Southern Quarterly* 21 (Summer 1983): 23–37; Paul Binding, "Anne Tyler," in *Separate Country: A Literary Journey through the American South* (New York and London: Paddington Press, 1979), 198–209; Margaret Morganroth Gullette, "The Tears (and Joys) Are in the Things: Adulthood in Anne Tyler's Novels," *New England Review and Bread Loaf Quarterly* 7 (Spring 1985): 323–34 and chap. 5, *Safe at Last in the Middle Years: The Invention of the Midlife Progress Novel* (Berkeley: University of California Press, 1988); Bradley R. Bowers, "Anne Tyler's Insiders," *Mississippi Quarterly* 42 (Winter 1988–89): 47–56; and William K. Freiert, "Anne Tyler's Accidental Ulysses," *Classical and Modern Literature* 10 (Fall 1989): 71–79.

6. Anne G. Jones, "Home at Last, and Homesick Again: The Ten Novels of Anne Tyler," *The Hollins Critic* 23 (April 1986): 1–14; Anne R. Zahlan, "Anne Tyler," in *Fifty Southern Writers After 1900: A Bio-Bibliographical Sourcebook,* Ed. Joseph M. Flora and Robert Bain (Westport, Conn.: Greenwood Press, 1987), 491–504; Mary Ellen Brooks, "Anne Tyler," in *The Dictionary of Literary Biography,* vol. 6, *American Novelists Since World War II* (Detroit: Gale Research, 1980), 336–45; and Sarah English, "Anne Tyler," in *The Dictionary of Literary Biography Yearbook: 1982* (Detroit: Gale Research, 1983), 187–94.

7. David Klinghoffer, "Ordinary People," *National Review,* 30 December 1988, 49; interview with Alice Hall Petry (August 1989).

8. John Updike, "Family Ways," *New Yorker,* 29 March 1976, 110–12; "Loosened Roots," *New Yorker,* 6 June 1977, 130, 133–34; "Imagining Things," *New Yorker,* 23 June 1980, 97–101; "On Such a Beautiful Green Little Planet," *New Yorker,* 5 April 1982, 193–97; and "Leaving Home," *New Yorker* 28 October 1985, 106–8, 110–12.

9. Joseph C. Voelker, *Art and the Accidental in Anne Tyler* (Columbia: University of Missouri Press, 1989).

10. Karin Linton, *The Temporal Horizon: A Study of the Theme of Time in Anne Tyler's Major Novels* (Uppsala, Sweden: Acta Universitatis Upsaliensis, 1989).

11. C. Ralph Stephens, ed., *The Fiction of Anne Tyler* (Jackson: University Press of Mississippi, 1990): Virginia Schaefer Carroll, "The Nature of Kinship in the Novels of Anne Tyler," 16–27; Joseph B. Wagner, "Beck Tull: 'The absent presence' in *Dinner at the Homesick Restaurant,*" 73–83; and Doris Betts, "Tyler's Marriage of Opposites," 1–15.

12. Alice Hall Petry, *Understanding Anne Tyler* (Columbia: University of South Carolina Press, 1990).

13. Jorie Lueloff, "Authoress Explains Why Women Dominate in South," (Baton Rouge) *Morning Advocate,* 8 February 1965, sec. A, 11.

14. The similarities between Tyler's superstitious rituals and those of Jeremy Pauling are

examined in my *Understanding Anne Tyler* (Columbia: University of South Carolina Press, 1990), chap. 5.

15. Laurie L. Brown, "Interviews with Seven Contemporary Writers," *Southern Quarterly* 21 (Summer 1983): 11.

16. Quoted in Zahlan, 491.

17. Anne Tyler, "Still Just Writing," in Janet Sternburg, ed., *The Writer on Her Work* (New York: W. W. Norton, 1980), 13.

18. Brown, 4.

19. "Still Just Writing," 3–10.

20. Marilyn Gardner, "Figurines in a Paperweight," *Christian Science Monitor,* 10 February 1966, 7.

21. Orville Prescott, "Return to the Hawkes Family," *New York Times,* 11 November 1964, 41.

22. Katherine Gauss Jackson, "Mad First Novel, but Without Madness," *Harper's,* November 1964, 152.

23. Wendy Lamb, "An Interview with Anne Tyler," *Iowa Journal of Literary Studies* 3 (1981): 64.

24. Michaels, 43.

25. Barbara A. Bannon, review of *A Slipping-Down Life, Publishers Weekly,* 12 January 1970, 59.

26. Martin Levin, "Reader's Report," *New York Times Book Review,* 15 March 1970, 44.

27. Binding, 203; Brooks, 340.

28. Tyler speaks of her "little paper people" in " 'Because I Want,' " 7; her concern about the baby is mentioned in Zahlan, 494.

29. Barbara A. Bannon, review of *The Clock Winder, Publishers Weekly,* 14 February 1972, 68; Martin Levin, "New and Novel," *New York Times Book Review,* 21 May 1972, 31.

30. Elizabeth Easton, review of *The Clock Winder, Saturday Review of the Arts,* 17 June 1972, 77. Alleen Pace Nilsen lists *The Clock Winder* on her "1972–73 Honor Listing" of "Books for Young Adults," *English Journal* 62 (December 1973): 1298.

31. Sara Blackburn, review of *The Clock Winder, Washington Post Book World,* 14 May 1972, 13.

32. Clifford A. Ridley, "Anne Tyler: A Sense of Reticence Balanced by 'Oh, Well, Why Not?,' " *National Observer,* 22 July 1972, 23.

33. Betts, "The Fiction of Anne Tyler," 30.

34. Notes Zahlan, "To the reader's shock, the apparently sexless Jeremy not only lives in apparent harmony with the beautiful young woman but fathers children as well" (495). Tyler has since reconsidered her depiction of Jeremy: "As I look back upon that book I see that it must be hard for readers to credit Jeremy with any sexual capability, and that I really owed it to them to show how he managed it. But Jeremy is the character I've felt most protective of, and so I let the book down on that account" (interview with Alice Hall Petry, August 1989).

35. Jay L. Halio, "Love and the Grotesque," *Southern Review* 11 (Autumn 1975): 945.

36. See, for example, Susannah Clapp, "In the Abstract," (London) *Times Literary Supplement,* 23 May 1975, 577. Doris Betts takes the matter one step further, arguing that Jeremy's own "development from collage to sculpture seems to parallel Tyler's literary progress from story to more and more complex novel" ("The Fiction of Anne Tyler," 29).

37. Victor Howes, "Freedom: Theme of Pecks' Battle Hymns," *Christian Science Monitor,* 14 January 1976, 23; Lynn Sharon Schwartz, review of *Searching for Caleb, Saturday Review,* 6 March 1976, 28.

38. Philip Howard, review of *Searching for Caleb,* (London) *Times,* 13 May 1976, 16.

39. Martha B. Tack, "Pecking Order," *Village Voice,* 1 November 1976, 95.

40. Catherine Peters, "Opting Out," (London) *Times Literary Supplement,* 27 August 1976, 1060.

41. Betts, "The Fiction of Anne Tyler," 33; Gilberto Perez, "Narrative Voices," *Hudson Review* 30 (Winter 1977–78): 612.

42. "I'm very interested in day-to-day endurance. . . . The real heroes to me in my books are first the ones who manage to endure and second the ones who somehow are able to grant other people the privacy of the space around them and yet still produce some warmth" (quoted in Michaels, 43).

43. Anatole Broyard, "Tyler, Tracy and Wakefield," *New York Times Book Review*, 8 May 1977, 12.

44. Shelton, 857. "Tyler herself believes that the novel is generally misunderstood to be 'another Unhappy Housewife Leaves Home book, which was the last thought in my mind.' " Rather, she regards it " 'as the work of somebody entering middle age, beginning to notice how the bags and baggage of the past are weighing her down, and how much she values them' " (Brooks, 344, 343). Tyler further admits that it " 'was written before I realized what the pattern was—that a relationship as bizarre as a bank robber and hostage could become a bickering familiar relationship' " (Michaels, 43).

45. Nicholas Delbanco, review of *Earthly Possessions, New Republic*, 28 May 1977, 36.

46. Robert Towers, review of *Morgan's Passing, New Republic*, 22 March 1980, 28; Thomas M. Disch, "The Great Impostor," *Washington Post Book World*, 16 March 1980, 5.

47. Eva Hoffman, "When the Fog Never Lifts," *Saturday Review*, 15 March 1980, 38.

48. Shelton, 855.

49. Peter Grier, "Bright Novel That Overstretches Credibility," *Christian Science Monitor*, 14 April 1980, sec. B, 9.

50. James Wolcott, "Strange New World," *Esquire*, April 1982, 124.

51. Updike, "On Such a Beautiful Green Little Planet," 196.

52. Benjamin DeMott, "Funny, Wise and True," *New York Times Book Review*, 14 March 1982, 1

53. Jean Strouse, "Family Arsenal," *Newsweek*, 5 April 1982, 72.

54. Anon., review of *The Accidental Tourist, Antioch Review*, 44 (Spring 1986): 249; Updike, "Leaving Home," 108.

55. Larry McMurtry, "Life Is a Foreign Country," *New York Times Book Review*, 8 September 1985, 36. Anne R. Zahlan sees Edward as "the id in canine form" (500), a thesis she develops much further in "Traveling Towards the Self: The Psychic Drama of Anne Tyler's *The Accidental Tourist*," in Stephens, 84–96. If Edward is indeed a physical manifestation of the troubled Macon's id, then the dog's "unaccountable neglect" in the last portion of the novel is actually a statement of Macon's psychic recovery.

56. Adam Mars-Jones, "Despairs of a Time-and-Motion Man," (London) *Times Literary Supplement*, 4 October 1985, 1096.

57. Updike, "Leaving Home," 108; Anon., review of *The Accidental Tourist, Virginia Quarterly Review* 62 (Summer 1986): 90.

58. Jonathan Yardley, "Anne Tyler's Family Circles," *Washington Post Book World*, 25 August 1985, 3.

59. Robert Towers, "Roughing It," *New York Review of Books*, 10 November 1988, 41.

60. Marita Golden, "New Wives' Tales," *Ms.*, September 1988, 86.

61. Robert McPhillips, "The Baltimore Chop," *Nation*, 7 November 1988, 465.

62. Klinghoffer, 49.

63. Wallace Stegner, "The Meddler's Progress," *Washington Post Book World*, 4 September 1988, 1.

64. Susan Gilbert, "Private Lives and Public Issues: Anne Tyler's Prize-winning Novels," in Stephens, 136–45.

65. DeMott, for example, noted that "there's a touch of Dostoyevsky's 'Idiot' " in Ezra Tull of *Dinner at the Homesick Restaurant*, "a hint of the unposturing selflessness whose effect on people denied faith in the possibility of human purity is invariably to intensify cynicism" (14),

while Martin Levin pointed out that Tyler "fills her pages with . . . richly-idiosyncratic characters who amble about in Chekhovian fashion" ("New and Novel," 31). Robert McPhillips made a tentative suggestion about Tyler's indebtedness to Hawthorne by remarking that her fiction "belongs to the tradition of the American romance pioneered by Hawthorne far more than to that of the realistic or naturalistic novel" (464). Her possible kinship to the Russian masters and the Concord Circle is also examined by me in *Understanding Anne Tyler,* passim.

INTERVIEWS AND PERSONAL STATEMENTS

◆

Authoress Explains Why Women Dominate in South

JORIE LUELOFF

The slim brunette scrunched further down on the small of her back, rearranged her stockinged feet on the coffee table and nibbled a chocolate cookie.

"When I was in college, one of my professors said a woman should never try to write from a man's point of view, because a woman doesn't know how a man thinks. Now this is very galling!" she exclaimed, sitting up and reaching for another cookie.

Despite the advice, Anne Tyler went ahead and wrote the story of a young law student at Columbia University, Ben Joe Hawkes. He returns to his North Carolina home town in the belief that his family of women—widowed mother, grandmother, and a flock of sisters—needs him. His reactions to the visit—his mother's chilliness, his sisters' self-reliance and restraint, and his ensuing sense of isolation—are drawn in vivid detail by Miss Tyler in her recent book, "If Morning Ever Comes."

Not only was it acclaimed by the critics, but one male reaction was, "It scares me. How can a 22-year-old girl know so much about how a man feels?"

BORN IN NORTH

Although the young novelist, now 23, was born in Minneapolis she grew up in North Carolina, attended Duke University, and considers herself a Southerner through and through.

"There are so many women writing about the South," she says ruefully, "you begin to feel it's old hat."

Indeed, no other part of the country in recent years has produced so many women writers as the South.

Some such as Harper Lee, Taylor Caldwell and Carson McCullers, have names known even to the casual reader. A couple—Flannery O'Connor, Eudora Welty—are regarded as high priestesses by the literary set.

Reprinted from the (Baton Rouge) *Morning Advocate,* 8 February 1965, sec. A, 11, by permission of the Associated Press.

Status of Writer

The preponderance of women authors can be explained partially by the status of the writer in the South, Anne says.

"Somehow writing in the South is like painting china—it seems to be a woman's occupation," she says. "I have a feeling the man writer in the South is looked on as being somewhat effeminate."

In the books turned out by the Southern women there are some obvious similarities.

Many concern family and tradition; sometimes, but not always, race is involved; almost all are especially strong on detail, color and a regional atmosphere that permeates everything from setting to character.

Life in Contrast

And then, perhaps there's a similarity that's not so obvious—a certain awareness of the difference between the traditional stereotype of the South and today's South as it really is; an awareness of the contrast between an old, gracious way of life and life as it is.

"It occurs to me," Miss Tyler says, "that men are fooled more easily by what's on the surface. The women know something's underneath it and write about the difference between the two."

The theme is very much a part of Anne Tyler's book.

"The most Southern thing about Ben Joe," she says, "is his inability to realize that time is changing. This is a very typical Southern fault. People were trying to live on the surface as a family—the way it's supposed to be."

She emphasized the word "supposed."

Avoids Stereotype

Although other Southern women writers are concerned with the myth-versus-reality theme, Anne feels that they sometimes reinforce the dream instead of reality.

"I don't see that the South in the way most writers put it down," [sic] she says, grey eyes gazing out the window. "A lot of things that people stereotype the South as being—the picture just isn't true. I think my book gives the true picture. At least I could go South at this moment and find something happening like this any place."

At any moment in the South she could also find an almost irresistible source of material, she says.

Loves the South

"I love the South," she continues. "I could sit all day and listen to the people talking. It would be hard to listen to a conversation in Raleigh for instance, and write it without putting in color. And they tell stories constantly! I love the poor white trash—they're fascinating and everything about them is so distinct. And I love the average Southern Negro—they speak a language all their own. A Southern conversation is pure metaphor and the lower you get in the class structure, the more it's true. Up North they speak in prose, and the conversation doesn't have as much color.

"And in the North," she rushes on, "they don't tolerate odd people so much. In any Southern woman's novel there are quirks in the family that in the North would cause a person to be sent off to a rest home! There are so many freaks in Southern literature. It's full of dwarfs, hunchbacks, petrified men—terrifying, violent, almost bloody people."

Gentle Characters

Not so notorious, but just as important as the gruesome, freakish types, Anne feels, is another sort of character that the Southern women have put down on paper.

"It's the gentle or tactful people," she says, "who have been ignored by the Northern novelists. There aren't enough quiet, gentle, basically good people in a novel. Usually whole holocausts happen. But this delicate thing where you just walk a tightrope between people—that doesn't happen very often in a Northern novel. Most Southern novelists have concentrated on these little threads of connection between people."

Even though she spent a year in New York at Columbia Graduate School working for a masters in Russian and even though she lives in Montreal now, Anne considers the South her true home.

"I'd like to change my cast of characters a little more and my setting, but basically, I'll always write the same kind of novel. All I want is to stop being in a small, red clay town all the time."

Anne and her husband, Taghi Mohammad Modarressi, live in Montreal where she works in the McGill University library. When her husband completes two more years of residency at McGill, they plan to move to his native Iran where he will take charge of a psychiatric clinic and training center. Even there, Anne will continue to write about the South.

"It seems so silly to live in Iran and write about a place you came from 40 years ago," she says, "and yet I can't picture writing about a Persian market place."

Anne Tyler: A Sense of Reticence Balanced by "Oh, Well, Why Not?"

CLIFFORD A. RIDLEY

It's as hard to get a fix on Anne Tyler the novelist as it is to get a fix on her novels, which simply defy the critic's customary bundling and knotting: Try as you may to package them in tidy summaries, you're left with echoes and ambiguities and inconsistencies poking up here and there. Miss Tyler works very understated and controlled, deliberately tossing out scenes that threaten to call attention to themselves. Her "effects" seem over almost before they've begun, like crossroads settlements that one drives through in the blink of an eye, yet they resonate long after her books are finished. She is very much her own woman, her own voice.

Met in the sunken living room of the shaded old house on a north Baltimore street of shaded old houses where she lives with her psychiatrist husband, Taghi Mohammad Modarressi, and their two young daughters, Anne Tyler is still very much her own woman. Phoning a week earlier to ask about seeing her, I had met with something less than unbridled enthusiasm. She'd used to submit to interviews, Miss Tyler explained, but she'd been misquoted a time or two (the last time, she said, in this newspaper), and her days were so busy, and her personal life was her own business, and . . . "Oh, well, why not?" So here we were, clutching coffee mugs and cigarets while a protective collie wandered in and out, and Miss Tyler was pondering why her characters often make their most abiding decisions on unpredictable impulse.

REPEATED NOTE

"I suppose," she said, "it's because if things were done the other way, they wouldn't be worth writing about. But maybe it's partly me, too. There was a period in my life, starting at 17 or 18, when I seemed determined to do whatever seemed the most contrary thing. And I suppose that any decision I make is more or less like that even now. When I decided to get married, for instance, I remember thinking 'Oh, well, why not?' Fortunately, of course"—a smile—"it worked out." I said nothing of when I had heard the phrase before, but I hoped to myself that this afternoon, too, worked out.

But stop. "Who," I hear you ask, "is Anne Tyler?" It's a fair question. There really are two kinds of literary interviews: the ones you feel you *ought* to do, whether you like it or not (Norman Mailer, Irving Wallace, and the legions between), and the ones you simply *want* to do because you're in love with a body of work. Locked in communion with a certain sensibility, you want to experience it at close range, to see how it functions in personal terms. Well, that's what brought me to Baltimore; Anne Tyler has written four novels, and I adore each of them.

A Sense of Community

Which is odd, in one sense, because their physical world is not mine at all. Anne Tyler lived in North Carolina from early childhood through college (Duke), and she has set 3½ of her books there. (Her fourth, *The Clock Winder,* transpires half in North Carolina and half here in Baltimore; her fifth, now in progress [*Celestial Navigation*—Ed.], will desert North Carolina entirely.) They're steeped in the physical details of that world—the flatness, the heat, the parochialism, the laconic and offhand speech patterns—and steeped most of all in a sense of community and self-protectiveness that transcends race, class, age, and everything else. And that, come to think of it, may be what makes them so appealing to a 37-year-old kid from suburban Connecticut whose life has been passed in search of the kind of community that seems to sprout from every crack in Miss Tyler's sidewalks.

And now I guess there's nothing for it but to synopsize what the books are "about," and inadequacy take the hindmost:

If Morning Ever Comes—published in 1964, when its author was all of 22—could be Miss Tyler's *You Can't Go Home Again*. Ben Joe Hawkes, a student at Columbia, ups and returns to North Carolina when family crises loom, but once there he discovers that lives go on and must work themselves out in their own quirky ways. His own included.

The Tin Can Tree, published a year later, begins with the funeral of a little girl, who has died in a tractor accident, and tells of the succeeding days in the lives of her family and of the two brothers who occupy the other end of their three-family house. It tells of how we come to terms with things; it tells, too, of how caring for people can be the salvation of some, the slow death of others.

'A Cucumber Sandwich'

("I don't like either of my first two books," their author says firmly. "They seem so bland. Ben Joe is just a likable guy; that's all you can say about him.

I remember one reviewer said he was about as interesting as a cucumber sandwich, and I think he was right.

("I wrote the book in a way out of curiosity, out of wondering how it would feel to be part of a huge Southern family. Oh, there were four kids in our family, but we were spread out in years. I always felt isolated from the South; I always envied everybody. I used to work at tying tobacco and listen to all the farm wives strung out along a long table, talking all day long; they fascinated me.")

A Slipping-Down Life, published in 1970 after the birth of the Modarressi daughters and the quiet shelving of an unpublished novel that nobody liked [*Winter Birds, Winter Apples*—Ed.], is the toughest and tautest of Miss Tyler's books. It's the straight-ahead story of a lumpy, nebbish high-school girl who impulsively carves the name of a local rock singer on her forehead, becomes a sort of freak attraction at his performances, and eventually marries him.

'DIRECT INHERITANCE'

("Yes, it's a different kind of book; I felt as I was writing it that I was being braver. *If Morning Ever Comes* and *The Tin Can Tree* were so much alike; I think I'd gotten tired of my own voice. A long time earlier, I'd read a small newspaper story about a 15-year-old girl in Texas who'd slashed 'Elvis' in her forehead, and I never forgot it. And somehow I pictured the paper as saying she was a fat, homely girl, although obviously it wouldn't have said that. I still like the book; I love Drumstrings Casey, his family, everything about him. He's the direct inheritance of all the days on the tobacco farm.")

And finally *The Clock Winder,* just three months old, returns Miss Tyler to the kind of big, loving-bickering family she created in *If Morning Ever Comes.* But this is a bolder, broader-scaled book than her first, spanning 10 years in the lives of the Emerson clan of Baltimore's Roland Park and the diffident North Carolina girl, Elizabeth, who arrives as Mrs. Emerson's "handyman" and survives time and tragedy to marry one of the Emerson sons and hold the mad menage together.

'A SAD ENDING'

The question of caring for people—whether we can and whether we should—runs so strongly, and sometimes so contradictorily, through Miss Tyler's work that one is compelled to ask if it's a conscious theme. "Most of the time," she smiles, "I hope somebody will tell me what my theme is. But I must find the idea of taking care of others very attractive; there must be a place in life for people who do that. If I have to take a moral stand, though, I feel terribly strongly that nobody should do anything, that you should leave your hands out of other people's business. In many ways *The Clock Winder* condemns what it praises and vice versa; I think Elizabeth does herself irreparable damage in not going farther than she does, but on the other hand what she does is the best and happiest thing for her. I think of it as a sad ending, and I've been surprised that not everybody does.

"I think something that tends to come out in all my books is an utter lack of faith in change. I really don't think most people are capable of it, although they think they are. One reason I like *A Slipping-Down Life* is because it's the one book of mine in which the characters do change."

THIS AND THAT

Well, we talked for a while longer about this and that—influences (Eudora Welty, mostly), novels by liberated women ("I hate 'em all"), attitudes toward characters ("I don't care for writers who write about people they don't like"), affection for the elderly ("I'd like to spend the rest of my life writing about old men"). We didn't talk nearly enough about the short story, which is the lady's real passion, her "dessert" after finishing a novel: "You don't have to feel you're committing yourself over the long haul; you can say something for exactly as long as it pleases you and then drop it." But I had promised no more than an hour and a half, and I kept my word.

Anne Tyler handed me my unneeded raincoat and smiled. "That was almost painless," she said, and I felt better about busting in even as I concluded that the operative word was still "almost." I thought back to something Miss Tyler said when we began: "I'm getting a little more and more willing to expose more of myself with each book. There's more of *me* in *The Clock Winder*—not autobiography, but more that I feel." Yes, perhaps there is—and that, of course, is as it should be. A writer's dreams and fears and delights are all he has to sustain his work—and it is there in his writing, not parceled out by dribs and drabs to every passing busybody, that they can grow and assume shapes that will please or caution the rest of us. So it's no less than proper that the sense of privacy by which so many of Anne Tyler's characters define themselves should be their creator's means of defining herself as well. If God had meant authors to chatter, he would have given them talk shows. Back to work, Mrs. M.

Olives Out of a Bottle

Duke University *Archive*

The following is a partial transcript of a panel discussion with Anne Tyler held during Ms. Tyler's visit to campus last November. Other members of the panel were Reynolds Price, James Applewhite, Donna Landry, John Stevenson, and Tim Westmoreland. The audience was also invited to question Ms. Tyler.

Reynolds Price: I'd like to begin our part of the discussion by asking Anne a question that has concerned me a great deal just in the last few years. It seems to have taken me an inordinate amount of time to define what I think is the major problem for the first half of the careers of most young people who wish to become novelists, especially in America, in recent years, where they tend to have gone through fairly good high schools and quite good colleges and have had a good deal of encouragement in their teens and early twenties in their writing—perhaps the encouragement is not always as discriminating as it ought to be but they have been encouraged, generally, if they have any talent at all. And then they finish college and what normally amounts to something like eight to ten years of very difficult time follows. This seems to me to be the result of the fact that very few novelists really begin to write their particular brand of fiction, their good fiction, until they are in their late twenties or early thirties. Perhaps because fiction seems to be so much a function of maturity. As opposed to some things like painting and dance and perhaps even lyric poetry, I can think of very few really good first novels written by people under the age of twenty-nine or thirty. There are extraordinary exceptions and Anne happens to be one of the exceptions. And so I'd like to begin by asking Anne, since she was an exception, and published her own first novel when she was twenty-three or twenty-four years old, how she felt at the time about the beginning of her actual professional career as opposed to her student career when she was something of a local celebrity as a child-wonder and how she feels now, some ten years later, looking back on that period in her life, the particular problems it presented to you or problems that perhaps you see now looking back that you weren't even aware of then.

Anne Tyler: Well, I think that it's true that you get this sense of being just tossed out. You don't know what's expected of you next and suddenly there's nobody to discipline you from above. And I think one of the things

From the Duke University *Archive* 87 (Spring 1975): 70–79. Reprinted by permission of the editor of *Archive* and the Duke University Undergraduate Publications Board.

that it took me maybe five or six years to realize was that I would have to set up my own discipline and that it was necessary to get a pattern in my life. I think also that I would know now the minute I left college, it's not necessary to go to graduate school, it's more necessary to get a boring job. And to find some way of scheduling your life around a job that takes a minimum of time and doesn't drain you in any way. Anything that emotionally drains you I think—I don't know how you can teach and write (gesturing to Reynolds Price)—but anything that takes something out of you so that you can't put it into writing would make it very hard for me to come home in the evening and write.

Price: And you had jobs as a librarian in those years.

Tyler: Yes, and that was very boring (*laughter*).

Price: And then how did you organize your writing around that?

Tyler: Well, that was the hardest period of time. If I worked from nine to five I would have to write in the evening which isn't a good time.

Price: You're tired then.

Tyler: Yes. And also, my mind doesn't function in the evening at all (*laughter*). But I think if you could choose the ideal thing you should have a part-time job if it could sustain you and that it should be—well I suppose different minds work better at different times of day—but if you could somehow write first, make that the pattern of time. Write in the morning, work in the afternoon—that would work better for me, I think.

Price: I don't know if we asked John Knowles about this last year when he was here, but I remember his telling me personally that, when he was writing *A Separate Peace* that he was working a full-time job at *Holiday,* in Philadelphia, on the magazine, and that he would get up at five in the morning and write from five to eight, every day of the week, before he would go in and do his nine-to-five job at *Holiday* because he couldn't come home at night and write. And this was certainly I think my pattern when I first came back—when I first met you (gesturing to Anne Tyler) in 1958—when I came back here to teach. The thing about teaching though is that, as my old landlord, who used to be a country school teacher said:—name three good reasons for being a school teacher—June, July and August. (*laughter*) And you do have these three months in the summer. No other job in the world gives you three months vacation—plus two weeks at Christmas and a week at Easter, plus a week off between semesters. Plus the fact that very few teachers at good colleges teach more than two or three days a week. And I think that that is one of the reasons that teaching has been so popular with writers is there's an awful lot of free time. There really is.

But there was a short period there of waiting before your first publications began. Did you have those terrible fears that you were a fraud, that everyone had misled you, that none of this stuff was ever actually going to eventuate in books? Did the book, as a physical reality, seem unattainable to you?

Tyler: Yes. It went beyond the stage of fear. I think I just gave up on it. There was at least a year and a half when nothing came to me automatically by inspiration, which was what I was expecting of course wouldn't happen and Dr. Blackburn or you weren't there to say you have to have something by Monday so I didn't do anything. And it seemed to me, as time passed, I just decided, well, that was a stage of my life and I guess it was for nothing and now I'm going to be something else. I don't think actually I ever would have taken it up again except that I had a period of time when I was really thrown on my own more because we moved to a city where I didn't know anybody and for about six months I couldn't get any job at all. And there was nothing to do so I wrote the first novel in that time. Also, there, I had too much time. In fact, one thing I think is really important, is to know when to quit on schedule too. Rather than go on because things are going well. It's best to quit when things are going well, at an appointed hour.

Price: How do you know when to quit?

Tyler: When the children come home from school (*laughter*). Well I think that probably if you don't have something like that to deliberately end your time, at least if you know that something is down on paper so you won't forget what you had in mind and yet it's not finished up so that you still have something sort of hot to come back to. It's a mistake I think to finish everything you wanted to say and when you come back it's going to be cold. . . .

Price: Hemingway says that, do you remember? I think in the *Paris Review* interview with him, he says always stop when you know what happens next, what's coming next. Because if you write to the end of your knowledge, on any given day, you've got this terrible problem the next day of cranking the machinery up from total inertia. I've found that tremendously true. The temptation is to rush ahead while it's going well. It's best to stop. And I often make a note in the margin to remind me of what the next two or three words are so that I can pick up the next day. Would you like to make this into a prescription then for young writers?

Tyler: No. (*laughter*)

Price: I would. (*more laughter*) Just in the sense that—They've got to learn that writing is something that occurs every day and probably should occur at the same time every day and the hard thing to learn is to go to a certain place where there aren't telephones and aren't pleasant distractions and to sit there and do the work. That's what I had to learn to do.

Tyler: I'm not sure that it would be universally true, though. I question. . . .

Price: Did you ever know a novelist who didn't do that?

Tyler: I don't know any novelists (*laughter*). But I think there are some who are known to . . . Well, the ones who drink and—sort of in little sprees of writing and then sprees of drinking. That's surely not a very disciplined . . . And they manage very well.

Price: Yes. Except that you read Blotner's biography of Faulkner and you find out that Faulkner wrote all the time but also drank all the time. I thought that Faulkner had been a spree drinker. But it turns out that he drank every day of his life and wrote every day of his life. I think Fitzgerald and Thomas Wolfe were sort of spree drinkers and spree writers. But Faulkner and Hemingway seem to have combined the two. It probably wasn't ideal in either case but they did it.

John Stevenson: Well I was going to ask you something which seems to me to be along the same lines as far as what the young writer or young artist needs to learn if he's going to make his life in part out of art. It's a question that's brought up, I think, by *Celestial Navigation,* by having your hero there, if I can use that term, be an artist. That is, how much of what you say about Jeremy in that novel, that a man who ends up being terribly isolated and cut off and who makes sort of thwarted, ineffectual attempts to find other people—how much of that is a part of the artistic condition? You seem to be sort of an exception in your own life because you do have a husband and a family as well as this career as a writer. How much privacy does the artist have to maintain, how much can the young writer expect to be a part of the world and still be a writer?

Tyler: Well, again, I think we see a lot of variations. There are very social writers. But I seem to need to . . . when I'm actually writing, I need to protect myself from experiences. I find in fact that I really don't want to see people, although it always seems to me that surely I should want to if I'm writing about them. But I just don't want to be influenced in any way by the outside and I think since part of a reason for writing is to put out on paper some of your own privacy that you've kept bounded in. So, well, you want to maintain the privacy while you're doing it. Jeremy has carried it too far, but in a lot of ways I feel like Jeremy about putting things out. I feel used up and burnt out if I'm working hard and I'm getting depleted all the time and then between I have to fill in by having a lot of experiences. And also I share with him the feeling that whatever you produce is like olives out of a bottle, that you don't have any choice. If someone were to say, Well I don't like this novel and we won't publish it, I still wouldn't feel that it had been wasted because I had no choice. It had to come before the next thing came. It seems to be a progression that's expected.

James Applewhite: May I ask what relation to reading is carried on. You say, you don't want to see people. Are you able to read things as you're writing or do you have to be cautious about that?

Tyler: If I'm really in the planning stage, or any stage when I'm not sure about what I'm doing, then I think it's really dangerous to read. I think I try and protect myself from getting influenced by somebody. And if I try to read I find my mind just wanders, I can't even take it in.

Applewhite: But once you're well-launched, you're able to read?

Tyler: Oh, yes.

Applewhite: Read fiction?

Tyler: Yes.

Applewhite: You mentioned, in our class I think, *A Hundred Years of Solitude*. Did you read that while writing a book?

Tyler: No, fortunately I didn't because that would have seeped into anything, I think. That was when I wasn't writing anything.

Price: Part of the trouble is just that novelists tend to be born mimics, isn't it? If you listen to anyone talking a certain way, you just tend to mimic it.

Tyler: Yes.

Applewhite: One of the reasons I asked the question is that frequently students who haven't read enough use as a defense that they are afraid of being influenced and I think that's a spurious rationale on their part at the time and yet there must be some legitimacy to it at least for you in the planning stages.

Tyler: Yes. I would think at the time they were students anyway they shouldn't mind being influenced for a little while.

Applewhite: Exactly. Right.

Price: My guess would be from the writers that I know that actually they've all been absolutely voracious readers when they were young and when they were apprentices and they've laid down these enormous strata of reading but that once they get their own work really heavily under way they are not at all systematic readers and I think it's not an accident that almost every fiction, good fiction, writer I know is an addict of detective fiction but reads almost nothing else. It's kind of like dental floss for the brain (*laughter*). You can take a good detective novel and read and forget it by morning but if you really are trying to read *A Hundred Years of Solitude* or the latest good book by anyone, it's a terribly engaging process. So, I think, that's another tremendous reason why any apprentice writer's student period needs to be, to a large extent, a reading period. It's going to get awfully hard to do a lot of reading later. You said the other day something that I agree with entirely. You said it's terribly hard for you to finish a novel now. The novel really has to be good before you can finish it. When you're young you just think: Well, gee, you've got to finish novels. They arrest you if you don't. You can't imagine putting a book down without completing it.

Stevenson: The whole business about reading other people brings up the question of the writer's voice. And I was wondering if you'd care to talk a little bit about—as long as we're discussing this interim period, this early period in the twenties which seem to be probably when most people are finding their voice—how you went about it. Was it simply a process of writing or was it writing and finding that was wrong and trying something else? Could you talk about that a little?

Tyler: I don't think that's a conscious enough process for me to be able to talk about. I think whatever comes to me to write comes through my right ear to be explicit. It's just about here, coming in. I haven't thought about what voice to use. I just put down what comes in. It's not just dictated by an angel.

Stevenson: What I'm thinking of, specifically, in your later work there seems to be a different voice at work than in your earlier books and I was wondering if there was any kind of conscious understanding on your part about the change that went on.

Tyler: Oh, yes. I think every book I've trusted the readers a little bit more. First of all, I've trusted that they might possibly be intelligent and I don't have to explain everything, but more important, I've entrusted myself to them. I don't feel that I have to be on guard quite as much. I think that a lot of the vagueness I see now in the early books was just wrapping cotton wadding so that no one could see me in the book in any way. And now, I figure, well it won't matter all that much after all.

Price: They're not going to do anything to you anyway.

Tyler: I was afraid they'd hold it against me and remind me of it every year or something.

Donna Landry: Why do you think you write? When did you begin and was there ever a period in which you were not doing any writing?

Tyler: Well, I write for two reasons. First of all, I like to lie and that's an acceptable way of lying (*laughter*) and second I have this resentment that I have only one life. So that if I'm happily married I would like to see what it would be like to be unhappily married or what it's like to go live in a boathouse or whatever. And this is my way of doing it. In fact, I'm not sure I was conscious that this was why I was doing writing at first and I'm not sure that's the reason I was but before I think I was writing more for an audience and in the later books, I am writing more just so I could lead these other lives. And I have tried stopping after every novel and, right now, I would say I'll never do another novel except that I *know* by now, I've said it so often before. After about a month, I start feeling more or less useless. There's nothing for whatever it is in me, no place for it to go.

Tim Westmoreland: Back when you were in college how heavily did you draw upon Mr. Price's or your peers reinforcement of your writing and what did you do in the period he was talking about when there was just nothing, before your first novel came out when there is no reinforcement, no encouragement, no praise.

Tyler: Well, I drew very heavily on it when I was here but one of the things about Dr. Blackburn was that he would follow people after college. He would send these little reminders all the time (*laughter*) which ought to be a part of any creative writing course—a guaranteed one-year follow up (*laughter*).

Price: Mimeographed postcards (*laughter*). You talk about stopping, you're convinced always that that's it. I once heard someone say that he heard Robert Frost—a woman came up to Robert Frost after [a] reading at Wesleyan in Connecticut and said, "Mr. Frost, I've been sending my poems around for fifteen years now to magazines and working tremendously hard. It's my whole life and I've never had one accepted yet and I'm nearly at the end of my rope and I'm wondering what I should do. What do you think I should do?" And he said, "Try quitting." (*laughter*). And it's a very good prescription: if you can quit, you weren't a writer.

Tyler: Yes.

Landry: What is your daily work schedule? As a woman who has two children, how do you manage to work your writing in and all those other things other women are able to fill up their days with?

Tyler: Well, I get up between four and five and get the housework out of the way and I start writing when the kids leave for school and I quit when they come home. And I do that four days a week. If there's a day when nothing come[s] out at all, it just isn't working, I still have to sit there. I've tried thinking well, I'll just take the day off and it extends to tomorrow and the next day, too. So I have to sit there and have the paper in front of me and that's all I require of myself.

Landry: What did you do when the children were not in school? I noticed that there's a gap in the publishing dates of your novels. Were you really unable to get much accomplished when they were there?

Tyler: Yes. It was impossible to schedule so that I could write in the early part of the day. And also, one of the reasons there's a gap in the novels is because I did write a novel when I had the first baby and it never really gelled. And I think now it's because having children is one of those draining things like an interesting job (*laughter*). I just didn't have it.

I'm very conscious between writing periods of having to get filled up again. Which is done partly by accepting any kind of invitation that comes in for any kind of peculiar jaunt anywhere with the idea that something is filling me up then. Or writing short stories for me is almost like getting filled up because it's not an exhausting business to write short stories and you can sort of be playful in them. You don't feel that a year of your life is going to go into it. You're not committed in that way.

Westmoreland: So you do short stories only between novels.

Tyler: Yes.

Westmoreland: And not together.

Tyler: Oh, no. I don't know how people can do things simultaneously. Can you do things simultaneously? (*to Mr. Price*)

Price: No. Not at all. But I was just thinking about your schedule and it sounds like the schedule of a medieval serf (*laughter*) which reminds me that one of the favorite things I know that anyone ever said about the novel Scott Fitzgerald said to his daughter. He said: "In every great novelist there's something of the peasant." And that's what there is in novelists—they're donkeys. I mean they're beasts of burden—they really are. There's a wonderful sonnet of Auden's about that, called "The Novelist." He talks about poets being these glamorous, dashing hussars who rush around having dramatic, catastrophic, meteoric lives and novelists are just there [these?] rather dull people who stay home and do the work—peel the potatoes—and get on with the business of writing this gigantic thing called the novel. I think that's the hardest thing ever to convince any young person of. Or if you are yourself convinced that you are a writer it's the hardest thing to realize, that the way you make it happen is you sit there and a large part of what you're doing is training your unconscious mind and that's what I assume you're doing when you force yourself to sit in the room, you're forcing your unconscious mind to work for you. And that's another wonderful thing that Knowles said when he was here last year. He said, "The unconscious is like dogs and children. It loves routine and hates surprises." It loves for you to go into the room every morning at ten minutes to eight and to leave at 3:45. And it'll work for you, you, know, if you train it to work certain shifts. If you've got one to start with. That's what the *if* is.

Applewhite: I have one other question that follows the remark that Anne made about the impulse to want to lead more than one life. I don't address that necessarily to her but to anybody who wants to respond. It seems to me that one of the problems, or one of the traps, for someone of writerly inclination might be the difficulty of separating that impulse to want to lead more than one life into the sphere of imagination wholly or primarily. I wonder if any of you had any thoughts on that head.

Price: You mean the danger he might become autistic or schizophrenic? (*laughter*)

Applewhite: No. No. The sort of Hemingway myth. You know in the introduction to his collected short stories he tells about having gone out and gathered experience and perhaps blunted the instrument—meaning his head by having a plane crash in Africa. But he's come back having quarried out seven men's volume of experience from the jungles of reality. And I think many people following Hemingway, or perhaps their own inclinations, or Thomas Wolfe's passionate desire to know the emotions of all the people passing on a train can very well attempt to enact that impulse literally rather than imaginatively. But I wondered if you think the writer, does the novelist automatically know that that's to be done in imagination instead of actuality? Or maybe attempt to lead three lives in reality?

Tyler: No. I think that's what I mean about protecting yourself from experience. But there's only a certain amount of will to lead other lives and you learn where to channel it. I can either go out and live in a boathouse or I can sit home and write about it.

Applewhite: Well, with a novelist like Wolfe or Fitzgerald this very impulse that would make you want to lead other lives in fiction might make you also want to lead other lives in reality, mightn't it?

Tyler: Well, some of them manage both. Yes (*laughter*). I couldn't.

Price: But don't forget, Wolfe and Fitzgerald had died before they were my age. Well, I'm forty-one and, how old was Fitzgerald? He was in his early forties and Wolfe was forty when he died. Thirty-nine or forty. I mean they really did. I think they badly damaged themselves. Certainly Fitzgerald did and he knew it. Hemingway knew that he had badly damaged himself. But I think a large part of what we feel about those people is a lie that was perpetrated both by them and by the media of the time. If you've ever been to Key West and been to that lovely home that Hemingway lived in for over ten years you know that Hemingway spent ninety-eight percent of his life in a little stucco room at a little round table writing those books. With a series of wives in the house who were getting on with simplifying his daily life for him. But every now and then he would go off to Ketchum, Idaho or Tanganyika or somewhere and then *Look* magazine would go with him and then we'd get all these pictures of someone roistering around the world. And gradually as I think his inspiration, his unconscious mind, slowed down and ceased to offer him a great deal of work—perhaps because he had done so much drinking, I don't know, there may be a connection there—he spent much more time wandering around the world. But if you look at the lives—I mean of the really great big novelists in the history of the world—and we don't have one in American literature—but if you look at someone like Tolstoy, or Dickens, or Dostoyevsky, or someone like that, they're just guys who go to the office everyday, wherever the office happens to be. They're like bankers. Tolstoy was in the army as a young man but most young men in the world have been in the army when they were young men. Or a lot of them have. A very large proportion. They were rather ordinary people as a matter of fact. Supremely ordinary except they had this one thing about their lives that happened to be extraordinary, which was that they were geniuses. Tolstoy had something like thirteen children. Ten that survived him which meant that Countess Tolstoy had a pretty rough life. (*laughter*) That's a whole other story. And she told it—endlessly.

Audience: Let me ask a kind of technical question. Do you tend to do a great deal of rewriting or do you seem to get it right the first time around?

Tyler: Well, now, I get it more or less right the first time around. I've found that works better for me. But it means that every novel that I do requires a month of planning ahead of time, which is very frustrating because I don't have pages to show at the end of the day. If I sit and take that month and really think it out and get everything outlined[,] then I'm fairly sure where I'm going to go from beginning to end except that so far it's always turned out that I've been wrong about the end. But at least I thought I knew how it was going to end before I began it. And that means that I might juggle things a little bit, cross out here and there but I don't actually do a second draft or anything like that.

Audience: And is your pace pretty regular? What is a day's quota for you?

Tyler: It's not regular enough to answer that. Sometime it's even ten or fifteen pages a day of very small handwriting and other times it's literally just one page. It just depends.

Audience: Do you write your novels out in longhand? Not use a type-writer?

Tyler: Yes. Since I really do seem to do it by ear, if I'm typing I can't hear as well. The rhythm of the keys gets me and also I'm a very poor typist and I get angry and that doesn't do any good either (*laughter*). So I write it out in longhand, type it up chapter by chapter as I finish a chapter, and then type it all in a neat manuscript at the end.

Price: I always like to say that Shakespeare was a very poor typist, too. (*laughter*)

Tyler: Yes.

Westmoreland: You said the other evening you could no longer write a Southern novel. You really didn't feel that at home in Baltimore either. I want to hear why you feel you can no longer write a Southern novel, or a novel with Southern characters.

Tyler: Well, just that I don't feel that I'm really in touch with North Carolina anymore. This is the first time I've been back in years and they may be speaking differently, there may be little changes here and there that I just don't know about. I think it would be presumptuous right now to set a novel in North Carolina unless I came back for a month or something and really got into it. I suppose theoretically, I could set a novel in San Francisco, where I've never been but I think sometimes if you're really on a long novel that will show through. Maybe a short story.

Price: Have you ever written a novel which you essentially made up from day to day as you went, getting started with a basic given situation and just winged it?

Tyler: Yes, the first one and the second one. And both of them show it I think. I have that sense of vagueness when I read them.

Audience: As long as we're talking about beginning. Would you say an axiom is also that you start out with a character in mind rather than say an incident?

Tyler: That's true for me but I think writers really seem divided into two camps. Some start out with a plot and have to work for the characters and I start out with the characters and have to work for the plot.

Price: You never feel over-planned? And then it's like a coloring book that you're filling in the outlines?

Tyler: No. It takes one sheet of paper to plan and it has like ten little headings and then I always know that I'm surely going to change some place, so it's flexible.

Price: So it's really not an elaborate scene by scene outline.

Tyler: No. That wouldn't work.

Applewhite: I'd like a little more on sort of the nature of the flashes that come. It's not in terms of place then—it's in terms of people? Do you see images in your mind's eye of the characters or just what is the nature of the flashes?

Tyler: Well, aside from a few little tiny events, I meant really tiny events—they wouldn't even be called elements of a plot—most of the flashes I get are voices of characters. Things that are said and that later I try to fit in, by hook or by crook.

Price: Be a little more specific about this. Is this like Joan of Ark's [*sic*] voices? (*laughter*)

Tyler: No.

Price: You're not actually hearing . . . You said angelic dictation, but . . . just how is this coming to you? Is it an aural phenomenon or . . .

Tyler: No. You know how when you think, if you happen to be thinking in words, your own voice is thinking in your mind. Well, it's my own voice and I know that my own brain is producing it but it's sort of on a subconscious level, someone will just take over and start talking.

Price: So dialogue is the easiest thing for you to write?

Tyler: Yes. In fact dialogue is one of those things where if I'm writing it and go down to get a cup of coffee it's keeping on going in my mind and I have to hurry back because I'm losing it as it goes. The part that is tedious to me is getting people from one room to the next. (*laughter*)

Audience: Have you learned anything at all from the craft of other writers?

Tyler: Yes. I think most obviously and visibly from Eudora Welty because I just knew her by heart when I was in high school. But, also—I really think majoring in Russian helped. A lot of the really obvious techniques and craftsmanship in them that were brought to our attention when we were studying them, I've remembered and I see it coming up in my own stuff sometime.

Price: Do you ever consciously reach a difficult point yourself and go hunting back through favorite writers looking to see how they may have handled a similar crisis?

Tyler: No, I would be scared to do that. If I found out from them how to do it I wouldn't want to use it because I would worry that it wasn't mine.

Price: I sometimes look in Tolstoy for things like that. I used to feel guilty about it and said this to my tutor in graduate school, who was a man named Lord David Cecil, and he said "Oh never worry about being influenced by Tolstoy. That's like being influenced by God." And it is.

Landry: It seems that most writers have at least one other person to lean on since writing is obviously a very draining experience. A woman writer like Virginia Woolfe [*sic*] has a husband who is able to devote just incredible amounts of love and time. Someone who can play the wife . . .

Tyler: I could use a wife. (*laughter*)

Landry: As a wife, how do you manage, really?

Tyler: I probably shut off a good deal of my wifely attention. You know, I think I take less interest in the children and everything if I'm in a really pressing point in the novel and I don't think it's hurting them yet.

I think it would bother me to feel that I was leaning on anybody that much. I think there's some kind of pride in writing, you know that, here I am, all alone in this room with this impossible problem. I'm never going to get them out of this situation in any believable way. And I don't want to talk to anybody about it or ask anybody or even have someone say "There, there." because I'd like to think at the end that I did it all myself.

Landry: Well this really relates to that theme of privacy and the inadvisability of intrusion by anyone else.

Tyler: Yes. Anything I've ever written I've wanted to know how much dependency is allowed between people, how much right people have to want to change other people. All that business. And I resent the fact that blurbs on my books always say I'm concerned with lack of communication because I don't think communication is really all that hot between people. I don't think it's necessary or desirable in a lot of cases.

Anne Tyler, Writer 8:05 to 3:30

Marguerite Michaels

"Two plus nine is eleven, carry the one," Mrs. Anne Tyler Modarressi says as she bends over 9-year-old Mitra and her math paper. "I don't think you should write down the one you carry—it's too confusing." Used cereal bowls and signs of school lunches already packed are scattered around the kitchen. Dinner is in the oven, but morning tea is still brewing as Mitra and her older sister Tezh slam the front screen-door on their way to school. It's 8 A.M.

At 8:05 Anne Tyler is walking up the stairs to her study. "I've learned over the years that I can't even put the dishes in the dishwasher," says Tyler. "As I close the door on the kids I go up to my room—like one of Pavlov's dogs. Otherwise I'll get sidetracked."

Thirty-five-year-old novelist Anne Tyler, mother of two and author of seven, resents being referred to as a housewife who writes. "Is John Updike a father of four who writes?" From 5:30 in the morning to 8 she is Mrs. Modarressi: wife, mother, cook, housecleaner, laundress. From 8:05 to 3:30, when school's out, she is Anne Tyler: writer. Monday through Thursday. Friday is for "groceries and snow tires."

"I have perfect control of time," says Tyler, "and I can organize it." Five minutes for a peanut butter sandwich lunch. Thirty minutes for "the high-light of my day"—the mail. A junk catalogue freak—"you can't imagine what people are selling"—Tyler knows all the mailmen who work her east Baltimore neighborhood and their exact schedules.

Now working on her eighth novel, Tyler doesn't see herself building up to "the great book." "I think of my work as a whole. And really what it seems to me I'm doing is populating a town. Pretty soon it's going to be just full of lots of people I've made up. None of the people I write about are people I know. That would be no fun. And it would be very boring to write about me. Even if I led an exciting life, why live it again on paper? I want to live other lives. I've never quite believed that one chance is all I get. Writing is my way of making other chances. It's lucky I do it on paper. Probably I would be schizophrenic—and six times divorced—if I weren't writing. I would decide that I want to run off and join the circus and I would go. I hate to travel, but writing a novel is like taking a long trip. This way I can stay peacefully at home."

From *New York Times Book Review*, 8 May 1977, 13, 42–43. Copyright © 1977 by The New York Times Company. Reprinted by permission.

The housewife and the writer are connected by index cards. White and unlined. "Around the house," one card reads, "Cobb wears kneesocks with her housedress." There are cards scattered in almost every room of the house. And ball-point pens. The pen in the bedroom has a light on it. The cards—with their random thoughts trapped—are eventually filed in one of two small metal boxes. The blue box is the novel box. Divided by chapter number, the box also has "extra," "general," "look up," "short story" and "revise" sections. The second box is the short story box. Its categories are "details" and "first sentence." The Cobb kneesock card has a three in the left-hand corner, which means it goes to event three in the 11th chapter of the new novel.*

Other cards for chapter 11 are scattered across the black-and-white checkered daybed on which Anne sits—"on the small of my back"—to write. Her novels are written in longhand with a Parker ball-point pen on white paper attached to a clipboard. "I used to use Bics," says Tyler, "but after a few hours the ridges became painful."

Her study has two large windows, but her eyes fix on the wall opposite the daybed. It's covered with family photographs and an eclectic collection of pictures cut from newspapers and magazines: a sepia photograph of her great-grandfather playing a cello up in the hayloft door of a barn—the same photo of Caleb described in "Searching for Caleb"; bare, empty rooms in stark black and white; and a hand-copied poem by Richard Wilbur about sleeping, which reminds Tyler of writing[:]" . . . step off assuredly into the blank of your mind . . . something will come to you."

Everything on the wall is framed; extra frames are in the closet next to the stacks of white paper and the Parker refills. The pictures are moved and removed, and the only constants in the room are the daybed and the bookcases—filled with almanacs back to 1948, Time-Life history books decade by decade back to 1870 and several photography books "just to sink into," says Tyler. "To fill up on when I feel empty."

Still, time "for thinking" and "for hearing my characters" is as important as the plain white cards and paper. She does much of her hearing from two to four in the morning—"an inherited family insomnia." When her children were little she slept through the night from fatigue, "and I wasn't half as productive as I am now. Five years went by between the second and third novels."

Her working rhythms were a long time coming. Born in Minneapolis, she moved around with her family—her father is a chemist—until they settled in a Quaker community in Raleigh, N.C. Never planning to be a writer, Anne Tyler would tell herself stories just to get to sleep at night.

*In an interview conducted by mail in August 1989, Anne Tyler revealed to me that the work-in-progress described in this article was her "ditched novel," *Pantaleo;* she also admitted that she continues to use index cards in her work, "but only in the most complicated chapters do I, or did I ever, bother numbering them"—Ed.

Westerns, usually. At Duke University she majored in Russian but took the required English 101 with Reynolds Price. Before she graduated Phi Beta Kappa, Price introduced her to his literary agent. Then there was graduate school in Russian at Columbia in New York; library jobs at Duke and McGill University in Montreal; occasional short stories in the Saturday Evening Post, Harper's and The New Yorker; and marriage to an Iranian psychiatrist, Taghi Mohammad Modarressi. Not exactly in that order.

She finished her first novel, "If Morning Ever Comes," in 1964, but only after leaving the manuscript—almost on purpose—on a plane. She hates it and hates her second novel, "The Tin Can Tree." Her favorite is her fifth[,] "Celestial Navigation," possibly because its central character, Jeremy, who never leaves his Baltimore block and lives life from a distance, is the closest Anne Tyler has come to writing about herself.

And she hates to research. "I wanted to do a fortune teller—Justine in 'Caleb.' Haven't you ever been tempted to have your fortune told? It would have killed it off instantly if I'd ever gone to one. Instead I bought a little dime-store Dell book—just to pick up the names of some of the card formations. It's a lot more fun to make things up."

But the first month of a new novel, according to Tyler, is not much fun at all. "It seems to me that very often the way I begin a novel is that I have these index cards—say a hundred. They are things that at one time or another I thought I would like to explore, maybe a conversation I've overheard on a bus that I wondered where it was going or what did it really mean. At every fifth card or so a little click would go in my mind and I think 'boy that would be fun' and I start to expand on it and then I set the card aside. At the end I have maybe 10 cards, and they are such disparate things that the problem is how on earth am I going to get them all into one framework? I have to think a month before I can figure it out.

"Sometimes a book will start with a picture that pops into my mind and I ask myself questions about it and if I put all the answers together I've got a novel. A real picture would be the old newspaper clipping about the Texas girl who slashed 'Elvis' in her forehead [Evie Decker in "Slipping Down Life"]. With this novel, the one I'm working on now, a picture came very clearly into my mind from out of nowhere of a young man walking down a street of row houses in east Baltimore pushing an empty baby stroller from the 1940's—one of those blue things with little white canework insets. There he went, and if you ask who he is and why on earth he's pushing an empty baby stroller—is he a man trying to take care of a small child? What are the complications?—then you can see a novel.

"My interest is character. The real joy of writing is how people can surprise one. My people wander around my study until the novel is done. It's one reason I'm very careful not to write about people I don't like. If I find somebody creeping in that I'm not really fond of, I usually take him out. I end a book at the point where I feel that I'm going to know forever what their lives are like. You know what Charlotte [in "Earthly Possessions"] is doing now. I build a house for them and then I move on to the next house.

"I guess I work from a combination of curiosity and distance," says Tyler. "It seems to me often that I'm sort of looking from a window at something at a great distance and wondering what it is. But I'm not willing to actually go into it. I would rather sit behind the windowsill and write about it. So all my curiosity has to be answered within myself instead of by crossing the street and asking what's going on.

"I feel very strongly an urge to make a large space around myself at all times. I'm not terribly involved in a really tangled life and I have a lot of ways of saving myself—of simplifying life where it doesn't matter, so I have time for what does."

Anne Tyler calls her family her "anchors to reality." "The only reason I know anything about popular culture is because the children drag it into the house." But her reality is, in many ways, sparse. Just a few friends—who know not to call until after 3:30; bluejeans and size-10 dresses ordered out of catalogues "in four or five colors"; Saturdays are for the weekly family excursions to the library (to get stacks of classical records); one trip a year to Bethany Beach in Maryland; long brown hair that hasn't seen a beauty parlor since 1958; wide blue-gray eyes without makeup; evenings without television.

"The only real physical effect that writing a novel has on the household," says Tyler, "is that I get so uninterested in cooking. My family can always tell when I'm well into a novel because the meals get very crummy."

"I have no world view," says Tyler. "Reading Eudora Welty when I was growing up showed me that very small things are often really larger than the large things. I know that there are some central preoccupations that keep popping up over and over in my books. I'm very interested in day-to-day endurance. And I'm very interested in space around people. The real heroes to me in my books are first the ones who manage to endure and second the ones who somehow are able to grant other people the privacy of the space around them and yet still produce some warmth.

"I am not driven to write. I am driven to get things written down before I forget them. My work goes in two parts. The first part is the story, with my characters talking and surprising. But I still don't know what it's about, or what it means. The second part comes when I read it back, and suddenly it seems as if someone else is telling me the story and I say 'now I see' and then I go all the way back and drop references to what it means. I keep telling my husband to burn any manuscript if I die before I get to part two. It isn't mine until I see what my subconscious is up to. The story of 'Earthly Possessions' was written before I realized what the pattern was—that a relationship as bizarre as a bank robber and hostage could become a bickering familiar relationship. Anything done gradually enough becomes ordinary."

Living in a large cubbyhole house on a beautiful old street she refuses to leave, Anne Tyler never expects, and says she doesn't want, to be a huge commercial success. Last year, her best year, she made $35,000. She doesn't want the "intrusion" of fame—"although I would very much like to think that somebody's out there reading my books."

"Populating the town is what's most important," says Tyler, "but it does matter to me that I be considered a serious writer. Not necessarily important, but serious. A serious book is one that removes me to another life as I am reading it. It has to have layers and layers and layers, like life does. It has to be an extremely believable lie."

"Because I Want More Than One Life"

A̶nne Tyler is a 34-year-old novelist who lives in Baltimore with her husband and two daughters, aged 8 and 10. She has written six novels—a seventh, "Earthly Possessions," is due out from Knopf in the spring. Though none has sold well, they have prompted a one-word defense—'Literature'—from loyal followers. Ward Just, who discovered her work with a review of last winter's "Searching for Caleb," concluded that "it is not possible for me adequately to convey the magic of this book."

This is her account of the circumstances from which the magic springs.

By Anne Tyler

Mostly it's lies, writing novels. You set out to tell an untrue story and you try to make it believable, even to yourself. Which calls for details; any good lie does. I'm quicker to believe I was once a circus aerialist if I remember that just before every performance, I used to dip my hands in a box of chalk powder that smelled like clean, dry cloth being torn.

Maybe, in fact, I once was a circus aerialist.

One lie leads to another; the tangled web you weave gives birth to events on its own. But that's if things are going well. I can tell they're going well when the words start running ahead of themselves. If I set aside my work for a cup of coffee, the characters continue talking in my mind. Or I keep hearing my own rather sexless, neutral, narrator's voice spinning away at the story.

What comes, comes once; I have to either resign myself to losing it or forego [*sic*] my cup of coffee. I choose in favor of the coffee more often than I used to, though. It's begun to dawn on me that ideas are infinite in number, and more will always show up. I used to be afraid we had a limited lifetime supply.

But I'm talking about the easy part: the middle, when I know where I'm headed. The hard part is the beginning. I have to begin all over every day. I get up at 6 or 6:30 to clean the house, and feed the children, and cook our supper ahead of time, so that I can be perfectly free the instant the children leave for school; but then when they're gone I find I'd rather do almost anything than go into my study. The door is so tall and dark; it looms. The whole room smells like a carpenter's shop because of the wooden bookcases. Ordinarily it's a pleasant smell, but mornings, it makes me feel sick. I have to walk in as if by accident, with my mind on something else. Otherwise I'd never make it.

I write sitting cross-legged on a very hard couch. I use a retractable ballpoint pen, for which I keep a constant store of two dozen refills (fine-tipped, black) in case the Parker Company suddenly goes out of business and leaves me helpless. These are the little rituals that make novelists look neurotic. I don't type because then I wouldn't hear my characters' voices; and besides, I often have the feeling that everything flows direct from my right hand. (What if I got arthritis? It's my second greatest fear. Next to going blind, because it matters very much how the words look on the page.)

Also, there is only one room I can work in—a stern white cubicle. Most of the pictures on its walls (I realized one day) have to do with isolation: uninhabited houses, deserted courtrooms, stark old men staring into space. I hate to travel away from here. I hate even to rearrange the furniture, or start writing at an unaccustomed time. All these magic spells to get me going. And still, I spend the first half hour of every morning just clicking the point of my pen in and out.

What's the purpose of this? I think then. And it occurs to me that I'm really doing no more now than I did at age 3—telling myself stories in order to get to sleep at night. Except that now I tell stories in the daytime as well; they've taken over my life.

It's probably very unhealthy.

But then my thoughts will snag on something—some passer-by I remember from years ago, or some intricate family situation I've often idly wondered about. I haven't, since my teens, used an actual living person in any of my writing, but a number of characters have been born out of thoughts I've had while watching an actual person. (What would it be like to be that woman? To be the daughter of that man? And then what would happen if . . . ?)

I write because I want more than one life; I insist on a wider selection. It's greed, plain and simple. When my characters join the circus, I'm joining the circus. Although I am happily married, I spend a great deal of time mentally living with incompatible husbands.

Once your mind is caught on the right snag, there's nothing so hard about the mechanics of writing. (Though it's tedious walking your characters from the dining room to the living room; and don't forget you've given one a tray of pastries so she'd have a little trouble shaking hands.) What's hard is that there are times when your characters simply won't obey you. Nearly every writer I've heard of says that; not one has satisfactorily explained it. Where did those little paper people get so much power?

I'll have in mind an event for them—a departure, a wedding, a happy ending. I write steadily toward that event, but when I reach it, everything stops. I can't go on. Sentences come out stilted, dialogue doesn't sound real. Every new attempt ends up in the wastebasket. I try again from another angle, and then another, until I'm forced to admit it: The characters just won't allow this. I'll have to let the plot go their way. And when I do, everything falls into place.

No wonder I often feel, sitting alone in my study, that the room is overpopulated.

And sometimes I imagine retiring to a peaceful little town where everyone I've invented is living in houses on Main Street. There are worse retirement plans. After all, they're people I've loved, or I never would have bothered writing about them.

I work until the children come home—3:30 or 4 in the afternoon. If things are going well, I feel a little drugged by the events in my story; I'm desperate to know what happens next. When the children ring the doorbell I have trouble sorting my lives out. The children complain, regularly, that I'm not really paying attention when I let them in, and they're right. I save my afternoons for them, and feel lucky to have such indisputable, ultra-real ties to the everyday world; but still in those first few minutes I'm torn in two directions, and I often wonder what it would be like to live all alone in a shack by the sea and work 23 hours a day.

We bake cookies. Run the dog. Argue a lot. My characters grow paler and paler and finally slink away.

In the evenings, occasionally—between baths and bed and other sorts of chaos—a sudden idea will flash into my mind, a person or a plot or a snatch of dialogue. I write it down on an index card and take it to my study. The carpenter smell overwhelms me. In the dark I see those feverish pages scattered across the couch. I set the card beside them and wipe my hands on my apron. I feel I've made an offering to someone, another person entirely.

I sleep well at night, but I believe some sort of automatic pilot works then to solve problems in my plots; I go to bed trustful that they'll be taken care of by morning. And towards dawn I often wake up and notice, as if from a distance, that my mind is still churning out stories without any help from me at all.

Sometimes I think I'd rather do something else. I lean toward manual labor, mainly. I'd like to run a repair shop for toys. I'd like to start an herb farm. And it wouldn't be so bad working for one of those companies that takes on odd jobs for old ladies—driving them to their palmists, collecting their ground-rents for them. But I see I'm reverting; I'm wondering how it feels to be a palmist. A whole long kite-tail of thoughts flutters in. What would I do if I had nowhere to put my thoughts?

I wish I weren't a writer every time the writing's over. The bad part comes when you have to deal with galley proofs, publicity, biographical sketches. I am protected (I am positively cushioned) by a very understanding agent, but still I'm forced to see what I've overlooked until now; these daydreams I've been weaving are no longer my private property.

Good Lord, other people are going to read them.

It's hard enough just having to end the book. To send all my characters alone to New York City. (I picture my favorite hero, a shy, pudgy man, waiting hopefully by the railroad tracks with his clumsy little suitcase.) For weeks before I finish a novel I swear I'm going to celebrate the minute I've mailed it off—throw a party, take to strong drink. But when I come back from the post office the house seems so quiet, and I can't believe how white and bleak my study is.

You lose some things, too. You start off with one book in January and end up with another in December; nothing ever turns out the way you imagined it would. You lose stories that trail away and die just after the second paragraph, and others that look wonderful on Friday afternoon and terrible on Monday morning. And gradually, you lose the feeling that you might someday be another Tolstoy. I am 34 years old now and see that I have a ceiling; there are limits to what I should attempt. At 22, I didn't know that yet.

You lose friends who can't understand why you never seem to recognize them in the supermarket. (Supermarkets are good places for letting your mind wander.) And other friends who call during work hours and feel you're not holding up your end of the conversation. And still others who say, "Since you're just sitting home all day, could you please watch my children from 8 till 4?"

It seems to be a job where the actual doing matters more than the results. Certainly the results are pretty puny: one narrow book, after all that time, and on the very first page I find something I'd like to cross out. It's so distant now, the whole business; I'm already working on something else. But I suspect that the something else is often a form of protection. Caught up in a brand new story, I'm able to feel more detached about both good and bad reviews. In fact, I tend to read reviews as if they refer to a whole different person. Or sometimes, I read them to see if they can tell me what I was writing about. But I've never seen a review that answered that, and I admit it's expecting too much.

It would be nice to be rich; but anyhow, money makes me anxious. And I used to think I'd like to be famous but that was based on a misapprehension: I pictured fame as my entering other people's lives, not their entering mine. Besides, I've never been able to autograph a book without feeling like an imposter.

Because sometimes people send letters saying they sat up all night with my book and forgot to feed their cats. (These letters are rare; I don't mean to imply that they arrive every day, or even every year.) Then I see that they in their solitude, and I in mine, have somehow managed to touch without either of us feeling intruded upon. We've spent some time on neutral territory, sharing a life that belongs to neither of us.

That I do care about.

I have only been able to write this by pretending it's untrue. I pretend I'm a woman who writes books; I lead a happy, peaceful existence, inhabiting the same dense web of stories that surrounded me when I was 3. Sometimes I even get paid for it. Which seems stranger than a lot of other things I've invented.

I'm still waiting to see what I'll be when I grow up.*

*In an interview with me conducted by mail in August 1989, Anne Tyler reevaluated several of the points she had made in this 1976 essay. "I still feel very strongly that I have to write my novels in longhand," she reports, although she has made one high-tech concession: she then types the manuscript on her word processor. Rewrites, however, continue to be done in longhand.

Tyler's daily schedule has been modified slightly now that her two children have reached adulthood: "I adhere to a fairly firm writing schedule even now that my daughters are grown, just so my day will have some shape to it; but I'm slightly less rigid now, since I have more hours at my disposal."

Finally, she seems to have grown much more sensitive to reviews of her novels: "I don't read reviews at all. (I don't want to know how often I've missed connecting)"—Ed.

A Writer—During School Hours

Bruce Cook

Down in a high school classroom in Raleigh, North Carolina, there is a desk that usually sits unoccupied. The English teacher who holds forth there, one Mrs. Peacock, will point to it and tell her students that it is the desk at which Reynolds Price and Anne Tyler sat in an interval of a decade, and that only a student who shows a little of the same talent and potential may sit there now. The person who told me that was very proud because after a couple of years of trying, she had made it. She is still trying to live up to the awful obligation that the desk placed upon her.

Anne Tyler herself has always labored under a similar sense of obligation. Leaving high school and starting at Duke University, she became a student of Reynolds Price, who was even then—in his late 20's—one of the South's most promising novelists. Writing was what she would do, she decided then—and writing is what she has done.

And now, with the publication of her eighth novel, "Morgan's Passing," she is well established, having achieved a solid *literary* reputation—all too rare these days—that is based solely on the quality of her books and not on some spectacular movie or television mini-series based on one of them.

It is not a reputation that came easily. She received mostly good reviews right from the publication of her first novel, "If Morning Ever Comes," in the early '60's, but the notices were often relegated to the back pages of the book-review journals. It was not until novelist Gail Godwin enthusiastically called readers' attention to her fourth novel, "Celestial Navigation," in the New York Times, and John Updike did the same for her fifth, "Searching for Caleb," in The New Yorker that Anne Tyler became a Literary Figure. Now her books are reviewed in the *front* of the literary journals—and that means she is somebody to reckon with. No longer one of America's best unknown writers, she is now recognized as one of America's best writers. Period.

Now she feels a little more sure of herself. "Maybe 'Morgan' will be the first book where I don't read the reviews," she says. "I always say I won't, but I wind up reading them anyway. But I do feel good about this one."

We are talking in her home, a big old house on a tree-shaded side street off North Charles Street here in Baltimore, near the Loyola University cam-

From *Detroit News,* 6 April 1980, sec. E, 1, 3. Reprinted with permission of *The Detroit News,* a Gannett newspaper, copyright © 1980.

pus. She is a wife and the mother of two school-age daughters. She never goes to New York. ("The last time I did I had to come home because of morning sickness—and that child is 14 now.") She has only one "literary" friend, a woman who writes children's books: "She's sympathetic, but mostly we just talk about what's on sale at the supermarket." What she does is write.

How does she manage it? "My day is exceedingly partitioned," she says. "In the morning before the kids go off to school I don't think about writing at all. But the minute the door closes behind them I don't think about anything *but* writing. And then my day ends at three when they come home. Of course there's a certain leakage from one life into the other—when one of the children is sick or when we have house guests. But this partitioning is working better than it did five years ago.

"I guess this is the life that's best for me as a writer. I don't miss being in New York or at a university, seeing a lot of other writers and that sort of thing. I'm superstitious. I don't talk about writing. I don't show anything I'm working on until I'm finished with it. I feel so vulnerable about my work."

She writes a book through from beginning to end—never sending chapters off, as many writers do, to attract the interest of a publisher early, get a contract signed, and draw an advance. ("Do they really do that?" she asks in all innocence.) And it doesn't take much to discourage her. Once she wrote a novel through to the end and sent it off to her agent only to find him somewhat unenthusiastic about it—but of course, he assured her, he would send it on to her editor at Knopf. Rather than that, she simply scuttled the project right then and there—withdrew the manuscript and never gave another thought to it.

Thank goodness she didn't do that with "Morgan's Passing." If she had, we would all have been deprived of one of the finest, funniest, most delightful characters to pop up in American writing in an age. Morgan is at once superbly human and larger than life, the kind of man who finds real life so restricting that he is continually creating other lives and other identities for himself.

He's no Walter Mitty. True enough, he fantasizes a good deal, as all of us do, but Morgan acts out his fantasies, presenting himself in a variety of roles to whatever audience he can con. One day a call goes out at a puppet show—"Is there a doctor in the house?"—and Morgan steps forward confidently, prepared to do no more than drive Emily the pregnant puppeteer and her husband, Leon, off to the hospital for the delivery of their baby. But Morgan winds up delivering the baby himself—challenged, he has met the test.

That is just the beginning of his participation in the lives of Emily and Leon. His own life doesn't interest him much anymore, now that his daughters are growing up. While in the beginning he restrains himself to merely observing the young couple and the daughter he helped birth, soon he plays a more active—some might say disastrously active—role with them.

Is he just a man going through a mid-life crisis? "I think Morgan's whole life is a crisis," says Anne Tyler. "That's not Morgan chasing after young girls. That's him being a lot of different people. My big worry in doing the book was that people would be morally offended by him. He's not a full-fledged con man, though. He's not out to do harm. He's sort of amoral—but basically a kind man."

How in the world did she dream him up? "Well, I've always had a great interest in imposters, and we have one here in Baltimore. At various times he's impersonated a police chaplain and a doctor. He's even gotten on local TV talk shows in different roles. Informants will call and say, 'He's not who he says he is!' Right now I understand he's running a clinic in Mexico. He's got some elaborate machine to recharge the heart or something.

"But I really think my interest in imposters has to do with my being a writer. We go in and out of other lives all the time. But what if an imposter got into another life and couldn't get out again? The writing of 'Morgan' was fun. He became very real to me."

One last point—one that doesn't fit in neatly with anything we have talked about up to now. Anne Tyler's full name is Anne Tyler Modarressi and she is the wife of an Iranian child psychiatrist at Johns Hopkins. I have often wondered how she and her family have survived the last months as relations between the United States and Iran have become increasingly strained.

She is quite willing to discuss it. "Well, it's been very uncomfortable for us, of course. But it's been hardest on the girls, our daughters. The first time I thought about it was when our 12-year-old came home and said she'd heard kids whispering behind her at school. 'Pass it on. There's a rumor Mitra Modarressi is Iranian.' So she turned around and said, 'That's the truth!' And then she came home to us, confused, saying, 'Yes, I am Iranian—but no, I'm not. I'm American.' The girls' close friends don't think about it at all.

"As for myself, I just feel angry about the hostage business. My husband doesn't feel *that* angry about it all. He's seen so many of his friends tortured and killed by the Shah's people. It's the first time I've really noticed that we're not from the same country."

And maybe a book will come out of that someday, too.

An Interview with Anne Tyler

WENDY LAMB

Anne Tyler is the author of seven novels and numerous short stories. Her first novel, *If Morning Ever Comes,* was published in 1964; her most recent books are *Earthly Possessions* (1977), *Searching for Caleb* (1976), *Celestial Navigation* (1974), and *The Clock Winder* (1972). In 1977 she received the Award for Literature of the American Academy Institute of Arts and Letters.

Anne Tyler was born in Minneapolis, but grew up in Raleigh, North Carolina, and considers herself a southerner. She graduated from Duke University at 19, where she twice won the Anne Flexner Award for creative writing, and was elected to Phi Beta Kappa. She has done graduate work in Russian Studies. She and her husband, Taghi Mohammad Modarressi, a child psychiatrist, live in Baltimore with their two daughters.

The following interview took place in a car en route to the Cedar Rapids airport, concluding Ms. Tyler's 18 hours in Iowa City, during which she gave a reading, attended a party, held a special workshop for fiction students, and discussed *Earthly Possessions* with an undergraduate seminar.

The night before, she had read the fourth chapter of a novel about a middle-aged man with a large family, Morgan, who "gets into his clothes every morning as if they are costumes, and who has a terrible tendency to step into other people's lives—which you might also say, in a way, about writers. This Morgan and I have been wrestling together for so long that I'm not sure the novel is ever going to see the light of day."

Morgan, a man who "must get out of his life sometimes," reflects a theme common to much of Ms. Tyler's work. *Earthly Possessions* is the story of Charlotte, a woman in her thirties who decides—not for the first time—to leave her husband, her family, the house where she grew up. She goes to the bank to withdraw money for the trip and is taken hostage by a bank robber who forces her to accompany him on his flight south. In *The Clock Winder,* Elizabeth Abbott takes some time off from school, accepts a job as a handyman with an eccentric family, and finds their dependence on her not only overwhelming but tragic. Though she leaves, she finds she cannot escape the relentless affections and energies of the Emerson family. Jeremy Pauling, the central character of *Celestial Navigation,* is a sculptor of "simple humanity," though he himself

Reprinted from *Iowa Journal of Literary Studies* 3 (1981), 59–64, by permission of *Iowa Journal of Literary Studies.* Copyright © 1981 by The University of Iowa.

cannot bear to venture outside his Baltimore boarding house to confront "real" humanity. In *Searching for Caleb,* Justine, a fortuneteller, accompanies her 90-year-old grandfather on forays in his search for his brother Caleb, who disappeared in 1912. Justine and her grandfather Peck take well to travel, since Justine's husband, her first cousin Duncan Peck, finds a new job and home every year—seeking, in one sense, to escape the looming presence of the Peck family compound in Baltimore. In her review of *Searching for Caleb,* Edna Stumpf (*The Phildadelphia Inquirer*) defines this central concern of Ms. Tyler's books: "It's about the simultaneous lust to wander and to take root, to move and to stay. It's about trying, up till the moment of death, to discover what it was we rebelled against, what it was we adjusted to, what we loved and what we lost. Anne Tyler has made something magical out of common life, fulfilling our belief that it can be magical."

LAMB: In your article on writing in *The Washington Post* (8/15/76) you said that it "seems to be a job where the actual doing matters more than the results." Since you've just been in the midst of a writers' workshop, it seems fitting to begin by talking about the process of writing, and then, perhaps, a bit about the role of a writer. In other interviews and articles one reads, you give the impression of being an extremely confident writer; for example, you've said, "What comes, comes once," and that if you are in the middle of an idea you want to get up and have coffee, you have to choose between coffee and the idea; and that now, more and more, you find yourself choosing the coffee, because you realize that ideas are limitless, you'll always have another. Was that something you had to learn—possibly by regretting crucial "lost" thoughts along the way? How did you develop this confidence?

TYLER: I hesitate to answer that because I'm in a different state from the one I was in when I wrote all that. I'm more concerned about losing ideas—I'm not getting up for coffee as often. This new novel, Morgan's, is giving me a hell of a time. I'm not as confident now.

LAMB: How did you lose your confidence?

TYLER: After *Earthly Possessions,* I wrote a novel [*Pantaleo*—Ed.] that I ditched. A year's work, out the door.

LAMB: What made you decide to ditch it?

TYLER: Well, I sent it to my agent, who didn't like it; so I said, don't send it out. Now if I had really liked it myself, nothing would have stopped me. The problem was that it was boring. I've never gone back and read it, from a distance, though.

LAMB: But you do seem very confident about your characters.

TYLER: I'm always confident about my characters—that doesn't change. I'm not confident about plots, I always feel very fond of my characters. Before I start anything I spend about a month just thinking about them, and I end up knowing an awful lot about them, much more than I put in the book.

LAMB: You've also said that you have "an automatic pilot" that works while you sleep, solving the problems in your plot—implying that your characters, somehow, keep going without you, and that sometimes, when you have an event in mind, your characters will take over. They'll refuse to do something, and you'll have to "let the plot go their way. And when I do, everything falls into place." How? Do you sit back and "let go?" I imagine that must be painful, if you just sit there with your pen clicking in and out.

TYLER: I haven't always known how to let my characters go. But if I have something in mind and they're going to make it impossible to do it, I find it out pretty early. I've had several angry letters and calls from people who've wanted a happy ending for *Celestial Navigation*—they wanted the man and woman to stay together. All along I wanted that ending, too, and I was sure I'd be able to work out a way. I kept pushing toward it, but that writing felt wooden: my sentences were jerky when I looked back at them. In a way I felt I was trying to cover up a lie, and then I thought, I may as well tell the truth: the woman leaves the man. The problem in *Celestial Navigation* was that those characters were two absolutely separate people, and they couldn't possibly have stayed together.

LAMB: Did you ever have a character who refused to do what *you* had planned, and then wouldn't work it out on his own, either?

TYLER: No—because of all the thinking that comes before, I would have ditched such a character long before I began the book. I like every one of my characters; this is very important to me. My mother is shocked by this. She says, "How can you *like* someone like Jake (the bank robber in *Earthly Possessions*)?" But what I like is a sense of character, however spiky or difficult the person may be.

LAMB: Speaking of difficult characters, I'm curious about the way you portray ministers. Meg's husband in *Searching for Caleb,* Elizabeth's father in *The Clock Winder,* Charlotte's "Frankenstein" husband in *Earthly Possessions*— all of them seem to be portrayed as something that makes other characters shudder, as something to escape. Why is this? Is there a personal reason behind it?

TYLER: No real reason. The fact is I'm very fond of Saul, Charlotte's husband. I don't think of him as a horrible character at all. It's not that I have anything against ministers, but that I'm particularly concerned with how much right anyone has to change someone, and ministers are people who feel they have that right.

LAMB: This confidence you have in your characters would seem to contradict your remark in *The New York Times Book Review* last June—when asked to comment on your summer plans, you said you'd go off on vacation, return to your characters, and "hope they will not, after all, have crumbled away, as I always fear they will."

TYLER: I don't *really* fear for them—the fact that I'm willing to leave them means that I trust them. I know they'll be OK. But it's true that events threaten your characters. What's difficult is that any day that a child stays home sick, when I've just gotten someone where he's starting to go somewhere. You know, you'll have a rusty day, where nothing happens, and then a character will flower suddenly, and you don't want to leave him.

LAMB: Actually, from your description of your working environment in the *Post* article, "There is only one room I can work in—a stern white cubicle. I hate to travel away from here. I hate to even rearrange the furniture, or start writing at an unaccustomed time," I'm surprised that you can let yourself take vacations at all. *Can* you just quit for awhile?

TYLER: I quit for a month sometimes. Sometimes longer. After a month, of course, it takes a while before my characters come back. But there's nothing I can do about it, with children. Most of the summer revolves around getting them to camp. One summer, when I was working on Morgan, carrying him around, it just seemed there was one emergency after another, one child or the other, it was always something happening, and I could see Morgan in his broad-brimmed hat, fading away. It took me a week's work to get him back, but then he perked up. This probably sounds crazy, talking about these people I "carry around with me," as if they were real.

LAMB: Oh, no. Do you ever find new characters trying to push up while you're in the middle of a book? And that you have to say, go away, I can't do you yet?

TYLER: Oh, yes. Sometimes at the end of a book—I suppose it's a protective device, when I'm feeling panicky about having nothing more to work on—I hear a new voice saying, "Well, I was born in so-and-so," and I say, "Will you shut up? I'll get to you."

LAMB: Last night, when we were talking after the reading, you said your family thinks of you, most likely, as the author of *Searching for Caleb,* because the grandfather is your grandfather, but you think of yourself as the author of *Celestial Navigation,* because Jeremy is closer to your own personality—which describes you as a recluse.

TYLER: I'm afraid that is so. Last year, the paper reported an award, some small award, and it said, "Award given to Cynthia Somebody, poet, and Anne Tyler, recluse." I find this is more and more true. It didn't used to be that way. Before I was married, it seemed I was always on a train. I do agree with Jeremy, though—you know, in the beginning of the book he has this quote, of Emerson's I think, which says that a man could develop character by doing one thing he disliked every day of his life. Jeremy starts out thinking that this would be a good thing to try. But then he finds that even getting out of bed is difficult, for him. He's already done something he disliked before his day is even begun. But I'm outwardly more balanced than

Jeremy. I do manage to cope and get things done—though I can't imagine driving on the Beltway, as we're doing now. I can't merge. I feel that I've become increasingly closed down, self-protective. There are things I just refuse to do. I wouldn't go out and give some sort of talk. Not only because I'm nervous in public but because I feel that kind of thing is a drain. I'm very involved with my children, yet I've never been to a PTA meeting in my life. I feel, well, the PTA can get along without me.

LAMB: You do seem to be an author who survives quite well without the "literary community," conferences like Bread Loaf, teaching at workshops like Iowa. Have you ever participated in something like that?

TYLER: I feel a little scared about constant involvement with other writers—I don't like to talk about writing. It makes me nervous. There are times, though, when I'm having trouble, when nothing will go, and I'd like to have someone to call and say what a rotten time I'm having. But then, that person would be a writer, and I couldn't call her in the middle of the day because she'd be writing too. I have thought that it must be nice to go to one of those places, like Yaddo, where you have no responsibilities, they hang your lunch on the door and you don't see anyone until supper, when you have some sort of conversation. But I'm afraid that everyone would talk about what they had done that day, which would be writing. My husband is a Persian novelist, and when he talks about how it's going, it makes me very nervous. I'm afraid that it's going to evaporate; he might just fritter it away.

LAMB: When you'd like to have someone to call—would you ever call your editor?

TYLER: No.

LAMB: What role does your editor play in the process of your novel?

TYLER: As little as possible. I don't want to know about anything that goes on in New York. I feel totally out of it. People don't believe me when someone will call and say, I have this novel, where should I send it, and I tell them I don't know anything. I don't have a list of addresses.

LAMB: Would you ever consider teaching?

TYLER: I think if I had to make other money I'd do something more physical, less mental—maybe a carpenter. Just not something that took a lot out of my mind.

LAMB: How do you feel about your reviews?

TYLER: Ideally, you shouldn't read reviews, but of course you do. A bad review is bad for your writing; a good one is very bad for your writing, because you keep those opinions in mind when you work.

LAMB: In a way, your sense of your own detachment, reclusiveness, seems contradictory, because anyone who writes and publishes imposes himself on the outside world—it's an aggressive act, in some ways. Can you really ignore your audience when you write, work in a vacuum?

TYLER: I try to write everything as if no one was ever going to read it. Then at the end when I go back to polish, I see if a reader could make sense of it. But it's hard to escape the sense of someone looking over your shoulder—the self-consciousness. *Celestial Navigation* was the most difficult book to write. It took two years and it made me sick all the way through. I'd go into my study and think, I really need shoelaces. Then I'd get in the car and drive five miles to get those shoelaces. *Searching for Caleb* was the most fun. I loved writing about a huge family.

LAMB: But you know, not all those characters are lovable—Justin, the patriarch, or Caroline, Justin's mother—I didn't really like them. What is it that makes you feel this affection toward your characters? Does it spring out of some enormous tolerance? Or curiosity?

TYLER: They don't seem unpleasant to me. I think that what I most fear in people is intrusion, but it doesn't happen with those characters because on paper you control them, you guard against that intrusion. I can feel quite affectionate toward people on paper, whom I couldn't stand to be in a room with.

LAMB: I've just been reading *The Tin Can Tree*—

TYLER: Don't read that book. Stop. *The Tin Can Tree* and *If Morning Ever Comes* should be burned.

LAMB: Can I quote that?

TYLER: Please. They were formless and wandering and should never have been published.

LAMB: Why were they published?

TYLER: I really don't know. That was a lucky time for young writers—not like now. Publishers were actually soliciting work from young writers.

LAMB: You don't have any fondness for those first two books at all?

TYLER: No. I suppose they have the same problem as I saw in the book that I ditched just recently; I never analyzed whatever the faults were, except that I knew that I wanted to write something, but I didn't have anything to write with. I didn't have a pressing urge. When you finish a book, it feels like you've used up all your ideas—like cleaning out your drawers; then, slowly, it all fills up again.

LAMB: So you're saying you never feel that there's *nothing* you want to write—you always have a next something to go on to?

TYLER: Oh, once a week I feel I have nothing to write. But that's a different feeling, all clogged up, than the one you have when you've used up all your ideas on something, finished—all cleaned out.

REVIEWS

◆

If Morning Ever Comes

◆

Return to the Hawkes Family

ORVILLE PRESCOTT

You can't go home again. The title of Thomas Wolfe's novel has become part of our common speech. No one who has left his home and grown and changed elsewhere can ever go home save in a physical sense. But neither can he leave home permanently behind him. It is part of him and the need to understand it and to relive it in imagination can be imperious. That's one of the reasons why so many novels are written about childhood and youth. It was that need which drove Ben Joe Hawkes back to Sandhill, North Carolina. One chilly November day the cold winds of Morningside Heights and the boredom of his classes at Columbia Law School seemed more than Ben Joe could stand and he lit out for home. His bewildered seeking for he knew not what is the theme of a brilliant first novel, "If Morning Ever Comes," by Anne Tyler.

This is an exceedingly good novel, so mature, so gently wise and so brightly amusing that, if it weren't printed right there on the jacket, few readers would suspect that Mrs. [*sic*] Tyler was only 22. Some industrious novelists never learn how to write good fiction. Others seem to be born knowing how. Mrs. Tyler is one of these. Her touch is deft, her perceptions are keen, her ear for the rhythms and wild irrelevancies of colloquial speech is phenomenal. Her people are triumphantly alive.

Ben Joe at 25 may be suffering from a severe case of post-adolescent, emotional befuddlement; but he is a decent, likable young man. Mrs. Tyler

From *New York Times*, 11 November 1964, 41. Copyright © 1964 by The New York Times Company. Reprinted by permission.

knows him inside out. Her book is written entirely from Ben Joe's point of view, with never a false note. The occasional blurring of reality in these engaging pages is Ben Joe's fault; not Mrs. Tyler's.

"I don't understand a soul in the world," cried Ben Joe in a moment of intense frustration.

Part of his trouble might be that he was confused by having grown up surrounded by women and returning to a houseful of them didn't seem to solve anything.

The old house bustled with women. None of them needed Ben Joe to look after her, which was disappointing. There was his daft grandmother; his widowed mother; his eldest sister, who after seven years of marriage had left her husband and run away home with her baby girl; and five other sisters. Ben Joe loved them all, felt responsible for them all and was irritated by them all.

Just to make everything more complicated, others had come back to Sandhill, too. Ben Joe's first girl, whom he hadn't seen in years, was there, just as nice, sympathetic and comforting as she used to be. And grandmother's first beau, now 84, was there, come back to die in a home for the aged.

And the past kept popping up in disturbing flashbacks, particularly the memory of Ben Joe's father, an alcoholic doctor who deserted his wife and family and went to live with his young mistress in a dreary house down by the textile mill.

Too many novels about youth's age-old search for identity (it used to be called "finding yourself") are shrill, abusive and dull. Too often their young protagonists are so brutal and belligerent that they are mighty poor company to keep for several hundred pages.

"If Morning Ever Comes" is just as honest and accurate in its account of a confused young man; but it is gay and funny and touching. Ben Joe's womenfolk are a grand lot, as typically small-town Southern as can be, but each a courageous, self-reliant, stubborn, foolish human being. There are too many of them for all to be characterized in depth, but their collective personality is striking.

"If Morning Ever Comes" is a more complex novel than it seems at first. In addition to being about Ben Joe's emotional crisis, it is also about old age, love, death and family living—the unbreakable bonds of shared memories and experience and the serious matters no one ever mentions. Only a rarely talented novelist could have written this fine book.

The Tin Can Tree

◆

Closing a Family Wound

HASKEL FRANKEL

Anne Tyler was born in 1941. At twenty-two she published her first—and well-received—novel, *If Morning Ever Comes*. And now here she is again, still much too young, with *The Tin Can Tree* (Knopf, $4.95). Certainly, it is unfair to harp on the lady's age but difficult to ignore it. You read and you wonder. On page after page she offers proof of a maturity, a compassion and understanding one would expect to find only in a more seasoned heart than hers could possibly be.

The scrubby, little tin can tree of the title grows back of the three-family house shared by the Pikes in the Southern tobacco town of Larksville. The tin cans occasionally rattling in the wind are the last earthly token of six-year-old Janie Rose Pike's existence. Janie Rose, who decorated the tree with them during her "religious period," was killed in a tractor accident. Opening with the child's funeral, Anne Tyler's novel focuses, during the days immediately thereafter, on her family and their closest friends and especially on ten-year-old Simon Pike, Janie Rose's brother. This is a novel rich in incident that details the closing of a family wound and the resumption of life among people stunned by the proof of mortality. As one of the characters puts it: "Bravest thing about people, Miss Joan, is how they go on loving mortal beings after finding out there's such a thing as dying."

Not only because she is describing a family death and in part a child's

From *Saturday Review*, 20 November 1965, 50. Reprinted by permission of Omni Publications International, Ltd.

reaction to it, but also because of her ability to evoke the feel of summer in a small Southern town, does Anne Tyler's *The Tin Can Tree* call to mind James Agee's memorable *A Death in the Family.* She is too fine a stylist, too sure a craftsman to have her novel weighed against Mr. Agee's. However, the Agee novel does offer a clue to why one only respects *The Tin Can Tree* without being deeply moved by it. Mr. Agee gave us time to meet the father before death was allowed to remove him so that we could grieve for him with his family. Miss Tyler introduces us to the Pikes after Janie Rose's passing. We have never known her alive so cannot mourn her dead. We can observe and sympathize but we are still outsiders during the period of adjustment. As a result, what lingers longest in the mind when the last page of *The Tin Can Tree* has been turned is the savor of an author's talent rather than a novel's content.

A Slipping-Down Life

◆

[From "Art and Artificiality in Some Recent Fiction"]

ARTHUR EDELSTEIN

Located at the other end of existence, Anne Tyler's *A Slipping-Down Life* is rooted in adolescence. Homely, touching, stylistically conservative, its one eccentricity belongs to its heroine, motherless Evie Decker of Pulqua, North Carolina, "a plump drab girl in a brown sweater," who one day cuts into her forehead the last name of Bertram "Drumstrings" Casey, a local rock singer of dubious ability. That deed precipitates the main action of the novel, in which Evie, a testimonial in scar tissue, becomes a publicity feature at Casey's performances, ultimately marries him (after the most touchingly phlegmatic courtship in literature), loses her father to a heart attack, gets pregnant, and finally, swallowing her fear of loneliness, delivers Casey an ultimatum: either they abandon their marginal existence and move into her father's house or she will do so alone. In the end, that is, she has weathered the crucial season of adolescence, having discovered an identity within the loneliness of her skin to replace the one engraved upon its surface—has slipped down into life. And because the transformation is made with such authentic hesitation, awkwardness, doubt—is in keeping, that is, with the circumstances of her ungainly life—we believe in it and are moved by it.

Though this novel sounds the tone of a life, its resonance derives from the observation of a *way* of life, a way that is tacked upon teenage bulletin

Reprinted from *Southern Review* NS 9 (July 1973): 742–43, by permission of the author.

boards, sewn to dresses "decorated with poodles on loops of real chain," enclosed in high-school notebooks containing *Silver Screen* magazine. All of this gathers toward personification in the guitar-obsessed Casey, whose personality hovers at that point of fusion where cool- and dull-wittedness are one. And it finds oblique expression in his vaguely evangelical "speaking out," the platform mannerism that is his trademark:

> "My girl is at a hymn-sing.
> "What happened to double ferris wheels?"

And at the other end of the electric amplifiers, beneath the insect-laden lights, a congregation of finger-snapping listeners projects upon the spangled and shiny rock groups a glamor of their own imagining. That is the hope that simmers beneath the festive surface, to transcend the ordinariness into which they must sink—as Evie sinks, her scarred flesh the emblem of her scarred hope.

The Clock Winder

◆

[Review of *The Clock Winder*]

MARTIN LEVIN

Mrs. Emerson is an abstracted Baltimore dowager, rattling around in a Victorian mansion filled with eight-day clocks and deserted by her grownup children. Some of these filter back from time to time, stirring up tangential flurries of activity. All are as indeterminate as the mother, "secure in her sealed, weightless bubble floating through time," but not as indestructible. Timothy, a medical student, has self-destructive learnings. Matthew whiles away his days as assistant to an alcoholic country newspaper editor. Peter, a brilliant student, expends his promise teaching chemistry in a second-rate girls' school.

Miss Tyler fills her pages with other richly-idiosyncratic characters who amble about in Chekhovian fashion. To a degree, the center of attention is Elizabeth Abbott, a girl wanderer who becomes the Emersons' resident handyman and trouble-shooter. With or without her, the novel pursues a serpentine way, and any bend in the road might just as well be marked finis. Gentle charm is the author's stock in trade. Her characters have so much of it one wishes their story had more substance.

From *New York Times Book Review*, 21 May 1972, 31. Copyright © 1972 by The New York Times Company. Reprinted by permission.

[Review of *The Clock Winder*]

Sara Blackburn

Anne Tyler's successful first novel, *If Morning Ever Comes,* was written when she was 22; this one, eight years later, is her fourth, and it seems to me to have many of the virtues that we associate with "southern" writing—an easy, almost confidential directness, fine skill at quick characterization, a sure eye for atmosphere, and a special nostalgic humor—and none of its liabilities— sentimentality, a sometimes cloying innocence wise beyond its pretense, a tendency toward over-rich metaphor. The title character is 20-year-old Elizabeth, a strong figure who is both oddly timeless and perfectly contemporary; she arrives vaguely from Ellington, North Carolina, to manage and eventually become a loving part of the lives of an eccentric but not very unusual Baltimore family who have enormous and even agonizing trouble relating to one another.

The novel charts Elizabeth's arrival, and her early days as handywoman with the Emersons, their change under her influence, her return home to North Carolina after a terrible Emerson family tragedy for which she holds herself responsible, her almost-marriage, and how, much later, she's able to get it all together with the Emersons in the end. If the result smacks of a group of hurt and inept people propping one another up to live a bearable, cozy life—another quality, come to think of it, of "southern" writing—it's neither sentimental nor intrusive enough to detract from the strength of its delightful heroine: Elizabeth, in her ashamed passivity, her struggle against it, her bursts of energy and what prevents them, her wry, open humor, is a recognizable and even memorable character who encompasses many of the contradictions that women are seeking to resolve today. And the author has created a group of minor characters to surround her who ring absolutely true. Anne Tyler has a special talent; she is a solid writer with real skill, but modest about her reach.

From *Washington Post Book World,* 14 May 1972, 13. © *Washington Post;* reprinted by permission.

Celestial Navigation

♦

In the Abstract

SUSANNAH CLAPP

Jeremy is an artist. His creative urge finds expression in the construction of collages: a form which Anne Tyler seems to find sympathetic, since her book is made up, collage-like, of different though not incompatible views of life and Jeremy. From his sister we learn that Jeremy is a not immediately attractive recluse. "People have asked me," she says, "if he is an albino." His common-law wife, Mary, describes how she was at first bemused and vaguely repelled by Jeremy's shy abstraction, but later grew to love him. And Miss Vinton, a worthy spinster, explains that he is "a genius. Not some run-of-the-mill insurance salesman."

These views are not accorded equal weight. Since sister Amanda is seen to place a high value on sensibleness and dignity, and exhibits blanket disgust of "coloureds," beatniks, clutter and cosseting, her opinion of Jeremy's merits is presumably to be despised. And Mary, who produces five children before leaving Jeremy because he has forgotten their wedding day, is rather too good at breast-feeding and battling with germs to take full account of what Jeremy's abstraction might mean. It is Miss Vinton, who comes closest to being an alert and fully functioning person, who echoes the tone of those passages which retail Jeremy's activities in a supposedly detached third person. These lay stress on the quality of Jeremy's sensibility, remarking on the presence in him both of "shimmering joy" and "nameless fears"—where

Reprinted from the (London) *Times Literary Supplement*, 23 May 1975, 577, by permission of the *Times Literary Supplement;* © Times Newspapers Ltd., 1975.

others are merely content or worried. But, though convincing in its sketch of shyness and agoraphobia—and in its ending, which shows loneliness to be as important a part of Jeremy's make-up as creativity—the tendency of the novel is to suggest that an inability to manage the practical and human side of life indicates other, rarer qualities. "Sad people," Mary says, "are the only real ones," but *Celestial Navigation* does not prove her point.

[Review of *Celestial Navigation*]

GAIL GODWIN

Anne Tyler is especially gifted in the art of freeing her characters and then keeping track of them as they move in their unique and often solitary orbits. Her fiction is filled with displaced persons who persist stubbornly in their own destinies. They are "oddballs," visionaries, lonely souls, but she has a way of transcribing their peculiarities with such loving wholeness that when we examine them we keep finding more and more pieces of ourselves.

The hero of her fifth novel is a real artist with real artist's problems. Jeremy Pauling, a 38-year-old bachelor who lives with various boarders in a shabby Baltimore house left to him by his mother, makes sculptures of what his dealer calls "simple humanity." But he is so overcome by the complexity and untidiness and depressing aspects of this same humanity that he suffers nausea and vertigo whenever he ventures as far as the corner grocery store. ("The old ladies were rude and sniveling, the men lacked solidity somehow, and the children seemed to carry a threat of violence.")

He is awed when his dealer, Brian, tells of his plans to sail his new boat by celestial navigation, though, as Miss Vinton, a boarder, observes to herself: "Oh Jeremy . . . you too sail by celestial navigation and it is far more celestial than Brian's." Jeremy makes his sculptures the way other men make maps, "setting down the few fixed points that he knows, hoping they will guide him as he goes floating through this unfamiliar planet."

"Humanity" at last overwhelms Jeremy in the form of a mysterious young woman who comes to live, with her child, in his boarding house. Mary Tell is an unlikely blend of Earth Mother and Maverick. She has a voracious need to give birth to as many children as possible. She also wishes she could climb inside every passing person, learn everything about their lives, "see how and who their friends were, what they fought about." She and Jeremy have five children, though Jeremy can never quite believe he had a part in it.

He is baffled and a little frightened by these fearless creatures who shout and cheer and throw oranges and—unlike himself—brave the teeming streets. Like a man who foresees what is inevitable to himself, he commits them to memory, "preparing for some moment in the future when he could sit down alone and finally figure them out." When this sad moment does come, it is a tribute to the author's gentle genius in preserving the integrity of her people that we do not hate Mary Tell. And she succeeds in convincing us that Jeremy Pauling's first and final act of heroism—taking a bus across Baltimore to visit Mary and his children—is more valiant and terrifying for him than blasting off to Venus would be for an astronaut.

[From "Five Easy Pieces:
One Work of Art"]

ALAN PRYCE-JONES

Of these five novels, only Anne Tyler's need be considered as a work of literature. The others have their merits, but they are, after their fashion, transparent. They admit simple reactions, such as laughter, suspense, nostalgia. But *Celestial Navigation* refracts life through a personal lens.

Through five lenses, in fact, picked up in turn by the guiding hand of Tyler. There is Amanda, sister of Jeremy Paulding [*sic*]. There are Mary Tell and Olivia and old Miss Vinton. There is Jeremy Paulding [*sic*] himself, aged 38, a loner and an artist. Their story covers 13 years, and they tell it in relays.

Amanda begins. Her mother, who had run a seedy but respectable rooming house in Baltimore, has just died, and she arrives for the funeral. Jeremy clearly cannot cope. He cannot cope with anything except his extremely private gift. One by one we perceive the boarders, but all the time the real focus is on Jeremy—a concentration the more difficult because he is a man who "sees life in a series of flashes," handed to him, in Tyler's phrase, like photographs and at unexpected moments. He dares not leave the house. He is numbed by living at all, and yet we are to suppose that his gift is a real one.

Suddenly there arrives Mary Tell, in flight from her husband, deserted by her lover, anchored by a small daughter. It is the problem of Mary Tell that she has no staying power. At a whiff of danger she bolts. Jeremy and she have at least that in common: neither fits easily into a living world. And so they come together, an implausible but touching pair.

Yet when at the crucial moment, Jeremy, by sheer inadvertence, does not marry her—the act, simply because it involves action, is too hard for him—she bolts once more, though by now they have been together the better part of 10 years and Mary has children by him. Olivia, aged 18, tries to take her place, but only old Miss Vinton understands that his single link with reality is his art. The Baltimore house, and all it touches, becomes more and more opaque, as if hidden from the surrounding city by a scrim. The story of Jeremy ends neither with a bang nor a whimper. It sighs away into silence.

From *Washington Post Book World*, 24 March 1974, 2. © *Washington Post*; reprinted by permission.

The device of turning from person to person excludes Jeremy himself. The others speak in the first person singular: Jeremy remains "he." Throughout, Tyler's observation is exact and as detailed as a *trompe l'oeil* sketch. But in her fastidiousness, she stays too oblique. Who in her celestial navigation is sailing, and whither? Are we to think the stars always contrary? She must have designed a chart of some kind, but as soon as I tried to use it, I found myself off course, though I shall not forget the elegance of the script nor the collisions by the way.

Searching for Caleb

◆

Family Ways

JOHN UPDIKE

Out of her fascination with families—with brotherly men and auntly women, with weak sisters and mama's boys, with stay-at-homes and runaways—Anne Tyler has fashioned, in *Searching for Caleb,* a dandy novel, funny and lyric and true-seeming, exquisite in its details and ambitious in its design. She here construes the family as a vessel of Time. The Pecks, who live (as her families tend to) in Baltimore, are known for longevity. Great-Grandma Laura, the second wife of the clan's founder, Justin Montague Peck, lived to be ninety-seven, and at the age of ninety-three Daniel Peck, Justin's first son, is lively enough to be riding trains and buses in search of his half-brother, Caleb, who disappeared from Baltimore back in 1912. It is 1973, and Daniel is living with two of his grandchildren, Justine and Duncan, who, though first cousins, have married. The minister who officiated at the wedding remembers "the bride's and groom's joint family" occupying the front pews: "There was something dreamlike in the fact that almost everyone in the front section had the same fair, rather expressionless face—over and over again, exactly the same face, distinguished only a little by age or sex." The intensely blue Peck eyes—"those clear, level eyes that tended to squint a little as if dazzled by their own blueness"—run through the layers of this saga like a trickle of icy-pure spring water; the motif is distilled in the marriage of Justine and Duncan, "their blue eyes opening simultaneously to stare at each other across the pillow." In Miss Tyler's vision, heredity looms as destiny, and with the force of a miracle people persist in being themselves:

> But Duncan, who had changed her whole life and taken her past away from her, slept on as cool as ever, and on the crown of his head was the same little sprig of a cowlick he had had when he was four.

The family's conservatism and longevity defy time while embodying it; a nonagenarian father sits next to his elderly son on a couch, and "they might have been brothers. . . . In the end, the quarter-century that divided their generations amounted to nothing and was swept away. . . . Everything was leveled, there were no extremes of joy or sorrow any more but only habit, routine, ancient family names and rites and customs, slow careful old people moving cautiously around furniture that had sat in the same positions for fifty years."

Yet not all the Pecks hold fast to the household established by the first Justin in northern Baltimore after the Great Fire of 1904. Caleb, his second son, whose "tilted brown eyes must have snuck in from the Baum side of the family," literally gives his father apoplexy with his love of music—the old man's left side is paralyzed by the young man's defiance, and his mother tells Caleb, in one of this book's many astounding sentences, "You have killed your half of your father." Caleb repentantly works for a decade in the family shipping business, then vanishes, leaving the fortune and the dynasty to his brother, Daniel. There are other runaways. Daniel's wife, Margaret Rose, bears him six children, one a year, and in the seventh year leaves him and flees to her parents in Washington. The six children do what is expected of them, as the family business becomes law instead of trade, but of *their* children (and there are oddly few) Duncan, the oldest's son, runs away at the age of eighteen, and a little later Justine, the youngest's daughter, defies her parents and marries him, joining him in a life of job-to-job vagabondage in the small towns of Maryland and Virginia. Their daughter, Meg, defies them in turn and also marries to escape. And even old Daniel, the patriarch of Peckishness, allows himself in retirement to drift away in search of Caleb, and takes up residence with the shabby, fortune-telling, forty-year-old Justine, the one other member of the family willing to spend time "chasing rainbows on the Greyhound bus line."

Searching for Caleb is, among other things, a detective novel, with an eccentric detective, Eli Everjohn (he looks like Abraham Lincoln, "even to the narrow border of beard along his jawline"), and an ingenious unravelling; readers should be permitted unhampered enjoyment of the plot's well-spaced turns. Suffice it to say that, with the quest for Caleb as her searchlight, Miss Tyler warmly illumines the American past in its domestic aspect. Old Justine's turn-of-the-century illness evokes this:

Therefore he undertook his own cure. He had all the panes in his windows replaced with amethyst glass, which was believed to promote healing. He drank his water from a quassia cup and ordered Laura to send away for various nostrums advertised in the newspaper—celery tonic, pectoral soup, a revitalizing electric battery worn on a chain around the neck. His only meat was squirrel, easiest on the digestive tract.

Miss Tyler, who was twenty-three when her first novel was published and is now only in her mid-thirties, seems omniscient about the details of old Baltimore. When Laura finally dies, Daniel reflects that she was the one person who with him could remember "the rough warm Belgian blocks that used to pave the streets downtown." We are told that the 1908 Ford had "a left-hand steering wheel and splashless flower vases," and that in the 1900s women wore Pompeiian Bloom rouge, and little Caleb leaned out a window to hear an Irish tenor sing "Just a Lock of Hair for Mother." Such tender erudition never feels forced. Contemplation of the vanished induces in Miss Tyler a totally non-academic ecstasy:

> Whenever you heard distant music somewhere in the town, maybe so faint you thought you imagined it, so thin you blamed the whistling of the streetcar wires, then you would track the sound down and find Caleb straddling his little velocipede, speechless with joy, his appleseed eyes dancing.

The whistling of the streetcar wires is another motif that recurs, and the search for Caleb feels to become a search for the lyrical, mystical, irrational underside of American practicality. Duncan spouts facts but he rarely applies them, and Justine is, matter-of-factly, a fortune-teller. Her fortune-telling, along with Caleb's invisible presence, keeps this scrupulously exact novel of furniture and manners spooky and suspenseful. The career of fortune-telling—the methods and habitats of its practitioners—occasions another fine display of curious information, and of Miss Tyler's subtle psychologizing. Madame Olita, offspring of a gypsy and a high-school civics teacher, instructs Justine:

> ". . . you must think of these cards as tags. . . . Tags with strings attached, like those surprise boxes at parties. The strings lead into your mind. These cards will pull out what you already know, but have failed to admit or recognize."

So, too, Miss Tyler's details pull from our minds recognition of our lives. These Pecks, polite and snide and tame and maddening and resonant, are *our* aunts and uncles; Justine and Duncan's honeymoon, when they are "isolated, motionless, barely breathing, cut loose from everyone else," is everybody's escape from a suffocating plurality of kin into a primitive twoness; the America they truck their fraying marriage through is our land, observed with a tolerance and precision unexcelled among contemporary writers. Paragraph after paragraph, details kindle together, making heat and light. For, along with the power to see and guess and know, Anne Tyler has the rare gift of coherence—of tipping observations in a direction, and of keeping track of what she has set down. Reading letters from Baltimore as a newlywed, Justine notes that "each envelope let out a little gust of Ivory soap, the smell of home." A generation later, when her daughter, Meg—who in rebellion against her mother's rebellion has become a super-Peck, prim and conventional—leaves home, Justine in the girl's abandoned room takes "a deep breath of Meg's clean smell: Ivory soap and fresh-ironed fabric." Dozens of such strands of continuity glint amid the cross-woven threads of this rich novel of nostalgia and divination, genes and keepsakes, recurrences and reunions.

Miss Tyler does not always avoid the pawky. Her ease of invention sometimes leads her to overdo. The secret of Caleb's departure, she would have us believe, was harbored for sixty years by a family servant whom no one ever thought to ask and who therefore, with the heroic stubbornness of a Faulkner character, declined to tell. Such moonbeams of Southern Gothic, without a sustained sense of regional delirium, shine a bit stagily. In a note following the text, the author's biography sounds cosmopolitan (born in Minneapolis, married to an Iranian psychiatrist, herself once a graduate student of Russian), but she says she "considers herself a Southerner"; and she does apparently accept the belief, extinct save in the South, that families are absolutely, intrinsically interesting. Are they? Her Pecks contain not only their milieu's history but every emotion from a mother's need "to be the feeder" to an old man's perception that "once you're alive, there's no way out but dying." Does Miss Tyler share Daniel Peck's preference when he says, "I would prefer to find that heaven was a small town with a bandstand in the park and a great many trees, and I would know everybody in it and none of them would ever die or move away or age or alter"? No other kind of goodness is suggested in this book, except Justine's hopeful forward motion. Miss Tyler gives us a border South busy commercializing its own legends, a New South where the traditional slave-boy iron hitching post has had its face (but not its hands) painted white and where faith healers live in hideously slick decors of sculptured carpets and glass knicknacks. The America she sees is today's, but, like the artist-hero of her previous novel, *Celestial Navigation,* she seems to see much of it through windows. There is an elusive sense of removal, an uncontaminated, clinical benevolence not present in the comparable talent of, say, the young Eudora Welty, whose provincial characters were captured with a certain malicious pounce. Powerhouse and Old Mr. Marblehead and the narrator of "Why I Live at the P.O." have an outrageous oddity they would disown if they could decipher the fiction. Whereas we can picture Anne Tyler's characters reading through her novels comfortably, like Aunt Lucy in "her wing chair in which she could sit encircled, almost, with the wings working like mule's blinders. . . . The upholstery was embroidered in satin-stitch, which she loved to stroke absently as she read." Sit up, Aunt Lucy. This writer is not merely good, she is *wickedly* good.

Opting Out

CATHERINE PETERS

An American family chronicle of five generations of Baltimore respectability; a black sheep in each generation; an atmosphere of genteel, gradual decay. It sounds a predictable choice for the library list. But Ann [*sic*] Tyler's cool handling of her material is original and exceptionally funny.

Caleb Peck disappeared in 1912, but it was nearly fifty years before anyone seriously thought of looking for him. He had been a typical member of a family who knew their duty and did it. They wore the right clothes, ate the right food, used the right furniture in houses at the right address. The envelope for the bread-and-butter letter would be ready, addressed and stamped, before the visit took place.

Caleb's disappearance was so out of character that at first it was not noticed, and then, like any other eccentricity that could not be suppressed, quietly ignored. No one could ever suppress or ignore his great-nephew Duncan, a trouble-maker from birth. When he too broke out of the tightly introverted family his good little cousin Justine was dispatched to bring him back. Instead she married him, and they embarked on a wild nomadic life ruled by Duncan's determination not to be a success. Whenever anything he started looked like turning out well—goat farming, cabinet-making, selling pets or antique farm machinery—he found some way of wrecking the enterprise and moving on to a more hopeless and bizarre occupation. Justine, outwardly adjusted to living on takeaway pizza and hardly bothering to unpack the cardboard boxes between moves from one broken-down house to another, went along with Duncan's vagaries, conforming, as she had done all her life, to what other people expected of her. To her distress her daughter Meg, longing for a respectability she has never known, is trapped by a more obvious conformity into a dreary dead-end marriage. Nor does Caleb turn out to be the wild adventurer of their imaginings, but a small-town failure.

It becomes clear in the course of this robust, witty novel that Ann [*sic*] Tyler is concerned with an existential examination of the nature of freedom. The choices, between staying put and running away, conforming or rebel-

Reprinted from the (London) *Times Literary Supplement,* 27 August 1976, 1060, by permission of the *Times Literary Supplement;* © Times Newspapers Ltd., 1976.

ling, are not as simple as they seem, perhaps not in themselves important: it is the use made of them that matters. In the hands of a less imaginative writer, this dimension of the novel might have seemed irritating or obtrusive, but Miss Tyler's characters have too much vitality for that.

[Review of *Searching for Caleb*]

Katha Pollitt

It's hard to classify Anne Tyler's novels. They are Southern in their sure sense of family and place but lack the taste for violence and the Gothic that often characterizes self-consciously Southern literature. They are modern in their fictional techniques, yet utterly unconcerned with the contemporary moment as a subject, so that, with only minor dislocations, her stories could just as well have taken place in the twenties or thirties. The current school of feminist-influenced novels seems to have passed her by completely: her women are strong, often stronger than the men in their lives, but solidly grounded in traditional roles. Among our better contemporary novelists, Tyler occupies a somewhat lonely place, polishing brighter and brighter a craft many novelists no longer deem essential to their purpose: the unfolding of character through brilliantly imagined and absolutely accurate detail.

In "Searching for Caleb" she has invented a family whose very conventionality borders on the eccentric. The Pecks of Baltimore are wealthy, standoffish, stolidly self-satisfied. In their suburban enclave of wide lawns and spacious houses, four generations have lived quietly together, tactfully ignoring a world they consider loud and frivolous and full of rude people with outlandish surnames. To be a true Peck is to sink into a kind of lukewarm bath that is comforting but enervating, a perpetual childhood presided over by the brisk, formal, aging grandfather, Daniel. Only two have rebelled: Caleb, Daniel's dreamy, cello-playing brother, who disappeared without a trace 60 years ago, and Duncan, Daniel's grandson, a wild boy in love with scrapes and danger who grows into a strange, private, restless adult.

When Duncan marries his cousin Justine, hitherto an ardent Peck, she begins to discover her own thirst for adventure. For years the two careen through the small towns of Maryland and Virginia as Duncan quits one makeshift job for another. He refuses to acknowledge the past that propels them both into an ever bleaker and dingier future. Justine is pulled both forward and back: an amateur teller of fortunes who advises her clients always to go along with change, she remains in thrall to her own childhood. And so, when Daniel decides to find his lost brother, Justine is the one who joins him. For the old man the quest is a way of recapturing the past, but for

From *New York Times Book Review*, 18 January 1976, 22. Copyright © 1976 by The New York Times Company. Reprinted by permission.

Justine it becomes a search for the self she has mislaid. The outcome is marvelously ironic, since the answers to her questions are themselves enigmatic. Yet she emerges triumphant, her own woman at last.

Less perfectly realized than "Celestial Navigation," her extraordinarily moving and beautiful last novel, "Searching for Caleb" is Tyler's sunniest, most expansive book. While etching with a fine, sharp wit the narrow-mindedness and pettishness of the Pecks, she lavishes on them a tenderness that lifts them above satire. Consider Daniel Peck. A cold and unoriginal man, aging gracefully but without wisdom, he is yet allowed moments in which we glimpse his bewilderment at a life that has been in the end disappointing: "In my childhood I was trained to hold things in, you see. But I thought I was holding them in until a certain *time*. I assumed that someday, somewhere, I would again be given the opportunity to spend all that saved-up feeling. When will that be?"

Reading "Searching for Caleb," one is constantly being startled by such moments: gestures, words, wrinkles of thought and feeling that are at once revelatory and exactly right. But at the center of Tyler's characters is a private, mysterious core which is left, wisely, inviolate. Ultimately this wisdom is what makes Tyler more than a fine craftsman of realistic novels. Her complex, crotchety inventions surprise us, but one senses they surprise her too.

Earthly Possessions

◆

[Review of *Earthly Possessions*]

NICHOLAS DELBANCO

Earthly Possessions is Anne Tyler's seventh novel, and very much within the canon; she's staking out terrain. In a modest, offhand way—like one of her heroines, apologetic, forgetful, tugging at her sleeve until the handkerchief becomes pure silk and rabbits come leaping from hats—she's managed to appropriate a section of the South. Magic: it's a landscape in Maryland mostly, where old houses go to seed, whose occupants emerge to blink at the overstrong sun or waddle off to grocery stores, and which the protagonist flees. Artists or tinkerers drift through her pages as "victims of impulse"; they're all of them rooted, adrift.

Charlotte Emory, whose "marriage wasn't going well," goes to the bank to draw out her savings and leave. It is a journey she's been planning on for years, with no fixed purpose but escape: she's living in her mother's house, the center of a circle that seems to be contracting around her as it expands. She has planned to travel light, untrammelled by the furniture with which her preacher-husband—ironically, in terms of the title—filled the house. He had been her neighbor and seemed the spirit of adventure once, but his wanderlust is slaked. Theirs is the only residence left; the Clarion neighborhood sprouts gas stations on each corner as emblems of the road. But Saul—returned ostensibly to settle his parents' estate—settles instead in Charlotte's house and turn by turn brings his three brothers back. One of them builds

Reprinted from *New Republic*, 28 May 1977, 35–36, by permission of *New Republic;* © 1977 by The New Republic, Inc.

doll furniture, ever more miniature, that fills the living room; another begs her, ineffectually, to run away with him; her father dies and she takes up his photography business; her mother dies but she cannot break loose. Her husband and two children are as hostages to fortune; she has a half-forgotten hundred dollar traveller's check tucked into her billfold, and a "Keep on Trucking" [*sic*] medallion that fell from a cereal box.

Therefore when Jake Simms, Jr., demolition driver and prison escapee, takes her hostage at the bank she is only half-unwilling. Charlotte runs with him in a white blur that makes it to TV. She trades her house for another sort of shell—a stolen 1950s roadster with the passenger door padlocked by a men's-room chain. Anyhow she cannot drive; anyhow she comes to see, on their shabby madcap journey south, that "we *are* traveling."

Yet Jake is no god in a car. He has two destinations: a home for unwed mothers in Georgia where his girlfriend Mindy waits, the next a motel in Florida, where his one friend Oliver may possibly provide them help. Along the way they share Doritos and warm Coke and money for gas and their claustrophobic histories; they share, if little else, a passion for departure that predicates return.

The book is contrapuntal, alternating chapters of the present action with chapters of first-person flashback. The brief opening scene at the bank, for instance, hovers just on the edge of the plausible—but is buttressed and defended later by Charlotte's memory of having been kidnapped before. These juxtapositions to the narrative sequence are uniformly rich: the crazed refugee at a fairground who kept the seven year old Charlotte hostage with paper-dolls; the single day at college till her fat cousin Clarence fetched her home (because her father, returning in the pick-up, had had a heart attack); the intimate distance she keeps from her mother or her adopted second child, Jiggs—all of this is handled with a compassionate precision that's Anne Tyler's trademark now. The dialogue has perfect pitch, the visual detail seems astonishing yet apt.

Sometimes the eye is a touch self-congratulatory, winking at itself while it catalogues each item on a grocery counter or lists six salient details of clothing at once. There's a way in which eccentricity becomes its own system and demands that *every* character be somehow peculiar, particular; there's a rigidity to these seemingly random associations that can wear thin.

The problem of maternity is a schematic case in point. Charlotte's mother is a grossly overweight blonde who thought her pregnancy was a grapefruit-like tumor and was taken by surprise; the daughter grows up dark and lean and alien, suspicious of a mix-up at the hospital. She is someone else's daughter, she believes, and her true life is being lived elsewhere. So she spends much of her time constructing alternative mothers (the woman at the fairground; Saul's mother Alberta—who ran off, scandalously, with her own father-in-law). Then, a mother herself, she hunts the maternal instinct within and comes up with a photograph of her mother's own true daughter.

This turns out—in an otherwise moving death-bed reconciliation—to have been a photograph of her mother when an infant; there can be no further doubt as to authenticity.

This is all clever enough, and it does have resonance. But the true achievement of the novel resides elsewhere—in the conversations overheard and Founder's Day Parade ("ONE HUNDRED YEARS OF PROGRESS") witnessed, the liberation of Charlotte as hostage, the vulgar eloquence of Mindy as she pleads to keep her man. And somehow all the contriving—the mother's photograph that replicates Charlotte's childhood's own, linked subtly to the studio where Charlotte feeds off the escapist impulse of her clients yet "fixes" them forever—calls attention to itself. In a world where the chanciness of things seems central, such manipulation is inappropriate; the skein of coincidence points to no system but that of authorial control.

Nor do we know quite what Anne Tyler's trying to tell us. The book ends on a fade-out with Jake and Mindy safe—untouched by what must surely be the most inept police dragnet ever. And Charlotte, returning to Clarion and her puzzled husband, attains some sort of peace in stasis and refuses his proffered "trip."

"I don't see the need, I say. We have been traveling for years, traveled all our lives. We are traveling still. We couldn't stay in one place if we tried. Go to sleep, I say."

The aftertaste is bittersweet; she's glad to have done it, glad to have done with the doing. The moral would appear to be: if you find yourself life's hostage, may your fortune be propitious, with a robber not inclined to rape, and with a neat set of wheels.

Anne Tyler's standards are high; she works both hard and fast. Of her earlier novels, this seems most similar to *A Slipping-Down Life*—the antagonists and circumstance and action are equivalent—but *Earthly Possessions* is far better done. If not precisely a sequel to her previous works, it's nonetheless a companion-text; the narrative is supple and the world a pleasant place. Violence and lust are rare, or offstage; the characteristic emotions are abstracted ones—anger comes to us as vexation, bliss as a kind of contented release.

Yet I do not feel this novel represents advance. The wheels are a touch too audibly clicking, and inspiration seems second-hand. It's as if her sense of continuity overruled the chance of change; the book is programmatic and the program feels over-rehearsed. Still, anyone who wrote the splendid *Celestial Navigation* and *Searching for Caleb* should be allowed to take a breather—and, Ann [*sic*] Tyler's average work is more than good enough. *Earthly Possessions* is deft, good-humored and never less than engaging; one hopes its author, next time through, will once more be fully engaged.

Loosened Roots

JOHN UPDIKE

Anne Tyler in her seventh novel continues to demonstrate a remarkable talent and, for a writer of her acuity, an unusual temperament. She is soft, if not bullish, on America: its fluorescent-lit banks and gas stations, its high schools and low life, its motels and billboards and boring backwaters and stifling homes and staggering churches and scant, innocent depravities and deprivations are all to her the stuff of a tender magic, a moonlit scenery where poetry and adventure form as easily as dew. Small towns and pinched minds hold room enough for her; she is at peace in the semi-countrified, semi-plasticized, northern-Southern America where she and her characters live. Out of this peace flow her unmistakable strengths—her serene, firm tone; her smoothly spun plots; her apparently inexhaustible access to the personalities of her imagining; her infectious delight in "the smell of beautiful, everyday life"; her lack of any trace of intellectual or political condescension—and her one possible weakness: a tendency to leave the reader just where she found him. Acceptance, in her fiction, is the sum of the marvellous—or, as *Earthly Possessions* would have it, the end of travelling is to return. This is not untrue. Nothing Anne Tyler sets down is untrue. But the impending moral encloses the excitements of her story in a circle of safety that gives them the coziness of entertainment. It may be that in this Protestant land, with its reverence for sweat and constipation, we distrust artificers, peaceable cultivators of the imaginary. Miss Tyler tends her human flora for each book's season of bloom and then latches the garden gate with a smile. So, one could say, did Shakespeare; but in the tragedies, at least, the enclosure of final order is drawn around a group of chastened survivors, while Miss Tyler here gathers in to safety the very characters she has convincingly shown us to be sunk in "a rich, black, underground world . . . where everyone was in some deep and dramatic trouble." The depths that her lucid vision perceives through the weave of the mundane are banished, as it were, by a mere movement of the author's eyes. *Earthly Possessions* contains, for instance, a chilling portrait of a habitual criminal, Jake Simms, Jr., who blames every destructive and chaotic act of his own on someone else. He kidnaps our heroine, the surpassingly amiable Charlotte Emory, because while he was robbing a bank a bystander happened to produce a gun. "I could be clean free," he tells his victim, "and you safe home with your kids by now if it wasn't for him. Guy like that ought to be locked up." As the chase continues, and the kidnapping lengthens into a kind of marriage, he persuades himself, "It ain't *me* keeping you, it's them. If they would quit hounding me then we could go our separate ways. . . ." This is perfect loser psychology, the mental technology for digging a bottomless pit; but Anne Tyler would have us believe that Jake is saved from falling in by the doll-like apparition of a wee seventeen-year-old girl he has impregnated, Mindy Callender:

> She really was a tiny girl. The biggest thing about her was that stomach, which Jake carefully wasn't looking at. . . . She raised a thin, knobby wrist, with a bracelet dangling heart-shaped charms in all different colors and sizes. The pink stone in her ring was heart-shaped too, and so was the print of her dress. "Hearts are my *sign,*" Mindy said. "What's yours?"

With such a figure, the Shakespearean ambience of dark comedy turns Spenserian; we are travelling in an allegory, and Love (Mindy) on page 193 points to the Grail with one of those bursts of articulate insight that overtake even the dimwitted in Anne Tyler's animated world.

The excitements of *Earthly Possessions* include both headlong suspense and surprises of retrospective revelation. Charlotte, the narrator and heroine, tells in her wry, patient voice two stories; she describes, hour by hour, the few days of her southward flight with Jake Simms and, synopsized in alternating chapters, the thirty-five years of her life. The two accounts flow parallel, to the same estuary of acceptance. As in the author's previous novels, a fundamental American tension is felt between stasis and movement, between home and escape. Home is what we are mired in; Miss Tyler in her darker mode celebrates domestic claustrophobia and private stagnation. Charlotte is the late and only fruit of a very fat first-grade teacher and a faded, fussy "travelling photographer named Murray Ames." Ames stops travelling, and sets up a studio in his wife's "dead father's house," where a child is born with grotesque inadvertence: the mother's obesity and innocence have hidden the pregnancy. "One night she woke up with abdominal spasms. . . . All around her the bed was hot and wet. She woke her husband, who stumbled into his trousers and drove her to the hospital. Half an hour later, she gave birth to a six-pound baby girl." The little girl grows up lonely. The common American escape from home into the "whole new world" of public school is feelingly evoked:

> I hadn't had any idea that people could be so light-hearted. I stood on the edge of the playground watching how the girls would gather in clumps, how they giggled over nothing at all and told colorful stories of family life: visits to circuses, fights with brothers. They didn't like me. They said I smelled. I

knew they were right because now when I walked into my house I could smell the smell too: stale, dark, ancient air, in which nothing had moved for a very long time. I began to see how strange my mother was. I noticed that her dresses were like enormous flowered undershirts. I wondered why she didn't go out more; then once, from a distance, I watched her slow progress toward the corner grocery store and I wished she wouldn't go out at all.

From embarrassing parents Charlotte moves to an embarrassing husband. Saul Emory, a boy who had lived next door, returns from the Army, courts her, weds her, and abruptly announces that he has been called to preach, in the local fundamentalist Holy Basis Church. Charlotte is a nonbeliever; while her husband preaches she sits deafly in church scheming how to get him into bed. "He was against making love on a Sunday. I was in favor of it. Sometimes I won, sometimes he won. I wouldn't have missed Sunday for the world." They live in what has become *her* dead father's house; she diffidently runs the studio that she has inherited, and the house fills up with charity cases and Saul's brothers. Charlotte says, "I felt like something dragged on a string behind a forgetful child. . . . I gave up hope. Then in order not to mind too much I loosened my roots, floated a few feet off, and grew to look at things with a faint, pleasant humorousness that spiced my nose like the beginnings of a sneeze." Childhood fantasies of flight recur; she keeps giving away the furniture; she finally decides to leave, goes to the bank "to get cash for the trip," and is seized by Jake Simms. Her adventure begins.

Writing a self-description for the Washington *Post,* Anne Tyler said, "Mostly it's lies, writing novels. You set out to tell an untrue story and you try to make it believable, even to yourself. Which calls for details; any good lie does." Her details are superb, tucked in with quick little loops of metaphor:

When she was angry, her face bunched in now as if gathered at the center by a drawstring.

When he lifted me up in his arms I felt I had left all my troubles on the floor beneath me like gigantic concrete shoes.

Without pushing at it, she establishes her characters in authentic occupations. Murray Ames's photography and his daughter's continuation of it become very real, and a paradigm for art:

"Move that lamp off somewhat," he would tell me from his bed. "You don't want such a glare. Now get yourself more of an angle. I never did like a head-on photograph."

What he liked was a sideways look—eyes lowered, face slanted downward. The bay window displaying my father's portraits resembled a field full of flowers, all being blown by the same strong breeze.

The author's attention to American incidentals is so unblinking that we are rather relieved when she seems to nod, as when Charlotte observes the "snuff adds" ("ads," surely) in Georgia, or a "pair of giant fur dominoes" (dice, more likely) hung from a rearview mirror. Every bit of junk food the fugitives nibble as they drive their stolen car south is affectionately noted, and the subtle changes in scenery and climate are continental in their cumulative effect. When, having at last arrived in Florida, Charlotte says, "It was one of those lukewarm, breezy evenings that make you feel you're expecting something," we have arrived, too, and feel exactly what she means.

What else do we feel, after our two hundred pages with Charlotte Emory? She belongs to what is becoming a familiar class of Anne Tyler heroines: women admirably active in the details of living yet alarmingly passive in the large curve of their lives—riders on male-generated events, who nevertheless give those events a certain blessing, a certain feasibility. Jake comes to need his victim: "Charlotte, it ain't so bad if you're *with* us, you see. You act like you take it all in stride, like this is the way life really does tend to turn out. You mostly wear this little smile." Amos, a brother of Emory's who turns amorous, exclaims in admiration, "Now I see everyone grabbing for pieces of you, and still you're never diminished. . . . You sail through this house like a moon, you're strong enough for all of them." These intelligent, bustling, maternal, helpless moon-women trouble us with the something complacent in their little smiles, their "faint, pleasant humorousness." Their detachment has been achieved through a delicate inner abdication, a multiplication and devaluation of realities. Anne Tyler stated in the *Post,* "I write because I want more than one life." Charlotte Emory as a photographer poses her subjects in odd bits of costume, "absent-mindedly" holding feathers and toys, antique words and pistols; she has come to believe that such elaborations "may tell more truths than they hide." In the crisis of her mother's dying, Charlotte says, "My life grew to be all dreams; there was no reality whatsoever." Her life, from lonely childhood to lonely marriage, spent in an old house between two gas stations, photographing workaday people with dream baubles, has a terror and a sorrow of which the outlines are acknowledged but not the mass, the terrible heft. She seems less a character than a creator, who among the many lives that her fantasizing, emphathizing mind arrays before her almost casually chooses to live her own.

[From "The Insane and the Indifferent
Walker Percy and Others"]

WALTER SULLIVAN

Anne Tyler is a talented and prolific novelist, and I have praised her work at least twice before in this quarterly. She is good at creating old people and children and society's borderline cases, and there are times when her technical mastery of her material is absolutely breathtaking. But she works in a very narrow range, and unlike the bolder [Joan] Didion, she declines to go one-on-one against the main stream of human experience. Indeed, in her pursuit of the peculiar, she seems put off by the teachers and preachers and lawyers and businessmen who do their work and live their lives without nourishing eccentricities or trying to make a comic virtue out of failure.

Earthly Possessions starts well enough. Charlotte Emory, child of typically curious Tyleresque parents, gets fed up with her marriage to an impoverished but generous preacher and decides to escape. While she is in the bank trying to withdraw her mad money, she is taken hostage by a bungling robber, and so the flaky odyssey begins. Tyler likes to have her people on the road, demonstrating incompetence and doing mischief. These two make their way, getting lost, wrecking cars, and as the hours pass, learning more about each other. The novel dwells on the crazy honest past from which Charlotte is trying to escape and the crazy dishonest boob with whom she is making a mad, but slow, progress toward Florida. The boob—his name is Jake Simms—is, we are asked to believe, a nice fellow. He is a race-car driver by profession—his specialty is demolition derbies—but he has not won for a spell, and he needs money to get to the girl he has left in Florida. Mindy is pregnant and tired of being scolded by her mother and weary of the silly rules by which she is asked to live at the home for unwed mothers.

So, one sees, Jake has the best of motives. He is really morally superior to those decent people Charlotte has abandoned, and toward the end we discover that he has been betrayed by his best friend. Jake had hoped to receive succor from Oliver, but Oliver has renounced his immediate ways and married and settled down to make an honest living. We are invited to sympathize with Jake, but I find him less than engaging. His antics might warm the cockles of Tom Wicker's heart, but I take the position, quaint as it

From *Sewanee Review* 86 (Winter 1978), 155–57. Reprinted by permission of the editor of *Sewanee Review*.

is, that robbing banks is a crime and stealing a sin and people ought to keep their hands off other people's money. As for Charlotte, I do not think this trip is necessary. She declines her opportunities to escape, she helps Jake make his getaway, and finally she goes back home with neither herself nor her situation much altered by this silly adventure.

I think I see what all this is supposed to signify. The boundaries between good and evil, right and wrong, integrity and deceit are becoming increasingly blurred. Who can chart the demarcation between vice and virtue? I recognize this to be a profound theme, but one which is as threadbare as an old coat. Miss Tyler's treatment is not new but is all too familiar in its sentimentality. The characters and action are interesting enough, but what you see is what you get. Everything that is to be gleaned here is on the surface. The hours spent in reading *Earthly Possessions* leave you no wiser than when you began. You wind up empty-handed.

Morgan's Passing

◆

When the Fog Never Lifts

Eva Hoffman

Morgan's Passing, Anne Tyler's eighth novel, opens on a scene of low-keyed, inchoate strangeness. A puppet show staged at a Baltimore Easter fair is suddenly interrupted when a fragile-looking young man emerges from behind the flimsy curtain and urgently calls for help; his wife, who is the other puppeteer, is having intense labor pains. The summons is answered by a "Dr. Morgan," a burly, heavily bearded man who offers to drive them to a hospital. He does so without any sense of urgency, although he intently asks questions about the materials from which the puppets are made, and about Emily and Leon Meredith's life, which he hopefully imagines to be "footloose." When Emily goes into labor, Dr. Morgan, in a hazy, casual way, delivers the child in the back of his junky and junk-filled car.

Almost everything about this episode is out of kilter; the unplaceable setting, whose seemingly irrelevant details jump out at us without context or explanation; the troubling irresponsibility of Leon and Emily, who apparently have made no preparations for the birth of their child; and most of all, the behavior of Dr. Morgan, whose unworried vagueness is utterly inappropriate to the event in which he is involved. Such baffling dissonances and misplaced reactions pervade and inform the entire novel, and at first they arouse the reader's curiosity (what's going on here?). But about halfway

From *Saturday Review,* 15 March 1980, 38–39. Reprinted by permission of Omni Publications International, Ltd.

through, as these absurdist perplexities are neither clarified nor deepened, the curiosity turns into exasperation (what's going on here, anyway?).

On one level, the story is of a disturbed man, a man "who had gone to pieces," or who had "arrived unassembled." Gower Morgan, the novel's protagonist, is not a doctor at all, but someone who, for lack of an identity of his own, impersonates a ragtag assortment of selves. The actual circumstances of his life are ordinary with a vengeance. He lives in a Colonial brick house acquired with his wife's money and manages a hardware store by the grace of his wife's family; he has seven daughters, and he and his family share the house with his nearly senile mother and his doltish, dreamily sleepy sister. Morgan exists amid this abundance of concreteness in a state of permanent disconnection, and he views those near and dear to him through a kind of aphasic, derealizing blur. He catches on to the fact that one of his daughters is getting married, for example, only when her wedding reception is discussed; and he sometimes thinks that his wife once forgot to tell him about the imminent birth of a daughter—but he isn't sure.

To escape this messy amorphousness, and the dissolving formlessness of his own self, Morgan, each morning, steps into a different costume chosen from his extensive thrift-shop collection, and into a different role. At various times, he has posed as a glassblower, an orthodox rabbi, "a tugboat captain for the Curtis Bay Towing Company, and a Mohawk Indian high-rise worker." His encounter with Emily and Leon is the beginning of his most compelling fantasy, and the plot of the novel revolves around his secret pursuit of the young couple and his gradual insinuation into their lives. Emily and Leon are a stray and an unexceptional pair of waifs who have meandered into Baltimore and into their unlucrative occupation half-accidentally, but to Morgan the straitened and simple tenor of their life is a mark of the clarity and definition he so entirely lacks. And, when he finally stops spying on the Merediths from parking lots and enters into a triadic symbiosis with them, it turns out that he answers a need in them too; particularly to the cramped, anxious, literal-minded Emily, he seems an elf or a goblin, who introduces her to disarray, and who promises some wider, more exciting possibility.

The interplay of a drab, mediocre reality and of second-rate fantasies is an intriguing theme. It suggests what happens to the needs of the spirit when they have no outlet for expression; it hints at the comedy of an imagination without style, a madness without panache. The unlovely, prosaic texture of the protagonists' lives is best conveyed through masterfully detailed descriptions of urban landscapes and of commonplace objects. Morgan's house, for example—with its "particles of related people's unrelated worlds: his daughters' booksacks tumbling across the hall radiator, which also served as mail rack, sweater shelf, and message bureau; his wife's League of Women Voters leaflets rubber-banded into a tower on the living-room coffee table; and his mother's ancient, snuffling dog dreaming of rabbits and twitching her paws as she slept on the cold brick hearth"—is a triumph of tacky, commonplace dailiness.

But, like the disjointed tidbits of Morgan's house, or the fragmented elements of his character, the various pieces of the novel, although intriguing in themselves, simply refuse to jell, focus, or add up. Morgan's dissatisfaction is so without contours, his perceptions and flights of fancy so vapid and lacking in energy, that it is difficult to sympathize with his condition, or to understand why Emily, after an ardorless courtship, decides to leave Leon and marry Morgan. Because Morgan's peculiarity seems without purpose, it drives the reader to ask the most naive questions: What's wrong with him? What does he want? Why doesn't he do something? In fact, all the protagonists of *Morgan's Passing* are separated from their alienated, eccentric, or neurotic brethren who so thickly populate the pages of modern fiction by their lukewarm emotional temperature, the absence of delineation or intensity even in their pain. They are too lethargic, too passive, and the novel remains suspended in a chilly, murky, ozone-thin limbo—a bit as if Flannery O'Connor were writing in a fog. Without an exploration that would make the characters more familiar, and without a perspective that would make their estrangement significant, Anne Tyler is left with a story about weirdness—and weirdness, as a novelistic subject, is simply not enough.

A State of Continual Crisis

A. G. MOJTABAI

The story opens at a church fair in Baltimore. In the middle of a puppet show, Cinderella collapses. The Prince asks if there's a doctor in the house. Apparently not—the audience consists almost entirely of children under 5. Suddenly an unkempt bearded man steps forward. His name is Morgan Gower. Shortly after, he delivers "Cinderella's" baby in the back seat of his car. Cinderella's real name is Emily, the Prince's name is Leon; Morgan Gower is no doctor, and the story that follows is no fairy tale. Morgan's stealing of Emily and Leon, his hankering after "their pure, vagabond lives," consumes a period of 10 years and proves the undoing of his own marriage and theirs.

"Morgan's Passing" is a narrative replete with colorful and idiosyncratic detail, precise in its tenderness. And yet, for all its intentness of specification, the book—like its subject, Morgan Gower—eludes and continues to elude one. The reader stalks Morgan as Morgan stalks Emily and, always, Morgan is just barely out of reach, turning the corner or dipping into some doorway or flattening against a wall, as fugitive and remittent as the refrain from a song one can't forget yet can't quite remember.

Who is Morgan Gower? He is, first of all, a man of vivid presence: "He smoked too much . . . ate too many sweets (and exposed a garble of black fillings whenever he opened his mouth), scattered ashes down his front, chewed his cuticles, picked his teeth, meddled with his beard, fidgeted, paced, scratched his stomach, hummed distractingly whenever it was someone else's turn to speak. . . . He smelled permanently of stale tobacco. When he wore glasses, they were so fingerprinted and greasy you couldn't read his eyes."

This is characterization by enumeration, and very skillful; the accumulation of sharp detail yields a surface richly encrusted, but remains a surface nonetheless. The question persists: who is Morgan Gower?

Morgan is a problem, not only to friends and relations, but to author and reader as well. How does one grasp a life that is endless impersonation, a life so scattered, slack and unfocused that it has become a sort of lost-and-found of other people's lives?

From *New York Times Book Review* 23 March 1980, 14, 33. Copyright © 1980 by The New York Times Company. Reprinted by permission.

Item:

"They passed a woman painting her front door a bright green. 'Apple green, my favorite color!' Morgan called, and the woman laughed and bowed like someone on a stage. They passed an open window where Fats Domino sang 'I'm Walkin,' and Morgan spread his arms and started dancing."

Item:

"He was never truly happy if he felt that even the most random passing stranger found him unlikable."

Can anyone make sense of this? One or two attempts are made that sound plausible:

"His father had killed himself during Morgan's last year of high school. . . . Morgan had spent a large part of his life trying to figure out why. . . . Anything would have been preferable to this nebulous, ambiguous trailing off."

And Morgan's wife reflects:

"I blame it on his mother. . . . 'You can be anything,' she told him. He must have misunderstood. He thought she said, 'You can be *every*thing.' "

If this were a case history, perhaps these accounts would seem sufficient, but the novel demands something deeper—not explanation, exactly, but penetration, a sense of *intimate* particularity. Morgan is so intriguing that he cries out for capture, an act of imaginative possession. What we have are suggestions—scattered moments and the blur of passage. Morgan remains a problem, and Anne Tyler's relation to Morgan is perhaps part of the problem. She seems at once too casually fond of Morgan to subject him to a truly loving, yet deeply probing scrutiny, and too beguiled by his disorderly charm to give us any outside perspective on him.

"Everything he looked at seemed luminous and beautiful, and rich with possibilities." So the world seems to Morgan Gower at the start of the novel and at its close. There's a fine irony here, for Morgan is a man so enamored of possibilities, and so negligent of the actual, that nothing is ever really possible for him. The irony would be still finer if there were some external vantage point from which the reader could reflect upon it. Morgan's wife, Bonny, if anyone, should provide that vantage point. Yet Bonny, as well as everyone else, seems under Morgan's spell.

When Morgan walks out on his marriage (30 years and seven children) to go live with Emily, Bonny's response is simply to unload Morgan's mother, sister and dog on Emily, and to take up smoking. Her retaliation, when she starts up with another man, is to print Morgan's obituary in the newspaper, a rejoinder in kind to her husband's perpetual play-acting. It's as if, to echo Morgan, none of this is happening *really.*

There is much to praise in Anne Tyler's eighth novel. This might have been the story of a midlife crisis, a familiar tale, with steady, reliable associations, however tormented; but Miss Tyler chose instead to depict an unfamiliar state of continual crisis, a condition for which there exist no charts or manuals ready to hand. And Miss Tyler has scrupulously adhered to a moderate tone, shunning sensationalism and easy emotion. Yet there is a cost. Intimacy and anguish are stinted in this novel and the loss is felt. The author's undeniable skill and her level of engagement seem at odds here. The title "Morgan's Passing" may well be a play on "passing on," reminding us of the obituary, Bonny's last laugh, but there are too many laughs all around and the sense of the book is of Morgan always just passing by, gliding by, far too blithely.

Bright Novel That Overstretches Credibility

Peter Grier

By all accounts, Anne Tyler is prodigiously talented. Her last novel, "Earthly Possessions," drew rave reviews in papers ranging from the Los Angeles Times to the New York Times. And the crown prince of urban fiction, John Updike, has judged her work not merely good, but "wickedly good."

"Morgan's Passing," her eighth book, pulses with this talent only in spurts, like a jalopy with a dirty carburetor. At times the characters and plot seem to be stuck together with baling wire and chewing gum. But in the end, the book plops you at its promised destination as surely as if it were a purring limousine.

Morgan Gower—clear-eyed, black-bearded, angular as a carpenter's rule—lives in Baltimore with his mother, sister, wife, and seven daughters. To escape a household knee-deep in chaos, Gower spends most of his time trying on different professions as if they were hats. Never content to be merely Morgan Gower, hardware store manager, he searches his costume-stuffed closet each morning deciding "who to be today." He lurks on down-town street corners disguised as Reverend Gower, or an Arabian immigrant, or a Mohawk Indian high-rise worker, spying on other people's lives.

He is obsessed with roles and disguises, so when he meets Emily and Leon Meredith, a young couple who make their living as puppeteers, the clarity of their daily routine fascinates him. When Emily suddenly goes into labor prematurely during a church fair performance, Gower, posing as a doctor, leaps from the audience and delivers their daughter into the world.

From this chance meeting come the shifting relationships at the novel's core. Morgan is "awed by the Merediths—by their austerity, their certitude, their mapped and charted lives." He imagines their world to be as unclut-tered as their stark apartment, and he begins to follow them, popping up in their path unexpectedly, like an eccentric uncle.

Aloof at first, Emily and daughter Gina gradually develop a fondness for Morgan and his quicksilver character. They find that over the years his presence brings a whiff of vitality into their lives, while Leon's retreat behind a wall of pride sets in motion the novel's final chain of events.

"Morgan's Passing" is about puppets and freedom. Emily sews her Cinderellas and Snow Whites with loving care, finding a kind of creative release within the confines of her craft. Her life and work are almost synonyms for order.

Morgan, on the other hand, would like to cut all his strings; he's chasing pure freedom. "I just trust my muscles to tell me what I'm here for," he says. "To drop me into my true activity one day, I let them lead me." Yet he seems a puppet, nonetheless, acting out the drama of his own discontent, never free to shed his disguises. It is an ingeniously conceived irony.

Unfortunately, the book's execution does not always match its conception. Fiction doesn't have to be realistic, but it does have to be believable, and in "Morgan's Passing" the characters often have the lifelike ring of solid oak. Morgan's eccentricities are too cute to be convincing, and the chaos of his household seems more choreographed than described.

"Amy was doing something to the toaster. The twins were mixing their health food drink in the blender. A French book flew out of nowhere and hit Liz in the small of the back. 'I can't go on living here any more,' Liz said. 'I don't get a moment's peace.' "

Twins enter stage left, cue French book. With prose like this it's hard to forget there's a writer pulling the strings. Marriages unexpectedly founder, and just as unexpectedly begin. Lifelong actors become committed bank officers overnight. Well-adjusted adults turn unconvincingly into babbling neurotics. Tyler seems to be running a puppet show of her own, shoving characters around as if they had no inner life.

But a puppet show is still a type of art. Flat characters may be flimsy vehicles for a weighty theme, but in this case they're serviceable. Morgan is mired in disguises. Emily, open and undisguised, teaches him the freedom of simplicity. Like puppets, they seem too slick, too shiny. And like puppets, they represent archetypes—in which we often see a little bit of ourselves.

[Review of *Morgan's Passing*]

ROBERT TOWERS

Twentieth-century psychology has largely tainted the comfortable Victorian enjoyment of eccentric characters in fiction. Dickens's audience could laugh at Mr. Micawber without having to worry about his infantilism and his exceptional orality; they had no obligation to feel anything but unalloyed pleasure in the bachelor Mr. Wimmick's extreme attachment to his Aged P. or to speculate about the hidden anguish of a dwarf like Miss Mowcher. Today readers and writers alike can accommodate any degree of weirdness, neurosis, perversion, or madness but tend to jib at the droll, the quirky, the harmlessly odd. And for the most part with good reason—these terms are too often synonymous with self-conscious whimsicality or cuteness. No doubt there are exceptions, but for the moment I can think of only two first-rate current writers who have successfully evaded the ban on colorfully eccentric characters. One is the octogenarian V. S. Pritchett, who might be regarded (quite wrongly) as a holdover from another era, and the other is the decidedly contemporary Anne Tyler.

It would be hard to exaggerate the oddity of her new excellent new novel, *Morgan's Passing*. And equally hard to summarize its action in a way that will appeal to readers who take their literature seriously. Yet *Morgan's Passing* is at once appealing, entertaining, and serious. Let's glance at a few of its oddities.

A young girl-wife goes into labor while she and her boy-husband are putting on a puppet-show of Cinderella at a church fair in Baltimore in 1967. Her baby is delivered en route to the hospital by the member of the audience who claims to be a doctor and who certainly seems knowledgeable about childbirth—a tall, lank, 40-ish oddball of a man with a bushy black beard and masses of black curls bursting from beneath a red ski-cap with a pompom at the tip. The fake doctor—who lives in a tumultuous, hopelessly cluttered house with an imperturbable wife, seven daughters, his half-senile mother, and crackpot sister—attaches himself to the young couple and their child, following them, popping up at odd moments. Later, after they have all become friends, this attachment narrows, focusing upon the young wife, with unsettling consequences for everyone. The shaggy man's middle-aged

Reprinted from *New Republic*, 22 March 1980, 28, 30–31, by permission of *New Republic;* © 1980 by the New Republic, Inc.

wife, who has cheerfully put up with him for 30 years, responds to his desertion by dumping a great pile of his clothes (costumes, rather) and the family dog outside the hardware store where he works and then, figuratively, dumps his mother and sister upon him as well. Still later she plants his obituary in the newspaper of a small town where he is living in a trailer camp; it is her way of announcing that he is dead to her, and that she is ready to encourage another man.

The shaggy man is Morgan Gower, whose identity is so unfixed that he slips uncontrollably into whatever role happens to excite his fancy at the moment. He thinks of all clothes as costumes and has a closet full of them—sailor outfits, soldier outfits, riverboat-gambler outfits that appear "to have been salvaged from some travelling operetta." Sleeping in thermal underwear during the winter, it pleases him "to stagger off to the bathroom hitching up his long johns and rummaging through his beard like some character from the Klondike." Morgan at one point explains this excessive lability as a matter of muscles, a matter of following wherever they lead him.

> Have you ever gone out to the kitchen, say, and then forgotten what for? You stand in the kitchen and try to remember. Then your wrist makes a little twisting motion. Oh, yes! you say. That twist is what you'd do to turn a faucet on. You must have come for water! I just trust my muscles, you see, to tell me what I'm here for. To drop me into my true activity one day. I let them lead me.

to which his exasperated (but secretly amused) wife Bonny replies:

> He lets them lead him into saying he's a glassblower . . . and a tugboat captain for the Curtis Bay Towing Company, and a Mohawk Indian high-rise worker. . . . You're walking down the street with him and this total stranger asks him when the International Brotherhood of Magicians is meeting next. . . .

Fortunately, Bonny has not only the easy-going temperament to endure such a marriage but enough inherited money to keep the household going.

Given the feckless confusion of his own life and the clutter of people and objects by which he is surrounded, Morgan yearns for something pure, something stripped-down and uncomplicated. For this reason he seeks out the young puppeteers whose baby he delivered, assuming that they lead an itinerant, flower-child sort of existence. But Emily and Leon Meredith are not what Morgan imagines, and it is through the counterpointing of their reality with Morgan's intrusive fantasy of them that Anne Tyler brings about the subtle drama of her novel. A gloomy boy with a fierce temper, Leon, when we first met him, is in furious rebellion against his father, a right-wing banker from Richmond; Leon also happens to be a gifted actor, with a "bitter look" that comes across on stage "as a sort of power and intensity." Emily, who makes the puppets with which they perform, is a quiet, pale, simple-hearted girl, an orphaned Quaker from Virginia; year in and year out she wears the same clothes: a black, scoop-necked leotard and a black, wrap-around skirt. But they are not hippies. After leaving college together they have drifted into puppeteering and have made a good thing of it. In the background lurk Leon's wealthy parents, eager to lavish presents on their grandchild and to reclaim Leon for the world from which he emerged.

In following their lives over a 12-year period, Anne Tyler records, acutely and touchingly, the gradual deterioration of Leon's and Emily's marriage and the change of their daughter Gina from a robust, cherubic toddler to an insecure schoolgirl whose problems reflect what is happening to her parents. Love grows old and waxes cold. Meanwhile, Morgan's daughters grow up, leave home, marry, divorce, return home with small children whom the grandfather has trouble recognizing. A new love takes root in the heart of the ever-hovering Morgan, whose impatience with his own family has intensified to an almost unbearable pitch. A gentle sadness pervades much of the latter part of the book, a sadness arising from the disparateness of the needs and desires of these essentially good-hearted people. Though she treats her characters with considerable kindness, never lecturing or hectoring them—letting them *be,* so to speak—Anne Tyler is clear-sighted about them, unsentimental. Coexisting as it does with comedy, this element of sadness deepens the novel, adding a Mozartian wistfulness to the unfolding of events.

Anne Tyler has been rightly praised (by John Updike, among others) for her ability to infuse the homeliest details of our daily lives and environment with a kind of luminous intensity—a process in which extreme accuracy of vision is combined with a poet's instinct for startling possibilities. Here are several examples.

> Morgan went upstairs to his bedroom, but two toddler girls [his grand-daughters] were standing at the bureau trying on Bonny's lipstick. "Out! Out!" he shouted. They lifted their smeared faces to him like tiny, elderly drunks, but they didn't obey.

> . . . Behind the office, a dozen small trailers sat at haphazard angles to one another. They might have been tossed there by a fractious child, along with the items of scrap all around them—discarded butane tanks, a rust-stained mattress, a collapsed sofa with a sapling growing up between two of its cushions.

Most magically of all, Emily uses Cheerios as tiny doughnuts for the puppet's breakfast in a production of Cinderella. One effect of this oddly directed vision is to document the fantastic, to creative a palpably real garden for a number of imaginary toads. Hints of myth, of fairytale, abound in the novel—hints reinforced by the subjects of the puppet plays—Beauty and the Beast, Rapunzel, Sleeping Beauty, Cinderella. . . . Morgan is a protean figure, a shape-shifter, Emily an unawakened princess or a princess in rags, Leon a glowering beast, a truculent prince. Yet they are at the same time a slightly crazed misfit and a perfectly knowable young couple dwelling in the grime and bustle of modern Baltimore. The hints, fortunately, remain just that and are never allowed to rupture the book's finely textured realism.

Dinner at the Homesick Restaurant

◆

[From "On Such a Beautiful Green Little Planet"]

JOHN UPDIKE

Anne Tyler, too, has sought brightness in the ordinary, and her art has needed only the darkening that would give her beautifully sketched shapes solidity. So evenly has her imagination moved across the details of the mundane that the novels, each admirable, sink in the mind without leaving an impression of essential, compulsive subject matter—the phobia portrayed in *Celestial Navigation* being something of an exception. Now, in her ninth novel, she has arrived, I think, at a new level of power, and gives us a lucid and delightful yet complex and somber improvisation on her favorite theme, family life. *Searching for Caleb* is the earlier book it most resembles, in its large cast and historical reach, and even in the perky monosyllabic name assigned the central family: Peck in the first case, Tull in this. Both novels play with the topic (a mighty one, and not often approached in fiction) of heredity—the patterns of eye color and temperamental tic as they speckle the generations. But genetic comedy, in *Dinner at the Homesick Restaurant*, deepens into the tragedy of closeness, of familial limitations that work upon us like Greek fates and condemn us to lives of surrender and secret fury.

The book opens in the mind of Pearl Tull, dying at the age of eighty-five, in 1979. The principal facts of her life emerge in the course of her

From *Hugging the Shore,* by John Updike. Copyright © 1983 by John Updike. Reprinted by permission of Alfred A. Knopf, Inc., and André Deutsch, Ltd.

circling reverie. Born in Raleigh of good family, small and intelligent and fair, she was still unmarried at the age of thirty when Beck Tull, a tall blue-eyed man of just twenty-four, with wavy dark hair and a salesman's position with a farm-and-gardening-equipment concern called the Tanner Corporation, courted and wed her. For six years, on the move as he was repeatedly transferred, they had no children; in 1930 they had a son, Cody, then, after an attack of croup nearly carried this only offspring away, two more children, Ezra and Jenny. In 1944, while they were living in Baltimore, Beck abruptly announced that he was leaving Pearl and his family; at first believing that he would return, and indeed never explicitly announcing to the children that their father had left, she took a job as a cashier in a local grocery store, and there, in that job and in that Baltimore house, she stayed, raising her children, and eventually seeing two of the three through college.

By 1979—to anticipate the later chapters—Cody is married, with one son, Luke, and works as an efficiency consultant to various industries; like his father, he is a travelling man. Jenny has been twice divorced, has one child, Becky, and lives with a chap called Joe, who was recently abandoned by his wife and was left with their six children; Jenny, after being left by her second husband (she left the first one), finished her degree at medical school and enjoys a busy practice as a pediatrician. Ezra Tull did not go to college or marry; he lives with his now aged mother in the city and owns and runs a nearby restaurant, which he has called the Homesick Restaurant. The Tulls, in short, present a not untypical American family history, marred by abandonment and scattering but redeemed by a certain persisting loyalty and, after early privation, respectable success. And the telling of the Tull saga is soaked through, you may be sure, with all the deft geographical, topical, professional, and cultural specifics required to make it stick, from 1903 to 1979, to the landscape of the upper South and to the curve of national life as glimpsed in its wars and fads and fashions. This type of authenticity Anne Tyler has provided consistently; what she has not shown before, so searchingly and grimly, are the violences, ironies, and estrangements within a household, as the easy wounds given dependent flesh refuse to heal and instead grow into lifelong purposes. A bitter *narrowness* of life is disclosed through all the richness of detail as the decades accumulate, to claustrophobic and sad effect.

The novel leaves Pearl Tull's mind, and chapter by chapter gives us Cody's, Jenny's, Ezra's, and even young Luke's view of the branching consequences of the primal event—Beck Tull's abandonment, as abrupt and mysterious as his courtship, of his wife. In her own mind a doting and heroic mother, Pearl is seen by Cody as a "witch," a terrible-tempered mother who "slammed us against the wall and called us scum and vipers, said she wished us dead, shook us till our teeth rattled, screamed in our faces." Cody's own violences to his placid and harmless younger brother follow suit. Jenny, too, has seen how her mother's "pale hair could crackle electrically from its bun and her eyes could get small as hatpins," has felt her stinging slaps, has dreamed that her mother is raising her to eat her. Even on her deathbed, Pearl calls her children "duckers and dodgers." A perfectionist, a fanatic laundress and housekeeper, she strives to keep her bare clean house free of contamination. She disapproves of her children's friends and has few friends herself; the isolation of this embattled family, in its Baltimore row house, is dreadfully well felt. Of course, all children are somewhat embarrassed by their parents and their homes; Pearl is a witch but also our authentic heroine, and the novel ends with Cody's adolescent vision of her beauty, "his mother's upright form along the grasses, her hair lit gold, her small hands smoothing her bouquet." The paradoxes of the family, *Dinner at the Homesick Restaurant* suggests, include love that must for survival flee its object, and daily communication that masks silence—that deep resentful silence of those who live together. Ezra, the most loving of Pearl's children, yet turns cold-hearted when she falls sick, because, it is explained, "he had trusted his mother to be everything for him. When she cut a finger with a paring knife, he had felt defeated by her incompetence. How could he depend on such a person?" When Luke runs away from home, he is given rides by three persons who all have a horror story of family life uppermost in their minds—infants who die, daughters who are ingrates, wives who leave. The family, that institution meant to shelter our frailty, in fact serves as a theatre for intimate cruelties, and brims with the cruellest of invisible presences, time. As Pearl's memories accumulate in the course of the novel, we become dizzied by the downward perspective into a well of personal history wherein hereditary traits reverberate and snapshots and frozen memories gleam amid the blackness of loss. Pearl, blind in her last years, directs Ezra to describe old photos and read aloud her girlhood diaries. At last, near the bottom of the well, she finds what she has been looking for, the diary entry:

> Early this morning I went out behind the house to weed. Was kneeling in the dirt by the stable with my pinafore a mess and the perspiration rolling down my back, wiped my face on my sleeve, reached for the trowel, and all at once thought, Why I believe that at just this moment I am absolutely happy. The Bedloe girl's piano scales were floating out her window, and I saw that I was kneeling on such a beautiful green little planet. I don't care what else might come about, I have had this moment. It belongs to me.

The plot holds a number of such epiphanies and moves its extensive cast agilely along, with flashback and side glance, through ten chapters that are each rounded like a short story. Miss Tyler, whose humane and populous domestic novels have attracted (if my antennae are tuned right) less approval in the literary ether than the sparer offerings of Ann Beattie and Joan Didion, is sometimes charged with the basic literary sin of implausibility. To me, her characters seem persuasive outgrowths of landscapes and states of mind that are familiar and American. The principal characters in *Dinner at the Homesick Restaurant* have their tics but also real psychologies, which make their next moves excitingly unpredictable. It is true, no writer would undertake to fill a canvas so broad without some confidence that she can invent her way across any space, and some of Miss Tyler's swoops, and the delayed illuminations that prick out her tableaux, have not quite the savor of reality's cautious grind. But any reader who picks up a work of fiction enters into a contract whereby he purchases with credulity satisfactions of adventure and resolution that his lived life denies him. This novel does not abuse the terms of that contract; its entertainments become our recognitions.

Funny, Wise and True

Benjamin DeMott

New work by a young writer who's both greatly gifted and prolific often points readers' minds toward the future. You finish the book and immediately begin speculating about works to come—achievements down the road that will cross the borders defined by the work at hand. Anne Tyler's books have been having this effect on me for nearly a decade. Repeatedly they've been brilliant—"wickedly good," as John Updike recently described one of them. "Dinner at the Homesick Restaurant" is Anne Tyler's ninth novel; her career began in 1964 with a fully realized first novel (the title was "If Morning Ever Comes," and there are piquant links between it and her latest book); everything I've read of hers since then—stories, novels and criticism (Anne Tyler is a first-rate critic, shrewd and self-effacing)—has been, at a minimum, interesting and well made. But in recent years her narratives have grown bolder and her characters more striking, and that's increased the temptation to brood about her direction and destination, her probable ultimate achievement.

The time for such brooding is over now, though—at least for a while. "Dinner at the Homesick Restaurant" is a book to be settled into fully, tomorrow be damned. Funny, heart-hammering, wise, it edges deep into truth that's simultaneously (and interdependently) psychological, moral and formal—deeper than many living novelists of serious reputation have penetrated, deeper than Miss Tyler herself has gone before. It is a border crossing.

The setting, as in many of this author's fictions, is Baltimore. The focus at first is Pearl Tull, 85 and dying, whose ruminations on her sickbed center partly on a moment 35 years before, when her husband, Beck Tull, a traveling salesman, announced he was clearing out for good; partly on the years of her ferocious labor that followed this catastrophe ("an out-of-date kind of woman, frail boned, deep bosomed," more or less gently bred, Pearl went to work as a grocery-store checkout clerk, toughened her provisioning skills, struggled to nurture and civilize the three children she'd had with her husband in her late 30's); partly on the mystery of the character of those

From *New York Times Book Review*, 14 March 1982, 1, 14. Copyright © 1982 by The New York Times Company. Reprinted by permission.

youngsters, persons who are approaching middle age as their mother approaches her end.

In Pearl Tull's view, "Something was wrong with all of her children. They were so frustrating—attractive, likable people, the three of them, but closed off from her in some perverse way that she couldn't quite put her finger on. . . . She wondered if her children blamed her for something. Sitting close at family gatherings . . . they tended to recall only poverty and loneliness—toys she couldn't afford for them, parties where they weren't invited. [They] referred continually to Pearl's short temper, displaying it against a background of stunned, childish faces so sad and bewildered that Pearl herself hardly recognized them. Honestly, she thought, wasn't there some statute of limitations here? When [were they] going to absolve her?"

Pearl's doubts about her young remain, throughout, close to the thematic core of "Dinner at the Homesick Restaurant," but gradually the book's angle of vision widens so that we begin to know this home and hearth as Pearl's children themselves knew it. The body of the work is structured as a series of artfully paced life stories within which are embedded the images and episodes that shape each child's relationships with siblings, mates and parents. Cody Tull, the eldest of the children, is driven from early youth by a rage to dominate; he is endlessly cruel not only to his brother Ezra (he steals Ezra's girl, for example, on the eve of the man's marriage) but to his own wife and son, emerging in middle age as a rich, time-obsessed efficiency engineer whose embitterment stops barely short of self-destructiveness. Jenny, the second child, is a thrice-married pediatrician who buzzes with lively contradictions—witty, animated, forthright in speech, yet skeptically withdrawn from those who should be closest to her. (Miss Tyler has created, in her books, a half-dozen individual, idiosyncratically charming, completely believable young women; nobody I know of now writing matches this accomplishment.)

Ezra, the family baby, his mother's favorite, and (owing to Cody Tull's greed) a bachelor, runs an original, down-homey restaurant in inner-city Baltimore, dwells in the house he grew up in, ceaselessly imagines a world of affection freely exchanged, and regularly schedules splendid family dinner reunions at his eating place (they give the book its quirky-perfect title)—occasions that disintegrate, usually, into fearful rows. There's a touch of Dostoyevsky's "idiot" in Ezra, a hint of the unposturing selflessness whose effect on people denied faith in the possibility of human purity is invariably to intensify cynicism. "Cody hated the radiant, grave expression that Ezra wore sometimes; it showed that he realized full well how considerate he was being. 'What do you want for Christmas?' Cody asked him roughly. 'World peace?' "

On its face "Dinner at the Homesick Restaurant" is a book about the costs of parental truancy (a subject that surfaces in Miss Tyler's first novel and elsewhere frequently in her *oeuvre*). None of the three Tull children manages to cut loose from the family past; each is, to a degree, stunted; each turns for help to Pearl Tull in an hour of desperate adult need; and Pearl's conviction that something's wrong with each of them never recedes from the reader's consciousness. But no small measure of the book's subtlety derives from its exceptional—and exceptionally *wise,* the word bears repeating—clarity about the uselessness of cost accounting in human areas such as these. Cody Tull suffers from obscure guilt (was it something I said, something I did that made my father go away?). Ezra Tull suffers from want of desire. Jenny Tull suffers from fear of connection. And the behavior and feelings of all three are linked somehow with the terrible, never-explained rupture: their father's disappearance.

But it's also the case that what is best in each of these people, as in their mother, has its roots in the experience of deprivation that they jointly despise. Jenny's outward exuberance flows from instinctive knowledge of how overwhelming the need for cheer can be among young or old. Ezra's movingly unconsidered kindness and generosity have a similar source. Even Cody, who for much of the story is perceived as an enemy of light, emerges at the end as a man elevated by what he's obliquely learned from his father's irresponsibility.

Adversity teaches? We advance well beyond that truism in "Dinner at the Homesick Restaurant." We arrive at an understanding that the important lessons taught by adversity never quite make themselves known to the consciousness of the learners—remain hidden, inexpressible. Outsiders stumble on them sometimes, and behave in their innocence as though the lessons couldn't be missed—but oh yes they can.

There's a nearly throwaway moment late in this book that exquisitely underlines the point. A child sees a grim-faced photograph of Jenny Tull at age 13 and insists to her that it's like a "concentration camp person, a victim," and that it can't be her. "It isn't! Look at it! . . . It's somebody else," he told [Jenny]. "Not you; you're always laughing and having fun. It's not you." Jenny glances at the picture showing "a dark little girl with a thin watchful face," an image of the mirthless youth she shared with her brothers—and then says dismissively: "Oh, fine, it's not me, then." It is Jenny Tull, of course; the wisdom of the moment resides in the perception of our impatience with the sight of our own discontinuity. If we pause too long in contemplation of a former self, studying some lesson or other, we run the risk of forgetting how to take our present selves for granted. And down that road there's a risk of starting to treat life as a mystery instead of the way smart people treat it—as a set of done and undone errands. No way, says Jenny, clearly one of us.

Will so much talk of wisdom hide the truth that "Dinner at the Homesick Restaurant" is, from start to finish, superb entertainment? I hope not.

Much as I've admired Miss Tyler's earlier books, I've found flaws in a few—something excessively static in the situation developed in "Morgan's Passing," for instance, something arbitrary in the plotting of "Earthly Possessions." But in the work at hand Miss Tyler is a genius plotter, effortlessly redefining her story questions from page to page, never slackening the lines of suspense. There are, furthermore, numberless explosions of hilarity, not one of which (I discover) can be sliced out of its context for quotation—so tightly fashioned is this tale—without giving away, as they say, a narrative climax. There are scenes that strike me as likely to prove unforgettable: Pearl Tull attempting, after years of silence on the matter, to explain to her adamantly inattentive children that their father isn't coming back; Jenny Tull revising and revising, as though aiming at a masterpiece in the mode of the laconic sublime, a letter accepting a marriage proposal; Cody Tull declaring his suspicion to his wife that his brother is the father of their son; and many more.

And everywhere there's a marvelous delicacy of finish, witness Pearl Tull's drifting remembrance as she falls off into her long sleep: "She remembered the feel of wind on summer nights—how it billows through the house and wafts the curtains and smells of tar and roses. How a sleeping baby weighs so heavily on your shoulder, like ripe fruit. What privacy it is to walk in the rain beneath the drip and crackle of your own umbrella."

Seriousness does insist, in the end, that explicit note be taken of the facts of this career. Anne Tyler turned 40 just last year. She's worked with a variety of materials, established her mastery of grave as well as comic tones. Her command of her art is sure, and her right to trust her feeling for the complications both of our nature and of our nurturing arrangements stands beyond question. Speculating about this artist's future is, in short, a perfectly natural movement of mind. But, as I said before, I'm reluctant to speculate, and I expect other readers, in quantity, will share my reluctance. What one wants to do on finishing such a work as "Dinner at the Homesick Restaurant" is maintain balance, keep things intact for a stretch, stay under the spell as long as feasible. The before and after are immaterial; nothing counts except the knowledge, solid and serene, that's all at once breathing in the room. We're speaking, obviously, about an extremely beautiful book.

[From "Strange New World"]

JAMES WOLCOTT

Anne Tyler is one of my favorite writers, and Baltimore is one of my favorite places, but the two of them have been locked in a crushing embrace for so long that it's time someone reached for a crowbar and pried them apart. Raised in North Carolina, Tyler has lived for a healthy spell in Baltimore, whose white-stooped streets have provided the setting for her most ardent and shapely novels (*Celestial Navigation, The Clock Winder, Searching for Caleb*). In photographs, Tyler seems to be all eyes, and her super-attentive appetite for wee detail—the sag of cupboard shelves, the worn lines around a worried mother's eyes—coupled with her secure sense of place, gives her best work its fine-grained sturdiness. But Tyler's previous novel, *Morgan's Passing,* was disconcertingly floppy and cuddlesome, doting far too affectionately on its title character's eccentricities. The book lacked muscle and a driving sense of purpose; its limp sweetness indicated that perhaps Tyler had squeezed Baltimore dry of fresh inspiration.

Now Anne Tyler has published a new novel, *Dinner at the Homesick Restaurant* (Alfred A. Knopf, $13.50), and the evidence is near-conclusive that she has licked Baltimore to a splinter. Unlike *Morgan's Passing, Dinner at the Homesick Restaurant* isn't whimsical or ingratiating; it's a glum, low-plodding, dogged novel, a study of people whose jaw muscles ache from nursing so many long-nagging resentments. *Dinner* is a work of unwavering integrity, but it doesn't exactly pop with exuberance and confetti. It's *conscientiously* dour.

Dinner at the Homesick Restaurant is hobbled from page one on by its rickety plot structure. As the novel opens, eighty-five-year-old grandmother Pearl Tull is shown lying on her deathbed, memories pricking at her fading mind; the bulk of the book consists of flashbacks from Pearl's life (courtship, marriage, motherhood) and the lives of her three put-upon children, Ezra, Cody, and Jenny. Deathbed retrospectives have been worked to the nub in fiction, and Tyler doesn't come up with any spiffy ways to soup up and customize her time machine. She simply creaks through her characters' pasts, scooping up mementos and scattering them across the table like a palmful of seashells.

From *Esquire*, April 1982, 123–24. Reprinted by permission of the author.

It seems a wearisome chore, this seashell collecting. When daughter Jenny gets married, we get a businesslike report:

> She married Harley late in August, in the little Baptist church that the Tulls had attended off and on. Cody gave Jenny away and Ezra was the usher. The guests he ushered in were: Pearl, Mr. and Mrs. Baines, and an aunt on Harley's mother's side. Jenny wore a white eyelet dress and sandals. Harley wore a black suit, white button-down shirt, and snub-nosed, dull black shoes. Jenny looked down at those shoes all during the ceremony. They reminded her of licorice jellybeans.
>   . . . Then Harley and Jenny took a train to Paulham University, where they'd rented a small apartment. They had no furniture yet and spent their wedding night on the floor. Jenny was worried about Harley's inexperience. She was certain he'd always been above such things as sex; he wouldn't know what to do, and neither would she, and they would end up failing at something the rest of the world managed without a thought. But actually, Harley knew very well what to do. She suspected he'd researched it. She had an image of Harley at a library desk, comparing the theories of experts, industriously making notes in the proper outline form.

Except for the licorice-black shoes, the details have no zing, the language is snoringly flat, and the vagueness about sex is coyly evasive. (Sex is always a flimsy rumor in Tyler's novels—she shies away from erotic heat, from all the randy, damp little itches of desire.)

I grew up in Maryland, so I get a happy tingle when Tyler refers to Ken Singleton's cheekbones or Timonium flea markets, and I do realize that it's presumptuous for a reviewer to offer a novelist advice. Still, *Dinner at the Homesick Restaurant* is so grindingly forced and unfelt that I'm compelled to urge Tyler to take a holiday from chronicling domestic strife in Baltimore and let her mind go carelessly ballooning off into the blue. Unexplored vistas are needed to rejuvenate Anne Tyler's novels; her last two novels are so suffocatingly cozy that her characters seem hammered into their lives, sealed off against the elements. The Homesick Restaurant may sound like a feeding hole across from the Hotel New Hampshire, but it's really a boarded-up prison—a roomy crypt. Bring on the trampolines and coochie dancers! Break out the fizz and brew! There's more to fiction than watching lives flicker and dim in the long Baltimore night.

The Accidental Tourist

◆

Watching Life Go By

PETER S. PRESCOTT

The markings on Anne Tyler's recent novels are as distinctive as those on a Japanese print, or on the back of a silver spoon. The first stands for "Baltimore." The next reads "delicate balance of comedy and pathos." The third: "tensions of domesticity." The last: "temptations of order and chaos." In "Morgan's Passing" and "Dinner at the Homesick Restaurant," eccentric or extravagant characters dream of a more orderly life. In "The Accidental Tourist," Tyler reverses her perspective: the orderly life, taken to an extreme, becomes a deadening cocoon; the dream of redemption involves a life of "color and confusion."

As the novel opens, Sarah Leary tells Macon, her husband of 20 years, that she wants a divorce. The previous year, their son had been murdered and Sarah is depressed by the world's evil. She thinks Macon doesn't care. Much later, she expands on her theme: "It's like you're trying to slip through life unchanged . . . You're like something in a capsule." She's right: there's something muffled about Macon's approach to living; he's a finicky, dithering man, fond of his little methods, reflexively correcting other people's grammar.

Most authors would be hard put to rouse sympathy for such a protagonist, but Tyler knows how: she makes Macon the author of a series of anti-guidebooks, books for the businessman who'd rather not leave Baltimore just to go to Rome, London or Paris. Macon's logo is an overstuffed armchair with wings. "Armchair travelers dream of going places," his publisher says. "Traveling armchairs dream of staying put." Macon's "Accidental Tourist" books tell a traveler how to see as little of a city as possible (they presume he'll never venture into the countryside). They tell him where to find American fast-food joints, how to avoid anything foreign. The only safe thing to eat in France, says Macon, is Salade Niçoise. On planes, eat little and "always bring a book, as protection against strangers. Magazines don't last. Newspapers from home will make you homesick, and newspapers from elsewhere will remind you you don't belong."

Nakedness: When Sarah leaves, Macon reverts contentedly to childhood, living with his sister and brothers, who avoid life just as busily as he. Any plot at this point needs a spoon to stir it; Tyler produces a familiar one. Muriel Pritchett, who trains Macon's dog for him, is one of Tyler's eccentrics. A ragged young woman with a damaged child, she's as appalling as she is appealing. Muriel embodies what Shaw called the Life Force. There's something heroic about the way she exposes her mangled past as if it were a book from which she must read aloud at once, something heroic, too, about the nakedness of her designs upon Macon. Macon moves in with her and her son, always keeping shy of commitment. But holding back won't work—not in life, certainly not in a novel.

It would be rash to say that "The Accidental Tourist" is the best of Tyler's 10 novels, but it's certainly as good as any she has done. Her comedies are of the very best sort, which is to say that they are always serious, that they combine the humor of a situation with a narrative voice that allows itself moments of wit. (Of a very young woman confronted by a children's game, she writes: "all the guests [joined] in except Brad's wife, who was still too close to childhood to risk getting stuck there on a visit back." Again: "Her face was a type no longer seen . . . How did women mold their basic forms to suit the times? Were there no more of those round chins, round foreheads, and bruised, baroque little mouths so popular in the forties?") Tyler cares for the frailty of her characters and exults in their resources. She knows that living is a messy business that will not long accommodate an antiseptic tourist like Macon. Macon must stop falling into his life; he must take charge of it. Tyler presents him with a fateful, clear-cut choice. Neither alternative is free from pain, nor from the pain he must cause another. The point is, he must choose and take the consequences, and he does. Like most novelists—think of Henry James, sending Isabel Archer back to her husband—Tyler spares us the sight of what happens next.

Anne Tyler's Family Circles

Jonathan Yardley

With each new novel—*The Accidental Tourist* makes 10—it becomes ever more clear that the fiction of Anne Tyler is something both unique and extraordinary in contemporary American literature. Unique, quite literally: there is no other writer whose work sounds like Tyler's, and Tyler sounds like no one except herself. Extraordinary, too: not merely for the quietly dazzling quality of her writing and the abidingly sympathetic nature of her characters, but also for her calm indifference to prevailing literary fashion and her deep conviction that it is the work, not the person who writes it, that matters. Of *The Accidental Tourist* one thing can be said with absolute certainty: it matters.

It is a beautiful, incandescent, heartbreaking, exhilarating book. A strong undercurrent of sorrow runs through it, yet it contains comic scenes— one involving a dog, a cat and a clothes dryer, another a Thanksgiving turkey, yet another a Christmas dinner—that explode with joy. It is preoccupied with questions of family, as indeed all of Tyler's more recent fiction is, but there is not an ounce of sentimentality to be found in what it says about how families stick together or fall apart. There's magic in it, and some of its characters have winning eccentricities, yet more than any of Tyler's previous books it is rooted firmly, securely, insistently in the real world.

That world is of course Baltimore, which in Tyler's fiction, as indeed in actuality, is both a place and a state of mind. By now Baltimore belongs to Tyler in the same way that Asheville belongs to Thomas Wolfe, Chicago to James T. Farrell, Memphis to Peter Taylor, Albany to William Kennedy; like these writers, she at once gives us the city as it really exists and redefines it through the realm of the imagination. When the protagonist of *The Accidental Tourist,* Macon Leary, drives along North Charles Street, he is on the map; when he arrives at Singleton Street, he is in uncharted territory. But there can be no question that Singleton Street, though fictitious, is real:

"He was beginning to feel easier here. Singleton Street still unnerved him with its poverty and its ugliness, but it no longer seemed so dangerous. He saw that the hoodlums in front of the Cheery Moments Carry-Out were pathetically young and shabby—their lips chapped, their sparse whiskers ineptly shaved, an uncertain, unformed look around their eyes. He saw that

From *Washington Post Book World,* 25 August 1985, 3. © *Washington Post;* reprinted by permission.

once the men had gone to work, the women emerged full of good intentions and swept their front walks, picked up the beer cans and potato chip bags, even rolled back their coat sleeves and scrubbed their stoops on the coldest days of the year. Children raced past like so many scraps of paper blowing in the wind—mittens mismatched, noses running—and some woman would brace herself on her broom to call, 'You there! Don't think I don't know you're skipping school!' For this street was always backsliding, Macon saw, always falling behind, but was caught just in time by these women with their carrying voices and their pushy jaws."

Singleton Street is not Macon's natural territory. Though by no means wealthy, he belongs to that part of Baltimore north of downtown where houses are detached, have yards, are shaded by trees; this is the world in which he grew up and in which until quite recently he lived all his life. But now, at the age of 43, he is finding that world come apart on him. A year ago something unspeakably awful happened: his 12-year-old son, Ethan, off at summer camp, was murdered in a fast-food restaurant, "one of those deaths that make no sense—the kind where the holdup man has collected his money and is free to go but decides, instead, first to shoot each and every person through the back of the skull." Now he has been left by Sarah, his wife of 20 years, who has been devastated by her son's death and believes that she must start life over because "I don't have enough time to waste it holing up in my shell," a shell she thinks Macon played a crucial role in constructing.

So there he is, alone in the house with Helen, the cat, and Edward, the rowdy little Welsh Corgi to whom he stubbornly clings because the dog was Ethan's. Macon is a creature of firm if peculiar habit who believes that a system can be devised to meet each of life's difficulties; his stratagems for breakfast, bedclothes and the laundry are nothing if not ingenious, even if they don't exactly work. Change and disruption frighten him, which makes him perfectly suited to be the author of guidebooks "for people forced to travel on business," accidental tourists who, like Macon, hate travel and much prefer to be at home.

"He covered only the cities in these guides, for people taking business trips flew into cities and out again and didn't see the countryside at all. They didn't see the cities, for that matter. Their concern was how to pretend they had never left home. What hotels in Madrid boasted king-sized Beautyrest mattresses? What restuarants in Tokyo offered Sweet'n'Low? Did Amsterdam have a McDonald's? Did Mexico City have a Taco Bell? Did any place in Rome serve Chef Boyardee ravioli? Other travelers hoped to discover distinctive local wines; Macon's readers searched for pasteurized and homogenized milk."

It is as Macon heads off on one of his research trips that his life begins to change. The veterinarian who has boarded Edward in the past now refuses to accept him—"Says here he bit an attendant," the girl tells Macon. "Says, 'Bit Barry in the ankle, do not readmit' "—so in desperation Macon pulls into the Meow-Bow Animal Hospital. There Edward is cheerfully admitted by "a thin young woman in a ruffled peasant blouse," with "aggressively frizzy black hair that burgeoned to her shoulders like an Arab headdress." Her name is Muriel Pritchett, and when Macon returns to reclaim Edward she tells him that she is a dog trainer on the side, with a specialty in "dogs that bite." As Edward's bad habits become steadily worse, Macon at last turns to her in desperation. It is the beginning of the end of his old world.

He'd been right on the edge. His grief over Ethan's death and the pain caused by Sarah's desertion had just about done him in, just about turned him into "some hopeless wreck of a man wandering drugged on a downtown street." Enter Muriel—Muriel with her "long, narrow nose, and sallow skin, and two freckled knobs of collarbone that promised an unluxurious body." Muriel babbling away like "a flamenco dancer with galloping consumption," Muriel with her bewildering array of odd jobs and her pathetic young son by a broken marriage and her run-down house on Singleton Street. Love at first sight it is not: "He missed his wife. He missed his son. They were the only people who seemed real to him. There was no point in looking for substitutes."

But life deals things out whether you're looking for them or not. Muriel, a fighter all her days, fights her way into Macon's heart: "Then he knew what mattered was the pattern of her life; that although he did not love her he loved the surprise of her, and also the surprise of himself when he was with her. In the foreign country that was Singleton Street he was an entirely different person. This person had never been suspected of narrowness, never been accused of chilliness; in fact, was mocked for his soft heart. And was anything but orderly." The accidental tourist has become a traveler— "Maybe, he thought, travel was not so bad. Maybe he'd got it all wrong"— whose journeys now are in the heart, whose world has grown larger than he had ever before imagined possible.

Where those journeys at last lead him is Tyler's secret, though it is no indiscretion to say that in the novel's final pages he faces wrenching, painful choices. But those choices are really less important than the change that has already taken place. Macon Leary has been given the gift of life. A man who had seemed fated to spend the rest of his days in a rut—"Here he still was! The same as ever! *What have I gone and done?* he wondered, and he swallowed thickly and looked at his own empty hands"—has been given new connections, with himself and with others.

This is the central theme of Tyler's fiction: how people affect each other, how the lives of others alter our own. As are her previous novels, *The Accidental Tourist* is filled with connections and disconnections, with the exaltation and heartbreak that people bring to each other; she knows that though it is true people need each other, it is equally true "that people could, in fact, be used up—could use each other up, could be of no further help to each other and maybe even do harm to each other." The novel is filled as well with the knowledge that life leaves no one unscarred, that to live is to accept one's scars and make the best of them—and to accept as well the scars that other people bear.

And in *The Accidental Tourist* there are many others: the large and bumptious Leary family, Macon's wonderfully unpredictable boss, the people of Singleton Street, and most certainly Edward, the funniest and most lovable dog within memory. They occupy what indisputably is Tyler's best book, the work of a writer who has reached full maturity and is in unshakable command, who takes the raw material of ordinary life and shapes it into what can only be called art. The magical, slightly fey and otherworldly tone of her previous books is evident here, but more than ever before Tyler has planted her fiction in the hard soil of the world we all know; *The Accidental Tourist* cuts so close to the bone that it leaves one aching with pleasure and pain. Words fail me: one cannot reasonably expect fiction to be much better than this.

Taking the Anne Tyler Tour

Joseph Mathewson

In Anne Tyler's new novel, *The Accidental Tourist,* the central character is a man named Macon Leary. Macon writes homespun travel books for people who don't want to travel, businessmen whose main concern is how to pretend they've never left home. "I am happy to say," runs a typical entry, "that it's possible now to buy Kentucky Fried Chicken in Stockholm." If Macon Leary himself were reviewing *The Accidental Tourist,* he might produce something like this:

"Anne Tyler is one of our most prolific and accomplished novelists. She has been turning out books on a pretty regular basis since 1964, when she was all of twenty-three years old. Her ninth and most recent was *Dinner at the Homesick Restaurant,* which made her famous.

"The many readers of that book responded to the warmth and poignancy of a story about a family who couldn't live with each other or without. Those readers will naturally expect to find Miss Tyler's hallmarks on anything else she writes: depth, compassion, a fine eye for details, language that wouldn't embarrass your grandmother, and, of course, a story set largely in Baltimore, Maryland, where Miss Tyler lives herself. Those readers will not be disappointed in her tenth novel, *The Accidental Tourist.* Far from it.

"But getting back to Baltimore, I would say that Miss Tyler doesn't just live there. She is at home there, and she makes us at home with a group of characters who are as real as your own family. And you know how it is with family. You grow up with them. You get a certain idea about your Uncle Fred, and that idea doesn't change much. You don't even want it to change. If Uncle Fred turns out to be a bank robber or a Republican—well, if that's the way he was going, that's the way he should go. Anything else would be too unsettling.

"And here is the one real reservation I have about *The Accidental Tourist:* Miss Tyler is just first-rate at creating these fully rounded people who all their lives have seen no reason to change, who have made resistance to change a sort of negative philosophy. Why, even the dog, Edward, who is a fully rounded dog, is also resistant to change. But the nature of life sometimes

From *Horizon,* September 1985, 14. Every effort has been made to locate all persons having any rights or interests in the material published here. If some acknowledgments have not been made their omission is unintentional and is regretted.

forces us into changing, whether we want to or not. That's one of the things Miss Tyler's story is saying. But she's done such a bang-up job of making me believe in the fixed qualities of her people that I had a few bad moments when some of the characters did begin to change, when the ice broke up around them and they started floating back to the mainstream of life, so to speak.

"For example, the central character hates the thought that he might get involved in talking to strangers on planes or trains. He always takes along a 1,198-page novel called *Miss MacIntosh, My Darling* and dips into it at random whenever trouble threatens. This strikes me as a highly practical idea; so, late in the book, on a bumpy flight, when this man actually engages in conversation with a frightened old lady and smiles to reassure her, I must confess to wishing that he still had his nose in *Miss MacIntosh*.

"This will tell you that I am a grumpy sort of a fellow and not easy to please. When I add that Miss Tyler does finally make me believe in the changes she's bringing about—cheer for them, almost—you will see how much she's accomplished. In fact, I will go as far as to say that, with the publication of *The Accidental Tourist,* the fall publishing season can be counted a success.

"*Dinner at the Homesick Restaurant* is a bigger book, and, in ways, more ambitious. But I had the feeling that the grown-up characters in it didn't have much relation to the children they were when Miss Tyler first introduced them. They were like wonderfully detailed portraits pasted over the snapshots of somebody else. In *The Accidental Tourist,* Miss Tyler is working on a smaller canvas, but the portraits are all of a piece.

"The new book is also very funny, much more so than its predecessor; and because it's a very touching book as well, there is something about the alternation of laughter and tears that puts me in mind of the great Victorian novelists. And I will go way out on a limb here and admit that the novelist I have especially in mind is Charles Dickens. There is almost that kind of size and eccentricity to Miss Tyler's characters. Her writing has a lot of Dickens's humanity, too, as well as a certain lack of fear, which came more easily to his own century than it does, alas, to ours.

"By this I mean that Miss Tyler isn't afraid to be sentimental—what other modern writer gives us views of dead characters enjoying a happy afterlife?—and she isn't afraid to be hopeful. Not exactly optimistic. This is a sober, elegiac hopefulness, but it's still in a class by itself. These days, the few good writers who also dare to be hopeful provide themselves with the safety net of an ultimate worldly cynicism (like John Irving). Miss Tyler does her act without the net.

"You will be wondering if this book has a plot, and so it does, mainly concerning the author of the *Accidental Tourist* travel guides. When his young son is murdered in a perfectly senseless fashion, the man's wife leaves him and the man himself returns to the bosom of his family—two brothers and a sister, all living in their grandparents' home.

"The brothers are both divorced, while the sister, who never married, is the kind of person who has her kitchen alphabetized, so that the allspice is next to the ant poison. After dinner, the siblings play Vaccination, a card game they invented as children which is so difficult that no outsider has ever gotten the hang of it. There, at home, our hero might linger till the end of his days, loveless, but safe—except for that well-rounded dog I mentioned, who has started biting people.

"And that's all I'm going to tell you. When traveling, it's all very well to be prepared for the road ahead. But there are some discoveries you'll enjoy more if you make them for yourself. One thing for sure, if you haven't discovered Anne Tyler yet, you should.

"*The Accidental Tourist* is being published by Alfred A. Knopf for $16.95, but a Berkeley paperback will be along eventually. A lot of Miss Tyler's books are already out in paperback, so you can read them while you wait."

Leaving Home

JOHN UPDIKE

Anne Tyler's tenth novel, "The Accidental Tourist" (Knopf; $16.95), manages to leave Baltimore; its hero, Macon Leary, writes a series of travel guides under the pseudonym "Accidental Tourist," and his creator, whose many virtues have not hitherto included cosmopolitanism, provides for him convincing, characteristically perky versions of London and Paris, Edmonton and Vancouver, as well as some vivid airplane rides. Transatlantic jet travel is authoritatively sketched:

> There was the usual mellifluous murmur from the loudspeaker about seatbelts, emergency exits, oxygen masks. He wondered why stewardesses accented such unlikely words. "*On* our flight this evening we *will* be offering . . ." [Macon] angled his book beneath a slender shaft of light and turned a page. The engines had a weary, dogged sound. It was the period he thought of as the long haul—the gulf between supper and breakfast when they were suspended over the ocean, waiting for that lightening of the sky that was supposed to be morning although, of course, it was nowhere near morning back home. In Macon's opinion, morning in other time zones was like something staged—a curtain painted with a rising sun, superimposed upon the real dark.

Real morning and real life are restricted to Baltimore, where Macon is one of four middle-aged siblings. His two brothers, Porter and Charles, after their marriages failed, moved in with their spinster sister, Rose, who still lives in the large house where they were raised by their grandparents; and Macon, after his wife leaves him and he breaks his leg, moves in also. There they complete their daily routines by playing a card game, Vaccination, which they invented in their childhoods and which is too complex for outsiders to learn. The point of Macon's guidebooks is to provide the unadventurous, "accidental" American traveller with information that minimizes the trauma of leaving home: where in Stockholm to get Kentucky Fried Chicken, what restaurants in Tokyo offer Sweet'n Low, how to avoid conversation in airplanes ("Always bring a book, as protection against strangers. Magazines don't last"). His guides constitute a parody of cautious, systematic self-

Reprinted by permission; © 1985 John Updike. Originally in *The New Yorker*, 28 October 1985, 106–8, 110–12.

protectiveness; Miss Tyler's lovingly detailed, lively procession, from novel to novel, of mild-mannered agoraphobes and habit-hugging families has in Macon produced its theorist and its own critic. The novel explores more forthrightly than any of its predecessors the deep and delicate conflict between coziness and venture, safety and danger, tidiness and messiness, home and the world, inside and outside, us and them.

Miss Tyler never fails to produce a fluid, shapely story sparkling with bright, sharp images drawn from the so-called ordinary world. Her Baltimore, though a city of neighborhoods and ingrained custom, is also a piece of the American Northeast and of Western culture; her fiction readily relays the brand names and pop tunes and fashions of the moment, with special attention paid to shoe styles. Yet, unlike some younger writers, she does not imply that these flitting fads and headlines are all the culture there is. She is a Southern writer in her sense of the past; her old people have a fine vitality, and some of her most moving pages reconstruct an older time, as in "Searching for Caleb" and "Dinner at the Homesick Restaurant." In her run of fiction since "The Clock Winder" (1972), she has made Baltimore, as a site for imaginative construction, her own—John Barth tends to stick to Maryland's Eastern Shore, and Mencken's city was a figment of his reminiscences. As a site, Baltimore is rich in characters and various in locale, yet with a cloistered and backward-gazing quality like that of a less drastic Yoknapatawpha County, with the same convenience to a microcosm-maker.

Miss Tyler's free rein there, with her artistic version of the metropolis unchecked by any other (compare the multiple shadows New York writers cast upon each other, or the way that Bellow must repeatedly shoulder Dreiser's ghost aside in dealing with Chicago), abets our impression of a toy city, manipulated a bit lightly. Her generous empathy and distinguished intelligence run toward moments of precious diminishment. In the course of this novel, the Learys, all in their forties, fall to making together a dollhouse extension, and the author's own delight breathes over their shoulders:

> The garage was convincingly untidy. Miniature wood chips littered the floor around a stack of twig-sized fire logs, and a coil of green wire made a perfect garden hose. Now they were working on the upstairs. Rose was stuffing an armchair cushion no bigger than an aspirin. Charles was cutting a sheet of wallpaper from a sample book. Porter was drilling holes for the curtain rods.

Her characters whittle away at playful hobbies, and tinker at witty inventions. The cuteness of the names invented, in "The Accidental Tourist," for fictional businesses savors less of mimesis than of literary foolery: Doggie, Do is an outfit that trains canines; Re-Runs names a secondhand-shoe store. Some of the Learys' behavior seems unlikely even for reclusive and order-obsessed eccentrics. Macon treads underfoot each day's dirty laundry while giving himself a shower, mounts a wash-basket on a skateboard, and sleeps in "a giant sort of envelope made from one of the seven sheets he had folded and stitched together on the sewing machine." His sister Rose, "had a kitchen that was so completely alphabetized, you'd find the allspice next to the ant poison," which gives the reader a laugh but keeps Rose at a distance. And are we seriously to believe of the Learys that four prosperous adults enjoy such tenuous connections with the world at large that they casually agree not to answer the telephone in their house, day after day? They just let it ring.

"The Accidental Tourist" is lighter than its wholly admirable and relatively saturnine predecessor, "Dinner at the Homesick Restaurant." Miss Tyler takes her time developing her story and fills much of the novel's first third with domestic slapstick of the alphabetized-kitchen, treading-the-wash variety. The story is a basic one of breakup and breakout. A year before the novel's first scene, the rude outside world has dealt Macon and his wife of twenty years, Sarah, a cruel blow: Ethan, their twelve-year-old son—"a tall blond sprout of a boy with an open, friendly face"—was senselessly murdered in a Burger Bonanza by a nineteen-year-old holdup man. Now Sarah announces that Macon has been no comfort and she is leaving him. Living alone, he breaks his leg and returns to his grandfather's house, where he and his three siblings play Vaccination and ignore the telephone. However, the misbehavior of his pet dog, an irritable Welsh corgi called Edward (and up to midpoint the novel's most sympathetic and intelligible character), brings into this airless situation a rasping breath of oxygen—dog-trainer Muriel Pritchett, who is younger, poorer, more vulgar and dynamic than Macon. That her brash and open world view shakes up the careful Leary ways is predictable, as is the revival of Sarah's interest when Macon makes himself at home with this new woman. But the turns and climaxes unfold with many small surprises, and after a high point (literally) where Macon panics at the revelation of distance afforded from what appears to be the top of the World Trade Center ("He saw the city spread far below like a glittering golden ocean, the streets tiny ribbons of light, the planet curving away at the edges, the sky a purple hollow extending to infinity") the book becomes a real page-turner. This susceptible reader, his eyes beginning to blur, stopped twenty pages short of the end, fell into a troubled sleep, woke before dawn, read to the end, and only then relaxed. It is a happy ending, as happy as one can be in a world where "after a certain age . . . you can only choose what to lose."

In a time when many woman [sic] writers find themselves quite busy enough proclaiming the difficulties of being female, Anne Tyler persistently concerns herself with the moral evolution of male characters. Though mild, passive Macon is not exactly macho, we live comfortably in his skin for three hundred and fifty pages and see through his eyes what he sees in both women—plump, solid Sarah with her "calm face, round as a daisy," skinny Muriel with her "spiky, pugnacious fierceness" and her eyes "very small, like caraway seeds." The wife is rather more winningly portrayed than the girlfriend, and Macon loves her with less effort, but he gropes beyond that:

"He began to think that who you are when you're with somebody may matter more than whether you love her." With Sarah, he has been, as she herself charges, "muffled." She tells him, "It's like you're trying to slip through life unchanged." Yet she herself confirms the basis of the Leary caution: the world is a terrible place. "Ever since Ethan died," she tells him, "I've had to admit that people are basically evil. Evil, Macon. So evil they would take a twelve-year-old boy and shoot him through the skull for no reason. I read a paper now and I despair; I've given up watching the news on TV. There's so much wickedness, children setting other children on fire and grown men throwing babies out second-story windows, rape and torture and terrorism, old people beaten and robbed, men in our very own government willing to blow up the world, indifference and greed and instant anger on every street corner."

Muriel takes Macon outside himself. And distinctly beneath his own social level. "The Accidental Tourist" is about, in part, crossing class boundaries. One doesn't have to be a Baltimorean to perceive that Singleton Street, where Muriel lives with her sickly and repulsive seven-year-old son, Alexander, and Timonium, where her parents dwell in a development called Foxhunt Acres, are a far socio-economic cry from North Charles Street, where Macon and Sarah had their home, and the unnamed avenue where Macon's grandfather, a factory owner, reared his four grandchildren. Macon went to Princeton, and nothing about Muriel exasperates him more than her solecisms—"eck cetera," "nauseous" when she means "nauseated," "enormity" when she means to talk of size, "da Vinci" when she should say "Leonardo," and (very subtle, this) "a nother," as in "I wish I was just a totally nother person."

It is Macon, however, who becomes another person: "In the foreign country that was Singleton Street he was an entirely different person." An accidental tourist within Baltimore, "he was beginning to feel easier here. Singleton Street still unnerved him with its poverty and its ugliness, but it no longer seemed so dangerous." The hoodlums hanging out, he perceives, are "pathetically young and shabby," and children and women bring a constant cleansing wind of "good intentions." The scruffy society of neighborhood women that collects in Muriel's kitchen comes to feel as cozy to him as a game of Vaccination; one wonders, indeed, whether he truly adjusts to this tawdry neighborhood or whether it has been simply annexed to the gaily colored, miniaturized precincts of Tylerville. "Macon saw Singleton Street in his mind, small and distant . . . and full of gaily drawn people scrubbing their stoops, tinkering with their cars, splashing under fire hydrants." A mugger accosts them, but Muriel swats him with her purse and tells him to run on home. Can Baltimore's underworld really be this easily disarmed? When Mrs. Soffel, in last year's movie of the same name, left her safe quarters in the warden's end of the Allegheny County Jail for disgrace and likely doom with an escaping criminal, that was de-domestication with a price tag. Macon doesn't so much leave home as change homes, and (retaining, of course, his money) he, like many before him, finds the slums livelier than the proper neighborhoods.

But yes, people are not evil. Or not *only* evil. And they prove more responsive and entertaining than a stay-at-home would suppose. Muriel has never travelled. When she tells Macon, "If I could go anywhere I'd go to Paris," he quickly informs her, "Paris is terrible. Everybody is impolite." Yet in the eventual event (not to give away Miss Tyler's slam-bang dénouement) Paris for Muriel abounds with polite, helpful, English-speaking persons, who guide her toward fantastic bargains in secondhand clothes. Throughout the book, people spontaneously open up and talk about themselves—taxi-drivers, airplane pilots, neighbors, camp directors. Miss Tyler's mankind is a race of compulsive fabulists: everybody in motion, talking. Looking out of a plane window as he takes Muriel for her first flight, Macon has "an intimate view of farmlands, woodlands, roofs of houses. It came to him very suddenly that every little roof concealed actual lives. Well, of course he's known that, but all at once it took his breath away. He saw how real those lives were to the people who lived them—how intense and private and absorbing." Though not every mugger can really be chased away with a purse, and not every Parisian is in fact polite to American yokels, an assumption to the contrary offers a basis for moving ahead. We should credit strangers and outsiders with a self-interest as intense and complex as our own—not an obvious fact to the initially timorous and solipsistic human organism—and with a benignity to match our own trust. If Anne Tyler strikes us as too benign, too swift to tack together shelter for her dolls, it may be that we have lost familiarity with the comedic spirit, the primal faith in natural resilience and the forces of renewal. Like the older, graver Iris Murdoch, Miss Tyler believes in love and art and the usefulness of a shaking-up. The constructive, tinkering, inventive, systematic side of our selves is not enough; he who would save his life must lose it. Macon's dreams are reported in this novel, as a necessary part of him, along with his struggles to fall asleep.

"It occurred to him . . . that the world was divided sharply down the middle: Some lived careful lives and some lived careless lives, and everything that happened could be explained by the difference between them. But he could not have said, not in a million years, why he was so moved by the sight of Muriel's thin quilt trailing across the floor where she must have dragged it when she rose in the morning." He cannot say, but the book itself slyly spells it out: Macon's mother, Alicia, glimpsed but rarely in the novel, is herself of the party of the careless. A woman of tempestuous and fleeting enthusiasms, she had been widowed in the Second World War and in 1950 remarried, to "an engineer who travelled around the world building bridges," and settled her four children with their grandparents in Baltimore. "They were met by their grandparents, two thin, severe, distinguished people in dark clothes. The children approved of them at once." Henceforth, "like some naughty, gleeful fairy, Macon imagined, she darted in and out of their lives leaving a trail of irresponsible remarks." When his sister marries, Alicia, now on her fourth husband, startles him by being at the wedding, displeases him with her gaudy outfit ("a long white caftan trimmed with vibrant bands of satin, and when she reached up to hug him a whole culvert of metal bangles clattered and slid down her left arm"), and links arms with Muriel. "Macon had a sudden appalling thought: Maybe in his middle age he was starting to choose his mother's style of person, as if concluding that Alicia—silly, vain, annoying woman—might have the right answers after all. But no. He put the thought away from him." But the thought is a good one. We are all, however careful, the children of chaos. Leaving home can be going home.

Life Is a Foreign Country

LARRY MCMURTRY

In Anne Tyler's fiction, family is destiny, and (nowadays, at least) destiny clamps down on one in Baltimore. For an archeologist of manners with Miss Tyler's skills, the city is a veritable Troy, and she has been patiently excavating since the early 1970's, when she skipped off the lawn of Southern fiction and first sank her spade in the soil which has nourished such varied talents as Poe, Mencken, Billie Holiday and John Waters, the director of the films "Pink Flamingos" and "Polyester."

It is without question some of the fustiest soil in America: in the more settled classes, social styles developed in the 19th century withstand, with sporelike tenacity, all that the present century can throw at them. Indeed, in Baltimore *all* classes appear to be settled, if not cemented, in grooves of neighborhood and habit so deep as to render them impervious—as a bright child puts it in "The Accidental Tourist"—to everything except nuclear flash.

From this rich dust of custom, Miss Tyler is steadily raising a body of fiction of major dimensions. One of the persistent concerns of this work is the ambiguity of family happiness and unhappiness. Since coming to Baltimore, Miss Tyler has probed this ambiguity in seven novels of increasing depth and power, working numerous changes on a consistent set of themes.

In "The Accidental Tourist" these themes, some of which she has been sifting for more than 20 years, cohere with high definition in the muted (or, as his wife says, "muffled") personality of Macon Leary, a Baltimore man in his early 40's who writes travel guides for businessmen who, like himself, hate to travel.

The logo on the cover of these travel guides ("The Accidental Tourist in England," "The Accidental Tourist in New York," etc.) is a winged armchair; their assumption is that all travel is involuntary, and they attempt to spare these involuntary travelers the shock of the unfamiliar, insofar as that's possible. Macon will tell you where to find Kentucky Fried Chicken in Stockholm, or whether there's a restaurant that serves Chef Boy-Ar-Dee ravioli in Rome. Macon himself is so devoted to his part of Baltimore that

From *New York Times Book Review*, 8 September 1985, 1, 36. Copyright © 1985 by the The New York Times Company. Reprinted by permission.

even the unfamiliar neighborhoods he visits affect him as negatively as foreign countries.

Like most of Miss Tyler's males, Macon Leary presents a broad target to all of the women (and even a few of the men) with whom he is involved. His mother; his sister, Rose; his wife, Sarah, and, in due course, his girlfriend, Muriel Pritchett—a dog trainer of singular appearance and ability— regularly pepper him on the subject of his shortcomings, the greatest of which is a lack of passion, playfulness, spontaneity or the desire to do one single thing that *they* like to do. This lack is the more maddening because Macon is reasonably competent; if prompted he will do more or less anything that's required of him. What exasperates the women is the necessity for constant prompting.

When attacked, Macon rarely defends himself with much vigor, which only heightens the exasperation. He likes a quiet life, based on method and system. His systems are intricate routines of his own devising, aimed at reducing the likelihood that anything unfamiliar will occur. The unfamiliar is never welcome in Macon's life, and he believes that if left to himself he can block it out or at least neutralize it.

Not long after we meet him, Macon *is* left to himself. Sarah, his wife of 20 years, leaves him. Macon and Sarah have had a tragedy: their 12-year-old son, Ethan, was murdered in a fast-food joint, his death an accidental byproduct of a holdup.

Though Macon is a grived by this loss as Sarah, he is, as she points out, "not a comfort." When she remarks that since Ethan's death she sometimes wonders if there's any point to life, Macon replies, honestly but unhelpfully, that it never seemed to him there was all that much point to begin with. As if this were not enough, he can never stop himself from correcting improper word choice, even if the incorrect usage occurs in a conversation about the death of a child. These corrections are not made unkindly, but they are invariably made; one does not blame Sarah for taking off.

With the ballast of his marriage removed, Macon immediately tips into serious eccentricity. His little systems muiltiply, and his remaining companions, a Welsh corgi named Edward and a cat named Helen, fail to adapt to them. Eventually the systems overwhelm Macon himself, causing him to break a leg. Not long after, he finds himself where almost all of Miss Tyler's characters end up sooner or later—back in the grandparental seat. There he is tended to by his sister. His brothers, Porter and Charles, both divorced, are also there, repeating, like Macon, a motion that seems all but inevitable in Anne Tyler's fiction—a return to the sibling unit.

This motion, or tendency, cannot be blamed on Baltimore. In the very first chapter of Miss Tyler's first novel, "If Morning Ever Comes" (1964), a young man named Ben Joe Hawkes leaves Columbia University and hurries home to North Carolina mainly because he can't stand not to know what his sisters are up to. From then on, in book after book, siblings are drawn inexorably back home, as if their parents or (more often) grandparents had planted tiny magnets in them which can be activated once they have seen what the extrafamilial world is like. The lovers and mates in her books, by exerting their utmost strength, can sometimes delay these regroupings for as long as 20 years, but sooner or later a need to be with people who are *really* familiar—their brothers and sisters—overwhelms them.

Macon's employer, a man named Julian, who manages to marry but not to hold Macon's sister, puts it succinctly once Rose has drifted back to her brothers: "She'd worn herself a groove or something in that house of hers, and she couldn't help swerving back into it." Almost no one in Miss Tyler's books avoids that swerve; the best they can hope for is to make a second escape, as does the resourceful Caleb Peck in "Searching for Caleb" (1976). Brought back after an escape lasting 60 years, Caleb sneaks away again in his 90's.

Macon, less adventurous than Caleb Peck, is saved from this immolation-by-siblings through the unlikely agency of Edward, the Welsh corgi. Unnerved by the dissolution of his own secure routine, Edward begins to crack up. He starts attacking people, including Julian and Macon's brothers too, one of whom, in a brilliant scene, Edward trees in the family pantry at the very moment that Macon is experiencing an anxiety attack in a restaurant on top of a building in New York.

Re-enter Muriel Pritchett, the dog trainer Macon had met earlier when forced to work out emergency boarding arrangements for Edward. Muriel is everything the Learys are not: talkative, confrontational, an eccentric dresser, casual about word choice. She lives with her sickly child, Alexander, in a Baltimore neighborhood that is not much less foreign to Macon than, say, Quebec. Muriel is also very different from Sarah.

Nonetheless, to the horror of his family, Macon moves in with Muriel. His indifference to his former life is so great that he doesn't even get upset when the pipes in his own house burst, ruining his living room. Muriel, despite her apparent unsuitability, "could raise her chin sometimes and pierce his mind like a blade. Certain images of her at certain random, insignificant moments would flash before him: Muriel at her kitchen table, ankles twined around her chair rungs, filling out a contest form for an all-expense-paid tour of Hollywood. Muriel telling her mirror, 'I look like the wrath of God'—a kind of ritual of leavetaking. Muriel doing the dishes in her big pink rubber gloves with the crimson fingernails, raising a soapy plate and trailing it airily over to the rinse water."

Macon, a fairly keen self-analyst, recognizes that while he does not exactly love Muriel, he "loved the surprise of her, and also the surprise of himself when he was with her. In the foreign country that was Singleton Street he was an entirely different person."

Surprise, however, is not quite enough; not to one so wedded to the familiar as Macon. Sarah, the not-yet-divorced wife, though a singularly articulate critic of Learys in general and Macon in particular, finds that all criticisms do not entirely invalidate Macon as a mate. She wants him back, Muriel wants to keep him, and a fierce tussle ensues, one in which Macon takes a largely spectatorial interest. He cannot entirely resist the suitable Sarah, nor forget the unsuitable but vivid Muriel.

The final scenes of this drama take place in Paris, where the two women manage to corner him. Even as Macon is making his decision, he is reassured by a sense that in a way it is only temporary, life being, in his scheme of things, a stage from which none of the major players ever completely disappear.

"The Accidental Tourist" is one of Anne Tyler's best books, as good as "Morgan's Passing," "Searching for Caleb," "Dinner at the Homesick Restaurant." The various domestic worlds we enter—Macon/Sarah; Macon/the Leary siblings; Macon/Muriel—are delineated with easy skill; now they are poignant, now funny. Miss Tyler shows, with a fine clarity, the mingling of misery and contentment in the daily lives of her families, reminding us how alike—and yet distinct—happy and unhappy families can be. Muriel Pritchett is as appealing a woman as Miss Tyler has created; and upon the quiet Macon she lavishes the kind of intelligent consideration that he only intermittently gets from his own womenfolk.

Two aspects of the novel do not entirely satisfy. One is the unaccountable neglect of Edward, the corgi, in the last third of the book. Edward is one of the more fully characterized dogs in recent literature; his breakdown is at least as interesting and if anything more delicately handled than Macon's. Yet Edward is allowed to slide out of the picture. Millions of readers who have managed to saddle themselves with neurotic quadrupeds will want to know more about Edward's situation.

The other questionable element is the dead son, Ethan. Despite an effort now and then to bring him into the book in a vignette or a nightmare, Ethan remains mostly a premise, and one not advanced very confidently by the author. She is brilliant at showing how the living press upon one another, but less convincing when she attempts to add the weight of the dead. The reader is invited to feel that it is this tragedy that separates Macon and Sarah. But a little more familiarity with Macon and Sarah, as well as with the marriages in Miss Tyler's other books, leaves one wondering. Macon's methodical approach to life might have driven Sarah off anyway. He would have corrected her word choice once too often, one feels. Miss Tyler is more successful at showing through textures how domestic life is sustained than she is at showing how these textures are ruptured by a death.

At the level of metaphor, however, she has never been stronger. The concept of an accidental tourist captures in a phrase something she has been saying all along, if not about life, at least about men: they are frequently accidental tourists in their own lives. Macon Leary sums up a long line of her males. Jake Simmes [sic] in "Earthly Possessions" is an accidental kidnapper.

The lovable Morgan Gower of "Morgan's Passing," an accidental obstetrician in the first scenes, is an accidental husband or lover in the rest of the book. Her men slump around like tired tourists—friendly, likable, but not all that engaged. Their characters, like their professions, seem accidental even though they come equipped with genealogies of Balzacian thoroughness. All of them have to be propelled through life by (at the very least) a brace of sharp, purposeful women—it usually takes not only a wife and a girlfriend but an indignant mother and one or more devoted sisters to keep these sluggish fellows moving. They poke around haphazardly, ever mild and perennially puzzled, in the foreign country called Life. If they see anything worth seeing, it is usually because a determined woman on the order of Muriel Pritchett thrusts it under their noses and demands that they pay some attention. The fates of these families hinge on long struggles between semiattentive males and semiobsessed females. In her patient investigation of such struggles, Miss Tyler has produced a very satisfying body of fiction.

Breathing Lessons

◆

Ordinary People

DAVID KLINGHOFFER

Though America's artist class has drawn many of its subjects and much of its financial support from America's middle class, our painters, sculptors, novelists, and poets have never quite learned to like that majority of Americans who are neither rich nor poor, powerful nor powerless, particularly sophisticated nor hopelessly parochial. Anne Tyler is a case in point, and her attitudes have affected the quality of her fiction.

For her much-acclaimed previous novel, *The Accidental Tourist,* Miss Tyler chose two out-of-the-ordinary characters as her protagonists: the highly eccentric Macon Leary, a Princeton-educated writer, and the highly marginal Muriel Pritchett, a single mother and poverty-stricken dog-trainer. Doing so, she produced a small prodigy of charm and warm humor. In *Breathing Lessons,* her latest, she has chosen to write about just plain folks: Ira Moran, owner of a Baltimore picture-frame shop, and his wife, Maggie, a housewife. For those who, after *The Accidental Tourist,* judged Miss Tyler one of America's best novelists, *Breathing Lessons* will be a disappointment. While Macon and Muriel were a gracefully drawn and highly sympathetic couple, Miss Tyler struggles to make Ira and Maggie halfway likable.

The whole of *Breathing Lessons* takes place during the Morans' trip to Deer Lick, Pennsylvania, for a friend's funeral. On the way up, they squabble and Maggie jumps out of the car in a huff. On the way back, they squabble

From *National Review,* 30 December 1988, 48–49. Copyright © 1988 by *National Review,* Inc., 150 East 35 Street, New York, NY 10016. Reprinted with permission.

and take a detour to visit their former daughter-in-law, Fiona, and her daughter, Leroy. Despite the tightly woven quality of its prose, like most books whose action spans only a day or so, *Breathing Lessons* staggers under an excess of narrative fabric: Miss Tyler gives Maggie three pages to maneuver her Chevy out of a tough parking space.

Miss Tyler is interested in the kinds of compromises people like Ira and Maggie have to make in order to raise children, to maintain a household, even just to stay together. Before the unplanned birth of their first child, for example, Ira had intended to study medicine. Instead, for a living, he ended up "cutting 45-degree angles in strips of gilded molding." When his son, Jesse, remarked once that he refused to believe he would die unknown, Ira, "instead of smiling tolerantly as he should have, had felt slapped in the face." Once, Maggie recalls, her daughter, Daisy, asked her if there had been "a certain conscious point in your life when you decided to settle for being ordinary?"

Though such compromises are built into the conventional system of marriage and parenthood, Miss Tyler believes we need not despair over the institution of the middle-class family. Climbing into bed at day's end, Maggie finds Ira playing a game of solitaire. Like solitaire, she reflects, a marriage starts out easy. But by now Ira had "arrived at the interesting part of the game . . . He had passed that early, superficial stage when any number of moves seemed possible, and now his choices were narrower and he had to show real skill and judgment. She felt a little stir of something that came over her like a flush, a sort of inner buoyancy, and she lifted her face to kiss the warm blade of his cheekbone." As the book concludes, Maggie has come to believe she *will* find happiness in her marriage, but only be doing her best to overcome the innumerable, mostly insurmountable, challenges the years are bound to present. In short, Miss Tyler turns the bored housewife into a kind of domestic Sisyphus.

Breathing Lessons is meant to end on a hopeful note—Camus, after all, said we must suppose Sisyphus happy. But it's too much to ask us to suppose the same of Ira and Maggie Moran. How could anyone be happy married to either one? On a couple of occasions Miss Tyler has Ira acting almost human. More typical, though, are the two scenes—one in real time, the other a flashback—in which he drives his son and daughter-in-law apart by loudly informing the latter that her husband is sleeping around. When Maggie needs him for support, she generally finds him deep and unreachable in a game of solitaire. When he's not playing solitaire, he's talking about auto routes or gas mileage.

Maggie, for her part, is pathetic. Twice in the space of perhaps three hours she resolves to leave Ira forever, and twice backs down entirely. She's stupid, too. Once, we're told, she spent a whole evening fretting over a wrong number:

"Hello?" she'd said into the phone, and a man had said, "Laverne, stay right there safe in your house. I just talked to Dennis and he's coming to fetch you." And then had hung up. Maggie cried, "Wait!"—speaking into a dead receiver; typical. Whoever it was, Ira told her, deserved what he got. If Dennis and Laverne never managed to connect, why, that was their problem, not hers. But Maggie had gone on and on about it. " 'Safe,' " she moaned. " 'Safe in the house,' he told me. Lord only knows what that poor Laverne is going through." And she had spent the evening dialing all possible variations of their own number, every permutation of every digit, hoping to find Laverne. But never did, of course.

These are not sympathetic characters—at best they evoke our pity. Some novelists can write successful fiction about people like Ira and Maggie. Flannery O'Connor could. John Updike can. Anne Tyler cannot. The Morans are just too middle-class for her tastes, and it shows. In Maggie's own words, they are the kind of people "you would classify in an instant and dismiss"; their creator plainly finds their lives dreary and dull:

Ira [sat] endlessly on his high wooden stool, whistling along with his easy-listening radio station as he measured a mat or sawed away at his miter box. Women came in asking him to frame their cross-stitched homilies and their amateur seascapes and their wedding photos . . . They brought in illustrations torn from magazines—a litter of puppies or a duckling in a basket. Like a tailor measuring a half-dressed client, Ira remained discreetly sightless, appearing to form no judgment about a picture of a sad-faced kitten tangled in a ball of yarn.

Indeed, from an "easy-listening radio station" to a "picture of a sad-faced kitten tangled in a ball of yarn," *Breathing Lessons* envelops its action in a dense atmostphere of depressing class signifiers. The author's distaste is palpable. So is her condescension. At one point, Fiona announces she has taken up the study of electrolysis: Leroy pronounces it "a genuine science," while Maggie "couldn't help feeling impressed. This was a highly technical field . . . something like dental hygiene."

Why Anne Tyler thought she could pull off a novel like *Breathing Lessons*—a novel that asks us to sympathize with and suppose happy a pair as unstintingly ordinary as Ira and Maggie Moran—is hard to say. The reader is left wondering what kind of contractual obligations the talented Miss Tyler had that convinced her to dig this one out of her manuscript drawer.

About Maggie, Who Tried Too Hard

EDWARD HOAGLAND

Anne Tyler, who is blessedly prolific and graced with an effortless-seeming talent at describing whole rafts of intricately individualized people, might be described as a domestic novelist, one of that great line descending from Jane Austen. She is interested not in divorce or infidelity, but in marriage—not very much in isolation, estrangement, alienation and other fashionable concerns, but in courtship, child raising and filial responsibility. It's a hectic, clamorous focus for a writer to choose during the 1980's, and a mark of her competence that in this fractionated era she can write so well about blood links and family funerals, old friendships or the dogged pull of thwarted love, of blunted love affairs or marital mismatches that neither mend nor end. Her eye is kindly, wise and versatile (an eye that you would want on your jury if you ever had to stand trial), and after going at each new set of characters with authorial eagerness and an exuberant tumble of details, she tends to arrive at a set of conclusions about them that is a sort of golden mean.

Her interest is in families—drifters do not intrigue her—and yet it is the crimps and bends in people that appeal to her sympathy. She is touched by their lesions, by the quandaries, dissipated dreams and foundered ambitions that have rendered them pot-bound, because it isn't really the drifters (staples of American fiction since Melville's Ishmael and "Huckleberry Finn") who break up a family so often as the homebodies who sink into inaction with a broken axle, seldom *saying* that they've lost hope, but dragging through the weekly round.

Thus Ms. Tyler loves meddlers, like Elizabeth in "The Clock Winder" (1972), Muriel in "The Accidental Tourist" (1985) and Maggie Moran in "Breathing Lessons," her latest novel. If meddlers aren't enough to make things happen, she will throw in a pregnancy or abrupt bad luck or a death in the family, so that the clan must gather and confront one another. She pushes events on people who don't want anything to happen to them, afraid that if the phone rings they may have to pick up a son at the police station, people accustomed to the idea that if anybody needs to move it usually means that he has lost his job. They don't get promotions; they hug what they have.

From *New York Times Book Review*, 11 September 1988, 1, 43–44. Copyright © 1988 by The New York Times Company. Reprinted by permission.

Though once upon a time they did look up the ladder, now they're mainly trying to keep from sliding into a catastrophe such as bankruptcy, a grown child taking to drink, a bust-up between brothers and sisters who have been smothering or battering each other. Clinging to a low rung of the middle class, they are householders because they have inherited a decaying home, not because they're richer than renters, and they remain bemused or bewildered by the fortuitous quality of most major "decisions" in their own or others' lives, particularly by how people come to marry whom they do: a month or two of headlong, blind activity leading to years and years of stasis. And whatever Ms. Tyler puts them through is going to be uprooting and abrasive before it is redemptive. "Real life at last! you could say," as Maggie tells herself in "Breathing Lessons." (The title refers to the various instructive promptings that accompany contemporary pregnancy.)

Maggie, surprised by life, which did not live up to her honeymoon, has become an incorrigible prompter. She doesn't hesitate to reach across from the passenger seat and honk while her husband, Ira, is driving. And she has horned in to bring about the birth of her first grandchild by stopping a 17-year-old girl named Fiona at the door of an abortion clinic and steering her into marrying Maggie's son, Jesse, who is the father and, like Fiona, a dropout from high school. Maggie's motives are always mixed. She wants to get that new baby into her now stiflingly lifeless house, and does succeed in installing the young couple in the next room, with the baby and crib being placed in hers. Jesse, in black jeans, aspires to be a rock star to escape the drudging anonymity he sees as his father's fate, in a picture frame store. "I refuse to believe that I will die unknown," he tells Ira (but eight years later is a salesman at Chick's Cycle Shop). Fiona, after the inevitable blowup, soon moves away to the house of *her* mother—the dreadful Mrs. Stuckey—where Maggie follows to spy on the baby.

Maggie is daring, enterprising and indulges her habit of pouring her heart out to every listening stranger, which naturally infuriates Ira, who, uncommunicative to start with, has reached the point where Maggie can divine his moods only from the pop songs of the 1950's that he whistles. Besides whistling, his pleasure is playing solitaire. He had dreamed of working on the frontiers of medicine, but after he graduated from high school his father, complaining of a heart problem, dumped the little family business on him, as well as the duty of supporting two unmarriageable, unemployable sisters.

The sisters and the father still live over the shop, and "for the past several months now," as Ms. Tyler confides, "Ira had been noticing the human race's wastefulness. People were squandering their lives, it seemed to him. They were splurging their energies on petty jealousies or vain ambitions or long-standing, bitter grudges. . . . He was fifty years old and had never accomplished one single act of consequence." In reaction, he has become obsessed in his spare time with the efficiency of motors, mechanisms, heaters and appliances, going over and studying them in people's houses where he and Maggie are visiting, or else plunging into one of his solitaire games, which also have at their crux efficiency.

Maggie, by contrast, is working quite happily as an aide at a nursing home, a job she started when high school ended. Her wishful notion that her son would make a good husband and father is based on her memory of him feeding her soup with a spoon once when she was sick. But Ira takes a far more "realistic," severely disappointed view of Jesse, and silently watches Daisy, their daughter—who at 13 months had undertaken her own toilet training and by first grade was setting her alarm an hour early in order to iron and color-coordinate her outfit for school—grow away from them and head off for college. As for Maggie, he does still love her, but quotes the brisk witticisms of Ann Landers ("Wake up and smell the coffee!") to her. Ira ought to have married Ann Landers, she thinks jealously. She also has "Mrs. Perfect"—the mother of one of Daisy's school friends at whose house Daisy spends every waking hour—to worry about. Not long ago Daisy had stared at Maggie for the longest time with this "fascinated expression on her face, and then she said 'Mom? Was there a certain conscious point in your life when you decided to settle for being ordinary?' "

The book's principal event is a 90-mile trip that Maggie and Ira make from Baltimore, where Ms. Tyler's characters almost always live, to a country town in Pennsylvania where a high school classmate has suddenly scheduled an elaborate funeral for her husband, a radio-ad salesman who has died pathetically soon after discovering that he had a brain tumor. In her grief and confusion Serena, the widow, expects the service to recapitulate their 1956 wedding, with Kahlil Gibran being read and Maggie and Ira singing "Love Is a Many Splendored Thing." The tumult of memories surrounding the funeral works Maggie into such a state that she gets Ira to lay his cards aside and make love to her in Serena's bedroom during the reception, until Serena catches them and kicks them out.

Ms. Tyler, who was born in 1941, has 10 previous books under her belt, which, as one reads through them, get better and better. Deceptively modest in theme, they have a frequent complement of middle-aged solitaire players, anxious grandparents, blocked bachelors, dysfunctional sisters or brothers, urgent snappish teen-agers wanting fame the week after tomorrow, unfortunate small children being raised by parents not quite fit for the project, or parents suffering the ultimate tragedy of the death of a child, and they have progressed from her early sentiment in "Celestial Navigation" (1974) that "sad people are the only real ones. They can tell you the truth about things." Maggie, although exasperating, isn't sad, and like the more passively benevolent Ezra Tull in "Dinner at the Homesick Restaurant" (1982), she is trying to make a difference, to connect or unite people, beat the drum for forgiveness and compromise. As Ira explains: "It's Maggie's weakness: She believes it's all right to alter people's lives. She thinks the people she loves are better than they really are, and so then she starts changing things around to suit her view of them."

In the amplitude of her talent, Ms. Tyler didn't hesitate to enjoy her apprenticeship by writing novels on subjects like what might really happen if a bank robber seized you as a hostage in a holdup ("Earthly Possessions"), or the mind of a girl who carves a rock singer's name on her forehead ("A Slipping-Down Life"). One lark of a book ("Searching for Caleb") starts out like this: "The fortune teller and her grandfather went to New York City on an Amtrak train, racketing along with their identical, peaky white faces set due north. The grandfather had left his hearing aid at home on the bureau."

But the fun of it all didn't prevent her from learning to stick right with her people, complicating their dilemmas, extracting their sorest memories and most tremulous delusions, not hastily moving on when their thought processes dragged or someone's fragile packet of self-esteem was shattered. In every book the reader is immersed in the frustrating alarums of a family—the Pikes, the Pecks, the Tulls, and Learys—and though Ms. Tyler's spare, stripped writing style resembles that of the so-called minimalists (most of whom are her contemporaries), she is unlike them because of the depth of her affections and the utter absence from her work of a fashionable contempt for life.

She *loves* love stories, though she often inventories the woe and entropy of lovelessness. She likes a wedding and all the ways that weddings can differ, loves to enumerate the idiosyncrasies of children's sensibilities and of house furnishings. Temperate though she is, she celebrates intemperance, zest and an appetite for whatever, just as long as families do stay together. She wants her characters plausibly married and caring for each other. We're not introduced to "any Einsteins"—as Serena puts it—in Tyler fiction, nor to the heroic theses typical of many authors in the pantheon of American letters. Her male heroes tend to have trick backs and deliberately give up, settle for decidedly less from life than they had anticipated. It is the amenities of survival that concern her: merciful love, decent behavior in the face of the laming misunderstandings that afflict personal relations. As in "The Accidental Tourist," she writes of worn, sad streets "where nothing went right for anyone, where the men had dead-end jobs or none at all and the women were running to fat and the children were turning out badly." Nevertheless, she loves the city, with its pearly-tinted sky over such a neighborhood, the whinnying of sound-track horses from the windows of the houses, the women who sweep their stoops even in the midst of a snowstorm and the lilac color of the air while they do so.

Maggie's mother, whose husband installed garage doors for a living but whose father was a lawyer, demands of her, "How have you let things get so *common*?" And indeed even the tomatoes Maggie grows turn out bulbously misshapen. Her son ("Mr. Moment-by-moment," as Ira calls him) is playing his guitar in clubs for no money, just "the exposure," and couldn't even follow through on building a cradle for his baby that he had promised Fiona—whose "shrimp-pink" blouses Maggie regards as low-class too. After the funeral and the fiasco of her latest plot to bring Jesse and Fiona back together, she recalls another agonizing instance of her meddling—putting Serena's mother in an old-age home dressed ridiculously in a clown costume because the evening when they were scheduled to arrive there had been Halloween. "I don't know why I kid myself that I'm going to heaven," Maggie tells Ira.

The literature of resignation—of wisely settling for less than life had seemed to offer—is exemplified by Henry James among American writers. It is a theme more European than New World by tradition, but with the graying of America into middle age since World War II, it has gradually taken strong root here and become dominant among Ms. Tyler's generation. Macon Leary, the magnificently decent yet "ordinary" man in "The Accidental Tourist," follows logic to its zany conclusion, and in doing this justifies the jerry-built or catch-as-catch-can nature of much of life, making us realize that we are probably missing people of mild temperament in our own acquaintance who are heroes too, if we had Ms. Tyler's eye for recognizing them. "Breathing Lessons" seems a slightly thinner mixture. It lacks a *Muriel,* for one thing: Muriel, the man-chaser and man-saver of "The Accidental Tourist," ranks among the more endearing characters of postwar literature. But Maggie Moran's faith that crazy spells do not mean life itself is crazy is an affirmation.

Because Ms. Tyler is at the top of her powers, it's fair to wonder whether she has developed the kind of radiant, doubling dimension to her books that may enable them to outlast the seasons of their publication. Is she unblinking, for example? No, she is not unblinking. Her books contain scarcely a hint of the abscesses of racial friction that eat at the very neighborhoods she is devoting her working life to picturing. Her people are eerily virtuous, Quakerishly tolerant of all strangers, all races. And she touches upon sex so lightly, compared with her graphic realism on other matters, that her total portrait of motivation is tilted out of balance.

Deservedly successful, she has marked her progress by changing her imprimatur on the copyright pages of her novels from "Anne Modarressi" to "Anne Tyler Modarressi" to "Anne Tyler Modarressi, et al." to "ATM, Inc.," That would be fine, except that it strikes me that she has taken to prettifying the final pages of her novels too. And in "Breathing Lessons," the comedies of Fiona's baby's delivery in the hospital and of Maggie's horrendously inept driving have been caricatured to unfunny slapstick, as if in an effort to corral extra readers. I don't believe Ms. Tyler should think she needs to tinker with her popularity. It is based upon the fact that she is very good at writing about old people, very good on young children, very good on teen-agers, very good on breadwinners and also stay-at-homes: that she is superb at picturing men and portraying women.

[From "Roughing It"]

Robert Towers

. . . [I]n Anne Tyler's novels, sympathetic recognition of her characters comes almost too easily, even as their expected oddity holds out the promise of small surprises. Like the *Rabbit* novels of John Updike, her books expertly render a familiar world in which our own observations are played back to us, slightly magnified, and with an enhanced clarity. Anne Tyler seems to know all there is to know about the surfaces of contemporary middle-middle- to lower-middle-class life in America, and if she chooses not to explore the abysses, she is nonetheless able to dramatize—often memorably—the ordinary crises of domestic life, of marriage and separation, of young love, parenthood, and even death. Though her style lacks Updike's metaphoric glitter, it has a strength and suppleness of its own. She can also be very funny.

In her recent novels—*Dinner at the Homesick Restaurant* and *The Accidental Tourist*—she has seemed at her best. The latter novel, particularly, is a luminous book. Beginning with the senseless murder of a twelve-year-old boy, it traces, with psychological cunning and humor, the steps of the boy's eccentric and obsessive father as he blunders his way toward a new life. Her eleventh novel, *Breathing Lessons,* strikes me as less substantial, more susceptible to the tendencies to whimsicality and even cuteness that sometimes affect her work. It is nonetheless shrewd in its insights and touching in its tragi-comic vision of familial hopes and disappointments.

Breathing Lessons begins in absurdity. A middle-aged housewife, Maggie Moran, goes to a repair shop to pick up their car so that she and her husband Ira can drive from Baltimore to a funeral in Deer Lick, Pennsylvania.

> She was wearing her best dress—blue and white sprigged, with cape sleeves—and crisp black pumps, on account of the funeral. The pumps were only medium-heeled but slowed her down some anyway. . . . Another problem was that the crotch of her panty hose had somehow slipped to about the middle of her thighs, so she had to take shortened, unnaturally level steps like a chunky little wind-up toy wheeling along the sidewalk.

As she is leaving the body shop, Maggie hears on the car radio what she takes to be the voice of Fiona, her ex-daughter-in-law, announcing on a talk

Reprinted with permission from *The New York Review of Books,* 10 November 1988, 40–41. Copyright © 1988 Nyrev, Inc.

show her intention to remarry—this time for security instead of love. Meaning to brake, Maggie accelerates instead and runs in front of a Pepsi truck that smashes into her left-front fender—"the only spot that had never, up till now, had the slightest thing go wrong with it."

Such is the start of what turns out to be a very full day in the lives of the warmhearted and scatterbrained Maggie and cranky, taciturn Ira. The funeral they are driving to is that of Max, the husband of Maggie's oldest, dearest friend, Serena. As they drive north along the highway ("The scenery grew choppy. Stretches of playgrounds and cemeteries were broken suddenly by clumps of small businesses—liquor stores, pizza parlors, dark little bars and taverns dwarfed by the giant dish antennas on their roofs"), Maggie begins a campaign to persuade Ira that on their way home they should stop off in Cartwheel, Pennsylvania, to see Fiona and their only grandchild, a girl named Leroy. Maggie has never been reconciled to the divorce between Fiona and their son, Jesse, or to being separated from her grandchild. She is convinced that Fiona and Jesse still love each other and she has schemed repeatedly to bring them together again, several times making secret, "spying" trips to Cartwheel to catch glimpses of Leroy. Unsentimental Ira, who has always been hard on his rock-musician son, regularly makes fun of her schemes. Fiona's publicly announced intention to remarry now lends a new urgency to Maggie's plea for a stopover in Cartwheel.

I can think of no one who captures the flavor of car travel in America today better than Anne Tyler—the attempt to pass an oil truck, disputes over directions, a stop at a roadside grocery-café ("The café lay at the rear— one long counter, with faded color photo of orange scrambled eggs and beige link sausages lining the wall behind it"), where Maggie, who loves to spill our her life's story to strangers, engages in a heartfelt conversation with a sympathetic waitress and in a long flashback recalls an elegant old man whom she had loved in the nursing home where she now works. The couple finally arrives at the church in Deer Lick where they are informed by the widowed Serena that she has invited to the funeral all of the old friends who had attended her wedding and that they are all expected to sing the same 1950s songs that they had sung then. When Maggie and Ira are asked to sing "Love is a Many-Splendored Thing," Ira balks. What follows is a comical set piece, including, after the funeral, the showing of a movie of Serena and Max's wedding years ago, and the attempt, which is interrupted, of Maggie and Ira to have a "quickie" in Serena's bedroom while the funeral reception is going on downstairs.

It was at this point that I felt that Anne Tyler had allowed her novel to slip into whimsy and slapstick. While the unconventional Serena, with her mixed feelings about her husband's illness and death, is carefully drawn, the funeral itself and its aftermath are simply preposterous. I was relieved to get back onto the highway, to see things from Ira's cooler point of view for a change, and to move on to the family drama involving Fiona, Jesse, and Leroy that occupies the final hundred and fifty pages of *Breathing Lessons*. We do not know until nearly the end whether Maggie's irrepressible determination to make everything work out is doomed or not.

Maggie is presented as a meddler in other people's lives but a lovable one. Tyler invites the reader to participate in Maggie's schemes, to laugh at her misadventures and miscalculations, but also to admire her resiliency. And for the most part one goes along. But Maggie sometimes seems too broad in relation to the much subtler handling of the other characters—she is too awkward, too silly, to carry the burden that has been assigned to her. The sentimentality in the conception of her character becomes an irritation.

Ira, on the other hand, displays that firmness of outline and richness of specification that we associate with Anne Tyler's most successful characters— especially her quirky men. Ira is presented as a gruff failure, frustrated in his ambitions, exasperated by this "whifflehead" wife, disappointed in his feck- less son, saddened by the humorlessness of his overachieving daughter. He had wanted to be a doctor but has ended up running a framing shop which he had to take over when his father, declaring himself disabled by heart trouble, gave up the attempt to support himself and his two incapacitated daughters. Ira now supports all three of them as well as his immediate family. He makes fun of Maggie's vagaries, plays solitaire, and maintains long silences. Yet he is shown to be capable of complex feelings of tenderness even when most irritated by his family.

> He had a vivid memory of Jesse as he'd looked the night he was arrested, back when he was sixteen. He'd been picked up for public drunkenness with several of his friends—a onetime occurrence, as it turned out, but Ira had wanted to make sure of that and so, intending to be hard on him, he had insisted Maggie stay home while he went down alone to post bail. He had sat on a bench in a public waiting area and finally there came Jesse, walking doubled over be- tween two officers. Evidently his wrists had been handcuffed behind his back and he had attempted, at some point, to step through the circle of his own arms so as to bring his hands in front of him. But he had given up or been interrupted halfway through the maneuver, and so he hobbled out lopsided, twisted like a sideshow freak with his wrists trapped between his legs. Ira had experienced the most complicated mingling of emotions at the sight: anger at his son and anger at the authorities too, for exhibiting Jesse's humiliation, and a wild impulse to laugh and an aching, flooding sense of pity.

It is writing of this authority and delicacy that justifies the admiration accorded to Anne Tyler's work—and redeems *Breathing Lessons* from the excesses of its whimsy.

The Meddler's Progress

WALLACE STEGNER

In the 10 novels that preceded *Breathing Lessons,* Anne Tyler demonstrated that you don't need exotic or violent or sexy action to make a novel, and that your characters needn't be psychopaths or satyrs. All you need—all *she* needs—are ordinary people going about their everyday affairs in ordinary cities such as Baltimore. Her people, a Dickensian gallery of oddballs, innocents, obsessives, erratics, incompetents and plain Joes and Janes, all see the world a little skewed, but their author sees them with such precision and presents them with such amusement and lack of malice that they come off the page as exhilaratingly human. First they surprise us, then we recognize them, then we acknowledge how much they tell us about ourselves.

Dinner at the Homesick Restaurant and *The Accidental Tourist* should have been hard acts to follow. Actually, so sharp is Anne Tyler's eye and so inexhaustible the field of her observation, *Breathing Lessons* shows us a writer who should have had trouble matching herself, surpassing herself. And Maggie Moran, who dominates the new novel, is a purely Anne Tyler creation—a woman with a cornpopper mind and an incorrigible capacity for self-persuasion, a scheming flibbertigibbet, a meddler whose misinterpretations and desperate cover-up lies belong in *Fawlty Towers,* but whose essential goodness and capacity for affection make us want to comfort rather than kick her. Even while we wonder how her husband Ira put up with Maggie for 28 years, we understand why the marriage has lasted, and will. Maggie's deviousness, underlain by emotional purposes as inexorable as heat-seeking missiles, is a form of innocence.

The central action of *Breathing Lessons* is a journey to the funeral of Max, the husband of Maggie's school friend Serena. All the friends who attended Max's marriage to Serena will be there for his funeral, and that very circumstance kicks Maggie's cornpopper into bursts of recollection, sentiment and regrets. But it is no straight-line journey. Since Maggie is involved, it is a journey of lost maps, detours, interruptions, quarrels, intimate conversations and reminiscences with strangers, cross purposes and the little white lies by which Maggie gets her way.

She starts with a characteristic misapprehension. Driving the family Dodge out of the body shop where its dents have just been rolled out, she

From *Washington Post Book World,* 4 September 1988, 1, 6. © *Washington Post;* reprinted by permission.

hears a female voice on a radio talk show say that, having married once for love, she is now going to marry for security. Instantly, erroneously, Maggie thinks: "Fiona!" and runs into a Pepsi truck and crumples another fender.

Fiona is the estranged wife of Jesse, Maggie and Ira's son, a rock musician who cannot carry a tune. It has long been Maggie's hope that she can get Jesse and Fiona back together. And since Fiona and her daughter LeRoy now live in Cartwheel, Pa., and Max's funeral is to be in Deer Lick, Pa., Maggie now has the ironclad intention of visiting Fiona and talking her out of this marriage for security. That intention involves persuading Ira, a realist, to detour to Cartwheel, and that persuasion involves some dissembling and a few white lies. Maggie and Ira's day is started on its crossthreaded course before they have even got the crumpled fender bent back up off the tire.

Only Anne Tyler, who is a master of the art, should be allowed to detail the mishaps of this funeral journey. It is enough to say here that Serena's whim of showing a film of her wedding at Max's funeral, complete with all the '50s popular songs and readings from Khalil Gibran, stimulates Maggie's cornpopper again and leads her into recollection of all the 28 not-so-romantic years of her marriage. Those recollections stimulate romantic feelings, leading to Maggie's erotic pass at Ira in a back room, and to their expulsion by a shocked Serena.

Never mind. Within minutes the missile is locked in on Cartwheel and the goal of reuniting Fiona and Jesse and preventing Fiona's marriage for security. It takes more than half the novel for Maggie to be disabused of her conviction that Fiona and Jesse really want to be together.

"Oh, Ira," Maggie cries on that glum evening, while her husband lays out a hand of solitaire. "What are we two going to live for, all the rest of our lives?"

Good question. The answer is implicit in Maggie's character. They are going to live for the day, from hour to hour and from misapprehension to bruising correction. They are going to cope as they have coped during this exhausting day. For look: within seconds of her lamenting cry, Maggie has got interested in the problems of Ira's solitaire hand. Thought goes through her like jolts down a line of freight cars. Bump—and now she is thinking about tomorrow, when they will drive their daughter Daisy to college. Plans suggest themselves. Schemes. With any luck, tomorrow's trip will be another Anne Tyler novel.

The Baltimore Chop

ROBERT MCPHILLIPS

In her ten novels, from *If Morning Ever Comes* through *The Accidental Tourist,*
Anne Tyler has staked out a comfortable, self-contained fictional landscape
recognizably her own. Having grown up in North Carolina and studied with
Reynolds Price at Duke University, Tyler initially considered herself a Southern writer. Her first three novels—*Morning* (1964), *The Tin Can Tree* (1965)
and *A Slipping-Down Life* (1970)—were set in North Carolina and bear, in
their focus on the eccentricities of family life and the strong influence of the
past upon the present, a resemblance to the Southern Gothic tradition of
William Faulkner, Flannery O'Connor, Eudora Welty and, especially, Carson
McCullers.

But Tyler never seemed fully committed to these conventions. If she is
concerned with family, history seemingly interests her not at all. She doesn't
share Faulkner's obsession with the South's perceived fall from an Edenic
state of grace, after the Civil War, perhaps simply because she was born in
Minneapolis. Neither is she attracted, like Faulkner and Welty, to the rich
allure of Southern dialect or to the potentially garrulous oral tradition so
common a staple of Southern narratives. Instead, her style is plain and gently
comic. Finally, she avoids the temptation to create the fully grotesque characters we associate with Southern Gothic. Tyler's best characters are, to be sure,
socially maladjusted flakes living with their own peculiar set of rules and
emotional ticks; but they are, by and large, in their own idiosyncratic ways,
approachable and familiar.

And so is Anne Tyler. The most benign of our novelists, she has forged a
kind of trust with her readers, who come to her novels expecting to be
comforted. And they invariably have been—at least up until now. *Breathing
Lessons,* Tyler's eleventh novel, represents a subtle but discernible shift in
tone that is likely to surprise her most devoted readers. Having long established a happy marriage with her readers, Tyler now forces them to face the
fact that such pacts are founded as much upon compromise as upon romance.
This novel's journey presents a vision of marriage as a very rocky road. Even
the most faithful of readers may find it a similar trip.

The first real breakthrough in Tyler's fiction came in *The Clock Winder*

From *The Nation,* 7 November 1988, 464–66. © 1988, The Nation Company, Inc. Reprinted by
permission.

(1972), the novel in which her tenuous connection to Southern writing is severed. In this book, Tyler dramatizes Elizabeth Abbott's decision to abandon North Carolina for Baltimore, Tyler's own adopted city and the site of her subsequent fiction. Elizabeth bears further comparison to her creator. She marries into a family of eccentrics for whom she functions as handyman and psychic caretaker. Tyler's imaginative marriage to Baltimore has left her similarly in care of a cast of fictional oddballs who manage to find a precarious sense of psychic balance, of family and home, within the city the author has remade in her own image. Tyler's Baltimore, however closely it represents the actual city, with its combination of urban decay and gentrification, remains largely immune to history. Her fiction belongs to the tradition of the American romance pioneered by Hawthorne far more than to that of the realistic or naturalistic novel.

Tyler's central concern with family as a kind of atemporal refuge where, for better or worse, long-lost children, siblings or even parents return for solace, is usually embodied in her novels by a central organizing metaphor. The most successful of these is the restaurant maintained by Ezra Tull in *Dinner at the Homesick Restaurant* (1982). It serves as a haven "where people come just like a family to dinner," one to which Ezra's father returns after the death of the wife he abandoned thirty-five years earlier. The fact that the Tulls are never able to finish a meal in this homesick restaurant merely serves to underline the complexity of Tyler's vision of family. Tyler's families are invariably not happy, or never precisely so. They nonetheless remain the only dependable unit against which to gauge one's identity. And they usually contain figures, like Elizabeth Abbott and Ezra Tull, who combine quixotic with pragmatic qualities, characters who, like Tyler as a novelist, are able to maintain, as if by magic, a sense of order in a universe prone to fragmentation and isolation.

In her best novels, Tyler convincingly expands the definition of family. *Breathing Lessons* shares many of the elements of these novels, though it is finally less sprawling and buoyantly comic, presenting a sourly diminished vision of the resilience of marriage. The action in this novel is limited to one day in the life of Maggie and Ira Moran, a couple in their late 40s, though it is an eventful one that will see both husband and wife reexamine the nature of their union. It is set in motion by the death of Max Gill, the husband of Maggie's closest friend, Serena. Despite the obvious gravity of this situation, Ira would prefer not to waste a Saturday making the ninety-mile trip north of Baltimore to Deer Lick, Pennsylvania, for the funeral. He considers it an unnecessary side trip, like so many of the activities he associates with his wife, one that will keep him away from his picture-framing shop on its busiest day. Ira, at once cynical and pragmatic, has long given up his dream of becoming an important doctor and accepted the dull routine of the shop and his responsibility not only to his wife and two disappointing children but to his ailing father and incompetent sisters as well. Maggie, who works in a nursing home, is, by contrast, unrealistically optimistic, impulsive, scatter-brained and meddlesome, though supremely well intentioned.

Tyler establishes these traits deftly in the novel's promising opening pages, which comically project the tensions that lie ahead. By the time the Morans hit the road, Maggie has already had an accident with a Pepsi truck—which she blithely drives away from—because she is so absorbed in listening to a discussion of "What Makes an Ideal Marriage?" on a phone-in radio show. Certain that she has heard the voice of her estranged daughter-in-law, Fiona, Maggie at once begins plotting a side trip for their drive from the funeral. Her intentions: to visit the granddaughter she hasn't seen in years and to attempt to rekindle the "true love" between Fiona and Maggie's son, Jesse, an unsuccessful and unreliable rock musician.

Tyler's strongest card is her ability to orchestrate brilliantly funny set pieces and to create exasperating but sympathetic characters. *Breathing Lessons*, in the first of its three sections, is strong on the former. A number of brief comic scenes—Maggie's accident, a stop at a coffee shop, an argument between husband and wife—build to the novel's strongest scene, Max's funeral and the reception that follows. Love and death are ingeniously juxtaposed when Serena insists that the funeral service re-create her wedding. This proves a mixed success. Ira refuses to sing his half of the duet that initiated their courtship and marriage, "Love Is a Many Splendored Thing," with Maggie. (A hammish old flame of Maggie's fills in for Ira, leaving her momentarily determined to drive back to Baltimore with him instead of her husband.) Similarly, Sugar, one of Serena's more snobbish friends, in the novel's most inspired comic touch, agrees to the scheme only if she can substitute another song for "Born to Be With You." Her choice is the hilariously sappy but apt Doris Day tune "Que Sera Sera."

At the reception afterward, the unexpected revival of Maggie and Ira's erotic life causes a fight with Serena and their dismissal from her house. This leaves a lot of the day left, and a lot of the novel. It also leaves one wondering how Tyler, after building to such an early and successful crescendo, will handle what is essentially a two-hundred page denouement.

Here the book falters. While the narrative continues to move at a whirl-wind pace (Tyler's control of her material as certain as ever), the material itself is less convincing. The novel's second section concerns another side trip instigated by Maggie, which centers around Daniel Otis, an elderly black man whose erratic driving, coupled with Maggie's own interference with her car's horn, causes Ira to swerve off the road. Maggie, determined to avenge this mishap, convinces Ira to pass the driver, whom she then informs that his front wheel is wobbling. Immediately repentant, however, Maggie insists they turn around and tell the driver, who has pulled to the side of the road, that they were mistaken. Nonetheless, the three end up at a garage because he is still convinced the tire is dangerous. Mr. Otis and Maggie exchange anecdotes on modern marriage that advance the novel's anatomization of that topic. But this episode underlines a weakness, inherent in Tyler's preference for the conventions of the romance over those of realism. Although Tyler's handling of this set piece is charming, it fails to confront directly to what extent both Maggie's aggression and guilt are racially motivated, while at the same time Mr. Otis eventually becomes merely a likable stereotype of the self-effacing black who defers to the greater wisdom of his white interlocutors.

Tyler has similar problems in a scene at an abortion clinic in the final section of the novel. Only this late in the book does the significance of its title emerge. It is Maggie, we discover, who took Fiona under her wing during her pregnancy, teaching her how to breathe properly during labor. First, though, she had to convince Fiona, at the ineffectual Jesse's urging, not to go through with a scheduled abortion. Maggie chooses to do so in front of a clinic being picketed by an antiabortion group. Here, she assumes the role of nurturer. But once again, confronted with a controversial public issue, Tyler seems unsure of herself. While trying to dissuade Fiona from having the abortion, Maggie also spouts liberal platitudes at the antiabortion forces. Her shallow political rhetoric is unconvincing. The failure of this set piece, coupled with Maggie's ultimate failure to reunite the myopically self-centered couple, make "breathing lessons" a far less resonant controlling metaphor than those in her best novels.

Finally, the characters in *Breathing Lessons* disappoint. Ira takes his disillusionment with life out on his family. Given to playing solitaire, communicating with his wife only unconsciously through the songs he hums to himself, Ira lacks any of the redeeming charm we find in Tyler's most engaging male characters like Jeremy Pauling, the reclusive painter of *Celestial Navigation,* or Macon Leary of *The Accidental Tourist,* who writes travel guides for people like himself who would prefer to stay home. Maggie, who haplessly tries to reorganize people's lives with her exaggerations and white lies—which are usually undermined, at crucial points in the novel, by Ira's compulsion to tell the truth, however painful—is at first sympathetic. But her skirmishes with reality outside the claustrophic confines of her family life make her resilience seem forced and finally insignificant. Tyler, moving outside of the conventions of the romance, fails in her attempt to invest Maggie with a genuine social conscience. This failure ultimately extends to the novel's more atemporal domestic realm as well. The Morans' two children, Jesse and Daisy—the latter remains largely off-stage as she packs to leave home for college the next day—as well as Fiona remain sullen and lifeless. Maggie's unflappable belief in their potential is not, alas, infectious.

Breathing Lessons is far less consoling and emotionally satisfying than any of Anne Tyler's novels since the slight *A Slipping-Down Life,* her weakest. While the reader is dazzled and entertained by the author's skillful manipulation of plot and her ability to continue to conjure up some of the funniest and most incisive scenes in contemporary American fiction, one is ultimately left feeling that Tyler has failed in her attempt to broaden her fictional universe, to combine successfully the conventions of social realism with those of the romance, as Hawthorne himself was able to do in *The Scarlet Letter, The House of the Seven Gables* and, somewhat more tentatively in *The Blithedale Romance*. In the past, Tyler has used her magic to illuminate seemingly drab lives. Here, she forces one to confront directly lives that even willful magic can't fully alleviate.

ARTICLES

♦

[From "New Faces in Faulkner Country"]

BRUCE COOK

. . . North Carolina notwithstanding, the South is fast becoming as urban-
ized as the rest of America. Not much of this has shown up in fiction by
Southern writers, however. That most atmospheric of all Southern cities,
New Orleans—perhaps of all cities, period—was done to a fare-thee-well by
John William Corrington in *The Upper Hand,* a fine novel that teems with the
sweaty, smelly life of the French Quarter. And in Charles Gaine's *Stay Hungry*
we get a good look at a younger and rowdier city, Birmingham—the New
South, such as it is. But no writer yet has staked out a claim on a Southern
city and made it his territory—as Farrell and Algren did Chicago—except
perhaps for Anne Tyler and her exploration of Baltimore.

That's Reynolds Price's opinion, anyway: "I think that she's the nearest
thing we have to an urban Southern novelist." The two go back a long way
together. At a space of several years they shared the same inspiring high
school English teacher, Phyllis Peacock, in Raleigh. And Anne Tyler was a
student in the first college course—basic freshman composition—ever
taught by Reynolds Price at Duke. In the South, altogether a smaller world,
coincidences of this kind are really not coincidences at all.

Is Anne Tyler a Southern novelist? She's not so sure. Born in Minnesota,
she lived through her early childhood in North Carolina in a number of
Quaker cooperative communities that were more or less insulated from the
surrounding country and people. It wasn't until she started high school that
her family moved to the outskirts of Raleigh, and she began to find out what
the South is like. It was like gazing on some newfound land: she was
fascinated.

"I actually don't consider myself Southern," she says, "though I suppose
I'm that more than anything else. Because if I did consider myself Southern,
then that would make me a Southern novelist—and I don't think there is any
such thing."

Not even Faulkner? "Well, I don't know. I remember reading him and
thinking, well, this must be what they mean by the Southern novel—and I
didn't feel any sort of identification with it at all. He is, after all, an
extremely masculine writer. There couldn't be a woman Faulkner at all.

From *Saturday Review,* 4 September 1976, 39–41. Reprinted by permission of Omni Publications International, Ltd.

Then, too, I guess I should make it clear that when I did get around to reading him, I had already started writing myself. And his whole approach to writing—obviously he was knitting off in all directions—was completely wrong for me. If it were possible to write like him, I wouldn't. I disagree with him. I want everyone to understand what I'm getting at."

Like Reynolds Price, she considers Eudora Welty the strongest influence on her own work. "Reading her taught me there were stories to be written about the mundane life around me. I'm really sorry that Flannery O'Connor seems to have taken something away from Eudora Welty—as though Eudora were too sunny to be counted important. I don't think that makes her less of a writer."

Anne Tyler's last two novels—*The Clock Winder* and *Celestial Navigation*, her fourth and fifth—are set in Baltimore. But is Baltimore a Southern city? "To me, Baltimore is the North—but then, when I go back to North Carolina today, so much of it seems like the North to me, too." The city's most famous writer, H. L. Mencken, described it as "touched by the Southern sun." And although the slave state of Maryland remained neutral in the Civil War, most old line Marylanders consider themselves Southerners. "There are ladies in the old houses in Roland Park who are like caricatures out of the Old South," says Anne Tyler. "But maybe they are the same way in Maine, too.

"Yes, I suppose I probably am the only writer who has written about Baltimore in a while, and it is wonderful territory for a writer—so many different things to poke around in. And whatever it is that remains undeniably Southern in me has made it easy for me to switch to Baltimore. I lived four years in Canada, and I could write practically nothing about it at all. It's taken me a while to settle in here, to get in a comfortable groove, which is the only way I can write, but now I feel right with Baltimore. I don't think I could write about North Carolina at all now. I've been away nine years."

The Individual in the Family:
Anne Tyler's *Searching for Caleb* and *Earthly Possessions*

STELLA NESANOVICH

In May, 1977, Anne Tyler was cited by the American Academy and Institute of Arts and Letters for "literary excellence and promise of important work to come." Just thirty-six years old, she has published seven novels and nearly forty short stories, almost all concerned with the intricacies of family relationships and the growth of the individual within the family. In her last two novels, *Searching for Caleb* and *Earthly Possessions,* she explores these themes in greater depth and with keener insight into human nature than she has previously shown, allowing us to see what indeed we can expect from a mature Anne Tyler. Clearly, important work is coming.

Both novels are set in Maryland, where Miss Tyler lives with her husband and two daughters. In *Searching for Caleb,* her sixth novel, she traces the development of five generations of the Peck family, residents of Baltimore's famous Roland Park. The Pecks are a staid, tradition-minded, and clannish group. Originally sired by Justin Montague Peck, "a sharp-eyed, humorless man who became very rich importing coffee, sugar, and guano during the last quarter of the nineteenth century," since 1912 they have been headed by Justin's oldest son, Daniel. A retired attorney and judge, Daniel embodies a number of Peck traits, including a joyless insistence on middle-class respectability and taste as well as the suppression of all emotional display. Interestingly, while the Peck family appears homogeneous in character, in point of fact it is dichotomous, with Daniel's younger half-brother, the Caleb of the title, representing the nomadic, free-spirited, and musical side of the family. Indeed, two of Daniel's grandchildren, Duncan and Justine, have inherited some of Caleb's waywardness. Married to one another, despite their first cousin relationship or perhaps being Pecks because of it, they have rejected the traditional occupations of the family as well as residence in Roland Park. Restless and mechanically inclined, Duncan has taken up a variety of occupations, from goat farming to selling antiques, while Justine, impulsive and intuitive, reads fortunes.

Reprinted from *Southern Review* 14 (January 1978): 170–76, by permission of the author.

As the novel opens, we accompany Justine and her grandfather on one of many journeys to locate Caleb—that is, to question the widows and children of former classmates and teachers of Caleb who might aid in locating him. Caleb, it seems, disappeared quietly one "Saturday afternoon in the spring of 1912," sixty-one years before the book's initial scene. In his quest for his long absent brother, Daniel has, with Peckish closed-mindedness, over-looked the most important clues to Caleb's personality: his unwillingness to follow the profession of his father and his taste for liquor and disreputable music. Possessed of a strong sense of family loyalty and a near blindness to the passage of time, Daniel, nearing ninety-three when the novel begins, has taken up residence with Duncan and Justine to facilitate his search. However, life with his grandchildren is not the orderly nor staid existence of Roland Park, nor is the search for his brother an easy one. At every turn, change is evident, and, unfortunately, the only remaining evidence of Caleb's exis-tence, apart from certain manifestations of his temperament in Duncan and Justine, is an old photograph showing him as he was in 1912, a young man seated in a stable loft door, a fiddle between his knees.

With these clues and in the company of some very amusing and delight-ful characters, Anne Tyler interweaves a kind of family adventure and record book, one that captures both the essence of "Peckishness" as well as the uniqueness of individual Pecks. The result is a novel that literally vibrates with vitality. Past eras are vividly evoked, and individual personalities emerge through the author's careful attention to the details of life. The memory of Caleb's presence, for example, and the idea of his character as representative of the nomadic, carefree, and imaginative side of the Peck family, is suggested throughout the novel by a recurring pattern of musical images and strains. At times, this pattern is merely the background of life, the sound of the trolley wires whistling overhead on a street in old Baltimore or the unceasing carousel music, " 'The St. James Infirmary Blues' spinning itself out among the cries of children and hot dog vendors" at a traveling circus owned by one of Justine's clients. However, as the search for Caleb draws closer to its goal, notes from ragtime pieces and whiskey blues tunes—the kind of music Caleb played—become audible, ultimately leading di-rectly to Caleb himself and forging a link with the songs that run constantly through his mind. Always, the music is evocative—of Caleb, his joyousness and rootlessness, and of the wayward side of the family character which he represents. Suggestive also of Caleb's life as a street musician in New Or-leans, the music provides another link, one that is temporal. It is a kind of continuum that unites not only Caleb and his two descendents, Duncan and Justine, but also his past and present.

With a gentle humor and a mild irony characteristic of her earlier fiction, Anne Tyler focuses on the adventures of these vagabonds, occasion-ally giving us views of life with the more inhibited Pecks. Her talent is multiple. We follow Duncan and Justine through their roaming from town to town in search of some type of permanently exciting and changeable employment—they "come to rest" finally as mechanic and fortune-teller for the traveling circus. Concurrently, we witness the growth and marriage of their daughter, Meg. Everywhere the ironic contrasts of individuals within the family are apparent, and so are the subtle, inescapable ways in which certain family traits reappear.

Meg Peck, for example, is a neatly groomed, serious, and orderly girl who, with her great grandfather, quietly suffers the disruptions that mark life with her parents. She has, in fact, inherited a good bit of the joylessness, the disapproving manner, and the insistence on respectability and stability that characterize the Pecks of Roland Park. Thus, in many ways, she is the antithesis of her parents. Present at a number of card readings, events which reveal the most intimate details of the lives of Justine's customers, Meg expresses annoyance at not being given her mother's attention, then shuts herself away in her well-kept room. Duncan's manner is jovial, Justine's intensely involved, Meg's serious. Grandfather Peck characteristically turns off his hearing aid, shutting out more of the world as he grows older. Significantly, the return of Caleb Peck, family bohemian and renegade, occurs only after the loss of Meg in marriage to a Milquetoast minister and the death of Daniel Peck, events that are, because of their timing, not only ironical but also suggestive of the incompatibility of the two sides of the family character.

But *Searching for Caleb* is not just a novel about family character and relationships. It is also, and perhaps more importantly, about the various ways in which people respond to life, the curiosity and involvement of some, the removal and caution of others. It is a novel about the *joie de vivre* and endurance of characters like Caleb Peck, the freedom of the human spirit to grow, and the choices which some people make to limit that growth.

Similar themes inform *Earthly Possessions,* Anne Tyler's seventh novel. Here, however, growth is limited more by the paradoxical and contrary nature of life itself than by human choice. Told in the first person by the central character, Charlotte Emory (a thirty-five-year-old, small town, Maryland housewife who longs to escape her life circumstances), the novel bears little external resemblance to *Searching for Caleb.* Its focus is smaller—one lifetime as compared with five generations of Pecks—the characters not quite as endearing. In fact, a certain flatness is evident, but so too is the magical Tyler manner that combines irony with a hint of stoicism and a brilliantly clear and enlivening prose style.

The principal character, Charlotte, is, paradoxically, the source of both the novel's flatness as well as its humor and insight. A bony, straight-haired woman who has lived her entire life in one town, indeed, in one house, Charlotte looks at the world around her with ironic detachment. Repeatedly bungled escape attempts have led her to "look at things with a faint, pleasant humorousness that," as she says, "spiced my nose like the beginnings of a sneeze." At times, she is almost cynical; always, she is strong, durable, and earthy.

Entrapped by a stunted family life, a marriage she believes isn't "going well," and a house cluttered with furniture and people, Charlotte has spent her life being strong and practical, caring for her mother and husband, and meeting the needs of other people. At the same time, she has been seeking to rid herself of all belongings and commitments that tie her to Clarion, her hometown. For her, life is a kind of "long foot-march" which she must make alone and empty-handed. Ironically, however, her own existence has been marked by a series of events and involvements that have served to multiply not only the number of people in her life but also the items of furniture and other odd earthly possessions that fill her house. Her stay at college was foreshortened to one afternoon by her father's ill health; her marriage to Saul Emory, because of his decision to stay in Clarion and study for the ministry of a local fundamentalist church, has led to more enclosure and clutter. Not only has Saul himself filled the house with his mother's furniture and possessions, but his brothers have also returned to Clarion to take up space in the Emory household. One is given to making doll furniture, small items that triplicate the furnishings that already crowd the halls and rooms of the house. In addition to their own daughter, Saul and Charlotte have adopted an abandoned infant, a child Saul brought home from his church, and various boarders—sinners from the mourners' bench at the Holy Basis—have also taken up residence. It is these relationships, including her marriage, which Charlotte is continually trying to escape, and it is the clutter of these people who fill her life, along with the leftovers of those who have died or moved away, which she is repeatedly giving away in order to free herself for her lone journey.

Like Justine Peck, Charlotte is an only child who grew up in a dark, closed house where "meals were strained and silent," the product of estranged adults. Her childhood was marked not only by a strong desire to escape this world but also by a belief that she was not her mother's "true daughter," that, in fact, there had been some mix-up at the hospital where she was born. Kidnapped at age seven, Charlotte was convinced that the dark-haired woman who stole her away was her real mother. Indeed, as a skinny, dark, and plain-looking child, Charlotte more closely resembled her kidnapper than she did the excessively obese and fair woman with whom she lived and the "stooped, bald, meek-looking," and moody man who said he was her father. Both are extremely unlikely parents for Charlotte, and her return to them after the kidnapping only serves to reinforce her notions about her identity. Like *Searching for Caleb*, *Earthly Possessions* is a novel about a quest for family identity and a sense of belonging, and Charlotte's family, like the Pecks, illustrates the frequent Tyler concern with the ironies of family life and resemblances. Fittingly, Charlotte spends her life until the time the novel opens looking for her true mother, at times investing various figures she meets with features she believes her real mother might possess. At one point in the novel, she adopts as an ideal her husband's mother, Alberta, a gypsy of a woman who elopes with her own father-in-law—clearly a figure whose wanderlust best matches Charlotte's own longings for freedom and escape. Ironically, the degree of freedom Charlotte possesses is directly tied to her knowledge of her real identity. Once she learns that she is her mother's "true daughter," an event that occurs just a few weeks prior to the novel's opening, she is freed of an idea that has kept her in bondage since childhood. She is not, however, immediately freed of her overwhelming desire to flee. Deliverance from this idea does not come until Charlotte at last takes the journey she has been planning most of her life. It is, in fact, the actualization of this lifelong desire which opens the novel. Having decided finally to leave her husband for good, her mother dead by a few weeks, Charlotte ventures to a Clarion savings bank to withdraw cash for her trip. There she is taken hostage by one Jake Simms, Jr., demolition-derby driver, county jail escapee, and inept bank robber.

As readers of *Earthly Possessions,* we accompany Jake and Charlotte on their dual journey. What puzzles us, and what the novel reveals, are the reasons for Charlotte's apparent willingness to run with her captor. Structurally, the novel balances each chapter recording Jake and Charlotte's flight south from Maryland with one revealing a segment of Charlotte's past life. We journey with Charlotte back and forth in time, grasping as we go the significance of her lifelong dream of escape, her coolness in handling unexpected situations, as well as her strength and skill in dealing with Jake, a nervous, restless, nail-biting man who keeps a gun poked in her ribs for at least a third of their three-day trek.

But *Earthly Possessions,* like Anne Tyler's earlier novels, is at heart an ironic and joyful book, and freedom is an elusive goal. Most of us are thrust or born into situations over which we have little or no control, situations which we did not choose but to which we must adjust. Such is the nature of family circumstances, the testing ground for almost all of Miss Tyler's characters. Such is the case for Charlotte Emory, a woman who, in her very bid for freedom, is taken hostage and locked in a stolen car with a man who chains her door shut, a man whose desperation and restlessness testify to his psychological and emotional imprisonment. Charlotte's adjustment to this confining situation, like her adjustment to life with her peculiar parents and her preacher husband, bears witness to Anne Tyler's faith in the ability of human beings to endure and even, in most cases, continue loving.

Like many of the characters in Miss Tyler's fiction, Charlotte and Jake are fully realized, vital though ordinary people who, despite the apparent drabness and inconsequentiality of their lives, confront confounding problems of freedom and commitment. A two-bit criminal and loser, Jake is nonetheless a triumphant portrait of yet another individual puzzled by the confining circumstances of his life: a man who comes to depend on his hostage because of her strength and durability. His bank robbery attempts net a fistful of one dollar bills only, and his best buddy, a former training school companion whom Jake sets out to find in Florida, has married and settled down. Even his girl friend, a seventeen-year-old, slender Kewpie doll named Mindy whom Jake rescues from a home for unwed mothers, has innocently planned to rope him into marriage.

Anne Tyler was born in Minneapolis and raised in the South, but her vision is hardly regional. In their dual struggle for freedom, Jake and Charlotte provide readers of *Earthly Possessions* with a clear insight into the curious disease of restlessness that has afflicted many mid-twentieth-century Americans, a disease whose symptoms are vividly reflected in the strings of fast-food restaurants, banks, and motels that litter the highway Charlotte and Jake travel. As the car they journey in comes to symbolize the unexpected confinement of most human relationships, including family life, so too the road they travel reflects the disjointed, random character of modern life. Significantly, the end of their journey together is a touching scene, one marked by pain and irony, for neither Jake nor Charlotte escapes unscathed by the ties that they have established in their brief sojourn together. Ironically, they have come to a kind of dependence and loving acceptance of one another, the kind most human beings share, despite the brevity of their stay or the hopelessness of their situation.

Family as Fate: The Novels of Anne Tyler

MARY ELLIS GIBSON

In a most interesting review of Anne Tyler's recent novel *Dinner at the Homesick Restaurant*, John Updike observes that Tyler's work has attracted "less approval in the literary ether than the sparer offerings of Ann Beattie and Joan Didion. . . ."[1] While Tyler's novels have had substantial popular appeal—in romanticized paperback covers—they are only now receiving the careful critical attention they deserve. This situation arises in part because Tyler's best work is her most recent, but also because her "spareness" is of a different kind than Joan Didion's; as Updike suggests, Tyler's novels are both "domestic and populous." In part, too, critical appreciation of Tyler's work may have grown slowly because her novels are neither stereotypically southern nor the stories of upwardly mobile suburbanites. Tyler's southern credentials—a childhood spent in North Carolina, study at Duke University under Reynolds Price, an avowed debt to Eudora Welty for her fictional territory—manifest themselves through an almost metaphysical intelligence which has often been overlooked by her reviewers. Nonetheless, as the varied and substantial praise for Tyler's latest novel makes evident, she has become a novelist seriously to be reckoned with.[2]

A careful reading of Tyler's recent work suggests a philosophical coherence and depth residing in aptly chosen domestic details. Like many writers, southern and otherwise, Tyler is obsessed with family, but this obsession does not fall into the familiar pattern of nature versus nurture, of maturity forged out of or against familial influences. Instead, for Tyler the familial becomes the metaphysical. Family is seen in the light of cosmic necessity, as the inevitable precondition of human choice. As Updike perceptively says of *Dinner at the Homesick Restaurant*, "genetic comedy . . . deepens into the tragedy of closeness, of familial limitations that work upon us like Greek fates and condemn us to lives of surrender and secret fury."[3] Updike is surely right to suggest that fatedness is at the center of Tyler's family fictions.

Yet fate is these novels is not precisely the fate of Greek tragedy. Tyler's fates lie somewhere between the classical Greek fates, or *moira*, who work our destinies in accordance with some cosmic order—those fates who preside over

From *Southern Literary Journal* 16 (Fall 1983): 47–58. Reprinted by permission of the editors.

Sophoclean irony—and the more oppressive fate or *heimarmene* of the gnostic dualists and their anti-metaphysical descendents the existentialists.[4] In Tyler's fiction, tragedy and comedy, or the mix of them, grow not from the conjunction of a hero's *hybris* and his fate but from the contest between human caring and nihilism. Again and again we see Tyler's characters, with their rootedness, their entanglements, and their inherited predispositions, come up against the possibility of change. Tyler's families live through a repeating pattern of desertion and reunion. Those who desert—or escape— inevitably carry their pasts with them; those who remain are in danger of becoming too passive, of awakening to find themselves in situations not of their making, of becoming dissociated from their own bodies and the physical world around them. In narrative structure, in characterization, and in the emblems through which she describes the human plight, Tyler works an intricate commentary on the nature of fate and on the importance of family to individual understandings of fate and responsibility.

These fundamental concerns come together with the greatest complexity in Tyler's most recent and, I think, her best novel, *Dinner at the Homesick Restaurant*. The novel opens at the bedside of Pearl Cody Tull, eighty-five years old, blind, and dying in a row house in urban Baltimore. Pearl's memories of the half-century since she married Beck Tull and left her genteel home in Raleigh, N.C., are interwoven with her three children's attempts to understand their father's desertion, their mother's love and anger, and their own responsibility for themselves. Cody, the eldest, has become a travelling man like his father, but a successful and driven efficiency expert rather than a two-bit salesman. Ezra, the middle child, watches faithfully at his mother's bedside, while she reflects that he "hadn't really lived up to his potential."[5] Never having gone to college, Ezra runs a restaurant on St. Paul Street, the Homesick Restaurant, where his greatest pleasure is cooking for others and his continually frustrated hope is for his own family to finish a celebratory meal together. The youngest child, Jenny, has become a pediatrician. She has left her first husband whom she married in order not to be "defenceless," and she has been deserted by her second. Almost by accident she stumbles into a third marriage to a man with a half-dozen children who feel as wounded by their own mother's desertion as Jenny does by Beck Tull's. Pearl Tull reflects that each of her children has an important flaw. In their turn, her children have inherited much of their mother's temperament, and their lives have been formed in response to her abuse. Like her mother, Jenny fears closeness with her own family; like his mother, Cody is prone to violent rages.

All these strands of the Tull's story are developed through a complex narrative structure. The careful weaving of past, present, and future is an advance on Tyler's earlier novels, and narrative structure here focuses more clearly then before on the present as a moment of crisis between past and future. While the Tulls' story suggests no overarching cosmic pattern or design, no future rewards or punishment, no justice on earth or hereafter, it

focuses our attention on moments of transition when the family comes together to celebrate or to mourn a change. For the Tulls, almost any moment
can be a moment of crisis, almost any conversation can be revealing. So it is
not surprising when Pearl thinks to herself on her deathbed, "You could
pluck this single moment out of all time . . . and still discover so much
about her children" (p. 33). Dwelling as it does on these moments of crisis,
the novel as a whole takes a shape analogous to what Hans Jonas describes as
the existentialist understanding of time: "Leaping off, as it were, from its
past, existence projects itself into its future, faces its ultimate limit, death;
returns from this eschatological glimpse of nothingness to its sheer factness,
the unalterable datum of its already having become this, there and then; and
carries this forward with its death-begotten resolve, into which the past has
now been gathered up. I repeat, there is no present to dwell in, only the crisis
between past and future. . . ."[6] In *Dinner at the Homesick Restaurant* each of
the Tulls is seen "gathering up" the past and carrying toward the future the
"unalterable datum" of what she or he has become.

The narrative structure of the novel as a whole is designed to bring past
and future together more subtly than in any of Tyler's earlier novels, except
perhaps *Searching for Caleb*. Tyler no longer relies on dated chapter headings
to peg down chronology, as she did in *Celestial Navigation* and in *Morgan's
Passing*. The third person narration of *Dinner at the Homesick Restaurant* allows
her to move easily from one character's thoughts to another's and to move
back and forth in time. Thus she avoids the sometimes jolting and mechanical transitions from past to present that characterize her first-person novel
Earthly Possessions.

The "Beaches on the Moon" episode of *Dinner at the Homesick Restaurant*
best illustrates the new subtlety of Tyler's narrative structure and the thematic coherence it makes possible. The novel begins in 1979, the year of
Pearl's death, moves backward in time to Pearl's childhood, to Beck's desertion in 1944, and to various events of the children's growing up and their
adult lives. Each episode brings us close to one of the central characters and
show us the family largely through his or her eyes. "Beaches on the Moon," a
chapter at the center of the novel, shows us Ezra'a "tragedy" through his
mother's recollections. Cody has "stolen" his brother Ezra's fiancee, Ruth
Spivey, a "country cook" from the West Virginia hills. Years later (in the
early 1970's) Pearl with Ezra's help keeps up her habit of spring cleaning
Cody's farmhouse—the place near Baltimore where he had once meant for
Ruth to live. The chapter is an intricate weaving together of past and
present. It carries us through the narrative of Cody's marriage and Ezra's
grief, but more importantly it brings us face to face with Pearl's most direct
meditation on the familial fate. This moment is made possible by the pattern
of Pearl's recollections; the present of Pearl's sweeping and cleaning becomes
the fulcrum between past and future.

The chapter begins several years before Pearl's death, before her encroaching blindness, but the image of Pearl at the beginning of the novel, blind and ill, presides over the view of her her. From present tense narration the chapter shifts to past perfect and then to past tense, as Pearl recalls Ezra's grief. Past and present alternate rapidly as the chapter follows both Pearl's cleaning and her relationship with Cody and Ruth after their marriage.[7] At the very end of the chapter Pearl is reminded of an incident still farther back in the past—back in the pre–World War I days when her school friend Linda Lou eloped with the history teacher. As the chapter returns to its predominant present, Pearl reflects that even Linda Lou's scandalous baby is an old man by now. Like Pearl herself and like Cody's farmhouse, he is greying toward death.

These complex recollections make possible and understandable Pearl's most direct confrontation with what she considers to be the family fate. As Pearl remembers Cody's marriage and his deliberate distance, she confronts the failure of her family. The narrative shifts to the present tense:

> Pearl believes now that her family has failed. Neither of her sons is happy, and her daughter can't seem to stay married. There is no one to accept the blame for this but Pearl herself, who raised these children single-handed and did make mistakes, oh, a bushel of mistakes. Still, she sometimes has the feeling that it's simply fate, and not a matter for blame at all. She feels that everything has been assigned, has been preordained; everyone must play his role. Certainly she never intended to foster one of those good son/bad son arrangements, but what can you do when one son is consistently good and the other consistently bad? What can the sons do, even? (pp. 184–85)

Pearl ends these reflections by encountering the force of time directly in the shape of her own aging face: "In the smallest bedroom, a nursery, a little old lady in a hat approaches. It's Pearl, in the speckled mirror above a bureau. She leans closer and traces the lines around her eyes. Her age does not surprise her. She's grown used to it by now. You're old for so much longer than you're young, she thinks. Really it hardly seems fair" (p. 185). Finally Pearl draws comfort from her futile spring cleaning, a present and future testament of her concern. Together, she thinks, she and Ezra will go on cleaning season after season, "the two of them bumping down the driveway, loyal and responsible, together forever." This view of Pearl, like the other episodes in *Dinner at the Homesick Restaurant,* implicitly shows us the importance of the past for shaping the present and the future, and vice versa; we know that even as Pearl herself is aging toward death her children, aging too, are devising ways of going on with their lives.

Tyler's concern with the weight of heredity, of fate and responsibility, is even more evident in characterization than in narrative structure; for her dialectic is the old one of fate versus the human will. The primacy of fate—not mere randomness but the pattern of necessary "accident"—in Tyler's work becomes especially obvious when we realize how many of her novels include fortune tellers. The heroine of *Searching for Caleb,* Justine Peck, becomes a fortune teller herself. In an early meeting with the woman who teaches her to read the cards, Justine asks questions about fate and responsibility.

"Madame Olita," [Justine] said, "if my fortune was to break my parents' hearts, it is true then that I had no way of avoiding it?"
"Oh, no."
"*No?*"
"Goodness, no. You can change your future. I have seen lines alter in a hand overnight. I have seen cards fall suddenly into places where they refused to appear at any earlier reading. . . . Otherwise . . . why take any action at all? No, you can always choose to *some* extent. You can change your future a great deal. Also your past."[8]

While Madame Olita's wisdom is instructive for Justine and a relief, Tyler shows the process of changing one's past and future to be difficult at best.

Virtually all of the major characters in *Dinner at the Homesick Restaurant* think of themselves as fated, though they may be equally mistaken in passively accepting or in willfully seeking to change their fates. At the first family dinner in Ezra's restaurant, when he announces his partnership in the business, Ezra reflects optimistically on the family gathering: "It's just like fate." (But the dinner is fated as always to end in a family quarrel.) Ezra's passivity is the consequence of his fatalism and of his misjudgment about the nature of his family's fates. Approaching forty at the end of the novel, Ezra thinks to himself, "He had never married, never fathered children, and lost the one girl he had loved out of sheer fatalism, lack of force, a willing assumption of defeat. (*Let it be* was the theme that ran through his life. He was ruled by a dreamy mood of acceptance that was partly the source of all his happiness and partly his undoing.)" (p. 266). Ezra is the most thorough fatalist in *Dinner at the Homesick Restaurant,* and in this he is somewhat like Jeremy Pauling in Tyler's earlier novel *Celestial Navigation.* Interestingly, Ezra is also Pearl Tull's favorite child—mother and son share a certain fatalism, but Pearl lacks Ezra's dreamy acceptance. She is all sharp edges, and while she is passive in important matters of concern to her children, she rebels at the one thing no one can alter, her encroaching blindness.

In contrast to Ezra's dreamy fatalism and Pearl's angry, self-justifying fatalism is Cody's relentless activity. Early in their acquaintance Cody catches Ruth reading her horoscope. "*Powerful ally will come to your rescue. Accent today on high finance,*" Ruth reads with a sneer. "I mean who do they reckon they're dealing with?" Cody determines to become himself Ruth's "powerful ally." Out of sheer desire to have whatever Ezra has, he will make Ruth's horoscope prove true. Yet for all his relentless will, Cody can't make himself accept what he has or who he is. After he is injured in an industrial accident and quarrels with his family, Cody thinks his life is like "some kind of plot where someone decided, long before I was born, I would live out my days surrounded by people who were . . . nicer than I am, just naturally nicer without even having to try. . . ." (p. 225). Cody tries with all his energies to have the world for himself; as an efficiency expert he is obsessed with the control of time. Yet even he feels, especially when presented with his family, that his life is plotted in a pattern he did not design. His very relentlessness seems fated, and it makes him less sympathetic than the more passive Ezra.

Jenny, in contrast, is the only character in the novel who comes to deny the family fate, though at one time she too has asked herself, "Was this what it came to—that you never could escape? That certain things were doomed to continue, generation after generation?" (p. 209) In her youth Jenny has tried to protect herself from fate. She marries partly in response to a fortune teller's advice that otherwise she will be "destroyed by love." Approaching middle age, she has learned to "make it through life on a slant" (p. 212), and she reflects ironically that the fortune teller was wrong—love cannot destroy her. She is alternately disengaged and engaged with life, ironically distant and yet taking responsibility for herself and her children. And she refuses to believe family determines future. As she tells one of her step-children, "I don't see the need to blame adjustment, broken homes, bad parents, that sort of thing. We make our own luck, right?"

Jenny could easily be taken to speak for Anne Tyler, who has herself said she tends to see life through a "sort of mist of irony."[9] But the novel suggests that even Jenny can't altogether make her own luck. As if to point to the problem clearly, Jenny's daughter repeats and enlarges her mother's flaws. Jenny, who is always eating lettuce and lemon juice, has a daughter who is anorexic. Analogously, Tyler's novel doesn't make its own luck either. In spite of comic moments, things are never resolvable into an unequivocally happy ending.

This interplay of fatalism and will is even more complex in Anne Tyler's novels than I have so far suggested. Fate is never reducible to a series of statements about it; and Tyler's work has the power to engage us seriously because she uses in her own quirky way the oldest emblems of the plight of humans who feel fated in destinies without meaningful cause.

The sense of having been thrown into an alien world may be expressed in nausea, in homesickness, or in what Annette Kolodny calls reflexive perception—the sense of finding oneself in a situation, of being dissociated from one's body or the world around one.[10] In Tyler's novels the problem of homesickness is presented concretely through minor characters; her novels are filled with hitchhikers and other waifs. More importantly, nausea, homesickness, and dissociation are the stuff of the lives of Tyler's central characters. These motifs permeate *Dinner at the Homesick Restaurant,* though their expression is less extreme here than in Tyler's earlier novels *Celestial Navigation* and *Earthly Possessions*.

In *Celestial Navigation* Jeremy Pauling is anything but at home in the world. Clinically he would be called an agoraphobic. A collage artist, pasting together bits of things and sending out for supplies, he cannot walk past the end of the block without experiencing overwhelming dread. He fathers a family with a woman, equally lonely, who happens to move into the boarding house he has inherited from his mother. For Jeremy fatherhood seems at least as much accident as action. When his wife leaves him he is locked in his studio, and he literally awakens two days later to find himself alone. He wonders, "Had he missed something? Had the days carried everyone else on by and left him stranded in some vanished moment?"[11] Jeremy's life is for the most part a series of such moments. At the beginning of the novel we see the improbable reward of these moments—Jeremy's art—as well as their price—his numbness. Tyler first introduces Jeremy this way: "Jeremy Pauling saw life in a series of flashes, startling moments so brief that they could arrest a motion in mid-air. Like photographs, they were handed to him at unexpected times, introduced by a neutral voice: Here is where you are now. Take a look. Between flashes, he sank into darkness. He drifted in a daze, studying what he had seen. Wondering if he *had* seen it. Forgetting, finally, what it was that he was wondering about, and floating off into numbness again."[12] Lonely, homesick, finding flashes of sight only to lose them again, Jeremy stumbles toward a final isolation.

The motif of homesickness and the device of reflexive perception are as important in *Earthly Possessions* as in *Celestial Navigation,* and equally extreme. The protagonist of *Earthly Possessions,* Charlotte Emory, is as much a stranger in this world as it is possible for a "normal"-seeming woman to be. She is virtually plunked down here out of nowhere, for her obese mother thought until the day of Charlotte's birth that her pregnancy was a prolonged attack of indigestion. Charlotte reacts to her mother's stories about her birth with the certainty that she isn't her parents' daughter.[13] She is homesick from birth. Charlotte also has a knack for finding herself in situations. Her marriage, for example, begins as a "trance," and she learns to survive her "hopeless, powerless feeling" by dissociating herself from her surroundings. "I . . . floated a few feet off," she says, "[and] look at things with a faint, pleasant humorousness. . . ."[14] At the beginning of the novel, Charlotte finds herself taken hostage in a bank robbery, and by the end of her farcical odyssey she speculates that if she signed her traveller's check "Charlotte Emory, hostage," the bank teller would think it her natural condition. Charlotte is the humorous hostage, providing connections and comforts without noticing it. At home she systematically tries to rid herself of earthly possessions, while her husband Saul, the preacher at Holy Basis Church, surrounds her with layers and layers of people and things. Ironically, Saul (not Paul) the fundamentalist preacher is less of a dualist than his atheist wife. Like Jeremy and like her customers in her photography studio (inherited from her father), Charlotte records "people in unexpected costume." Charlotte, with more saving humor and less radical isolation than Jeremy, concludes she has been travelling all her life. Both Jeremy and Charlotte are passive protagonists, buffeted largely by what fateful accidents bring to their doors. The one survives with distant humor; the other, unbelievably perhaps, survives for art.

Dinner at the Homesick Restaurant, I believe, goes beyond these earlier novels both in subtlety and humanity. While it retains the philosophical dimension of Tyler's earlier novels, it makes the situations of aloneness and homesickness meaningful through conditions which are, at least superficially, less unusual than those in the two earlier novels. But despite ordinary domestic appearancs, the characters' situations in *Dinner at the Homesick Restaurant* are extreme. (By implication, all of our situations are extreme.) All of the Tull family experience dissociation from themselves and their actions. Pearl, for example, says, "Sometimes I stand outside my body and just watch it all, totally separate" (p. 140). All the Tulls, too, live with loneliness and fear. None of this is glossed over, none of it is finally mitigated by the happenings of plot. Beck Tull at last arrives for a family dinner—but only on the occasion of Pearl's funeral.

And yet, Tyler manages to suggest that people do go on attempting to nourish each other. At the funeral dinner Beck looks down the table and exclaims in surprise, "It looks like this is one of those big, jolly, noisy, rambling . . . why, *families!*" Cody retorts, "You think we're a family. . . . You think we're some jolly, situation-comedy family when we're in particles, torn apart, torn all over the place, and our mother was a witch" (p. 294). In many ways Cody is right. Yet the Tulls *are* a family. The narrator of Tyler's novel never consigns them to total fragmentation and alienation, and the Tulls never quite give up on themselves. As the narrator observes, "In fact, they probably saw more of each other than happy families did. It was almost as if what they couldn't get right, they had to keep returning to" (p. 155).

Tyler never quite becomes either a fatalist or a nihilist, though both attitudes seem possible given the human situation as she sees it. The question of fate—of necessity without meaningful design—as it is developed in Tyler's narrative suggests that Tyler's fictional world is kin to those of gnostic dualism and of twentieth-century existentialism. Yet there is no superior wisdom to which Tyler's characters might awaken, and their choices are not so bleak as they are in the existentialist novel. Forlornness and ironies there are in plenty, but Tyler's irony is not mordant. Instead, it can be tinged with humor, as if to imply that ironic distance is as authentic as and more survivable than despair. As her latest title suggests, fatalism and despair are balanced by attempted human sympathy and nourishment; homesickness may make possible human efforts to connect. Tyler's world is in fact something like Pascal's, but without a god toward whom to make a leap of faith. In the *Pensées,* Pascal writes, "I am frightened and amazed at finding myself here rather than there; for there is no reason whatever why here rather than there, why now rather than then."[15] For Tyler's characters such fear and amazement are mingled, with fear often overpowering amazement. For the novelist herself, amazement predominates in the "setting-apart situation" she believes is necessary to art. "I am still surprised, to this day," she writes, "to find myself where I am. My life is so streamlined and full of modern conveniences. How did I get here? I have given up hope, by now, of ever losing my sense of distance; in fact, I seem to have come to cherish it."[16]

Tyler's recent novels, particularly *Celestial Navigation, Earthly Possessions,* and *Dinner at the Homesick Restaurant,* are structured by her investigation of what such a "sense of distance" means. She insists on asking directly questions of metaphysical dimension: Why are we here? How do we happen to be who we are? Tyler's characters long for a comprehensible design, a celestial pattern by which or toward which they might navigate. In their gropings toward explanations for their own motives and choices, the question of fate recurs with a singular urgency. It is the measure against which we see Tyler's ordinary families struggle toward a modicum of sympathy and grace.

Notes

1. John Updike, "On Such a Beautiful Green Little Planet," rev. of *Dinner at the Homesick Restaurant, The New Yorker,* 5 Apr. 1982, pp. 196–197.

2. On Tyler's background, see Tyler, "Still Just Writing," in *The Writer on Her Work,* ed. Janet Sternburg (New York: W. W. Norton and Co., 1980), pp. 3–16. Two important essays on Tyler are Benjamin DeMott's review of *Dinner at the Homesick Restaurant,* in which he observes that Tyler's latest work goes "deeper than many living novelists of serious reputation have penetrated," and Stella Nesanovich's review essay. See DeMott, *New York Times Book Review,* 14 Mar. 1982, pp. 1, 14; and Nesanovich, "The Individual in the Family: Anne Tyler's *Searching for Caleb* and *Earthly Possessions,*" *Southern Review,* n.s. 14 (1978), 170–176. Other useful reviews include: Gail Godwin, rev. of *Celestial Navigation, New York Times Book Review,* 28 Apr. 1974, pp. 34–35; Susannah Cheap [*sic*], rev. of *Celestial Navigation, Times Literary Supplement,* 23 May 1975, p. 577; Walter Sullivan, "Gifts, Prophecies, and Prestidigitations: Fictional Frameworks, Fictional Modes," rev. of *Searching for Caleb, Sewanee Review,* 85 (1977), 116–125; Gilberto Perez, "Narrative Voices," rev. of *Earthly Possessions, Hudson Review,* 30 (1977–78), 607–620.

3. Updike, p. 194.

4. On classical *moira* and tragic irony, see H. D. F. Kitto, *Greek Tragedy: A Literary Study,* 3rd. ed. (London: Methuen, 1961), pp. 125–149. Kitto observes that in Sophocles, "What we do, innocently or not, may have unpleasant consequences. . . . in Sophocles the fact that these things come to pass as they do is itself an indication that design of some kind lies behind them" (p. 148). For the best distinction between *moira* and *heimarmene* and for a suggestive treatment of the common motifs of gnosticism and existentialism, see Hans Jonas, *The Gnostic Religion: The Message of the Alien God and the Beginnings of Christianity,* 2nd. ed. (Boston: Beacon Press, 1963); see especially Jonas' "Epilogue: Gnosticism, Nihilism, and Existentialism." Also helpful on gnosticism and existentialism are William Barrett's *Irrational*

Man and Hayden Carruth's introduction to Jean-Paul Sartre, *Nausea,* trans. by Lloyd Alexander (New York: New Directions, 1964).

5. Tyler, *Dinner at the Homesick Restaurant* (New York: Alfred A. Knopf, 1982), p. 22. Further references are indicated parenthetically in the text.

6. Jonas, pp. 336–337. Jonas here is drawing heavily on a reading of the early Heideigger. He contrasts this view of the moment—a view without "metaphysics" or at least without traditional Christian cosmology—with the gnostic moment between the past and eternity, which is founded on a metaphysical dualism.

7. One can plot the chapter chronologically thus: it begins in the early 1970's; moves back to the 1950's when Cody steals Ruth; returns to the virtual present of Pearl's housecleaning (the 1970's); then moves back again to the years in the 1960's following Cody's marriage; returns to the virtual present; moves back to 1964 when Cody's son Luke is two years old; returns to the virtual present with some reflection on the immediate past; moves back to the 1910's; and ends finally in the virtual present (which predates Pearl's death by several years).

8. Tyler, *Searching for Caleb* (New York: Fawcett Popular Library, 1975), pp. 134–135.

9. Tyler, "Still Just Writing," p. 12.

10. Jonas describes these motifs in some detail, while Annette Kolodny finds the phenomena of "reflexive perception" particularly important in recent novels by American and British women. See Kolodny, "Some Notes on Defining a 'Feminist Literary Criticism,' " in *Feminist Criticism: Essays on Theory, Poetry and Prose,* ed. Cheryl L. Brown and Karen Olson (Metuchen, N.J.: Scarecrow Press, 1978), pp. 37–58. Perhaps the most famous and certainly one of the most extreme instances of reflexive perception in modern fiction comes early in Sartre's *Nausea,* when Antoine Roquentin writes in his journal: "A little while ago, just as I was coming into my room, I stopped short because I felt in my hand a cold object which held my attention through a sort of personality. I opened my hand, looked: I was simply holding the door-knob" (p. 4).

11. Tyler, *Celestial Navigation* (New York: Alfred A. Knopf, 1974), p. 188.

12. Tyler, *Celestial,* p. 43.

13. In a telling episode Charlotte is kidnapped by a refugee woman who tells her terrible tales of escape from some devastated country; Charlotte believes this woman to be her real mother.

14. Tyler, *Earthly Possessions* (New York: Alfred A. Knopf, 1977), p. 113.

15. Quoted and translated in Jonas, p. 323.

16. Tyler, "Still Just Writing," p. 13.

The Necessary Balance:
Distance and Sympathy in the
Novels of Anne Tyler

Frank W. Shelton

The artist needs and seeks distance—his own best distance—in order to learn about his subject.

The sharpest recognition is surely that which is charged with sympathy as well as with shock—it is a form of human vision. And that is of course a gift. We struggle through any pain or darkness in nothing but the hope that we may receive it, and through any term of work in the prayer to keep it.

—Eudora Welty, *The Eye of the Story*

Anne Tyler has frequently acknowledged her debt to Eudora Welty for demonstrating how meaningful literature can be made of the small and seemingly insignificant. Tyler also seems to have been influenced by Welty in establishing the ordering poles of her fiction: a sense of distance on the one hand and a gift of sympathy on the other. Every appreciative reader of Tyler's novels notes her warm sympathy and affection for her characters; at the same time, however, she observes those characters from afar and allows them their privacy. She has remarked, "I work from a combination of curiosity and distance." In her personal life, it is interesting to note, she maintains the same kind of dual perspective. In "Still Just Writing," she addresses a question often asked of her—how can she be wife, mother of two, and house-keeper, yet still be a prolific writer? She explains that she has put partitions around the part of her that writes by setting aside certain portions of every day for her writing. The rest of the time is for family, children, "real life." Far from resenting the demands her family and children have made on her, she declares, "It seems to me that since I've had children, I've grown richer and deeper. They may have slowed down my writing for a while, but when I did write, I had more of a self to speak from." Writing affords her a necessary

Reprinted from *Southern Review* 20 (Autumn 1984): 851–60, by permission of the author.

distance from everyday life, while her time with family and children nourishes her emotional roots.

Yet although Anne Tyler has integrated opposing qualities in her life, her fiction constantly, almost obsessively, deals with the vexing relationship between distance and sympathy or, in other terms, disengagement and engagement. Her characters often rebel against restrictive institutions, especially the family. Disengaging themselves from others in order to seek freedom, they struggle between the two poles of distance and sympathy. The indeterminate endings of her novels indicate that a balance is very difficult to find and that, in fact, the terms of that balance may shift in the course of a person's life. But the central issue in the Tyler canon remains the same: how can the individual retain the distance from others necessary for a modicum of personal freedom, yet at the same time achieve enough closeness to others to share necessary human warmth and sympathy?

Her first three novels, while relatively slight compared to her later works, show her approaching this problem from different angles. *A Slipping-Down Life* (1970) deals with her youngest protagonist, Evie Decker, a fat unattractive teenager who experiences the alienation typical of teenagers. Through the grotesque act of cutting his name in her forehead, she hopes to gain the attention of a local rock singer. Her attempts finally unsuccessful, she remains isolated; however, she has learned something about herself. *If Morning Ever Comes* (1964), Tyler's first novel, explores the reverse situation. The protagonist, though twenty-five years old and a Columbia University law student, cannot disengage himself from his family and so is constantly drawn back home to North Carolina. Yet like Evie he too makes some tentative steps toward adulthood and independence by the end of the novel. *The Tin Can Tree* (1965) focuses on two adult characters, James and Joan, who have rebelled against and left their own families and seek comfort with one another. While they never marry because of James's obligations to his sick brother, they do come to see that their affection for one another and those around them provides them with necessary sustenance and helps prevent the isolation threatening them all.

Not until *The Clock Winder* (1972) does Anne Tyler find her characteristic voice and the terms on which to treat her fiction with depth and complexity. From this point on in her career her novels have a heft and weight of very fine fiction. Typically they cover great expanses of time and are comprehensive in treatment of character and subject. *The Clock Winder* contains the distinct Tyler voice, as she focuses with wry humor and sympathy on the ordinary and mundane aspects of life which yield real meaning. It and *Celestial Navigation* (1974) can usefully be paired as her first explorations, from different perspectives, of the full potential of the theme of distance and sympathy.

In *The Clock Winder* Tyler presents clear representatives of both engagement and detachment, tracing how they affect one another in the course of the novel. The Emerson family, with its seven children, is typical of Tyler's fictional families in that it is a large clan. As one of them says, the family is "event-prone," full of crises and conflict and people pulling and tugging at one another. Mrs. Emerson nags her children and tries to hold them to her, while they, feeling confined by her, try to break away. The children, almost all of them grown, feel disconnected and are drifting through their lives. While trying to separate themselves from a dominating mother, many of them are unable to find a way of living independently and fruitfully.

Into this confusion comes Elizabeth Abbott, who has rejected her narrowly religious family and is happy to be traveling aimlessly. She becomes Mrs. Emerson's handyman, and though wanting to be helpful and useful, she keeps her distance and resists involvement in family problems. Open and easygoing, she treats everyone in a friendly but joking manner. She especially likes to surprise herself, so she accepts all invitations to go anywhere. Clearly the opposite of the Emerson children, who are trying to gain their freedom, she is determined to keep hers through separating herself from others. However with Timothy, the most directionless and troubled Emerson child, her attitude has unexpected consequences. Frustrated that she will not take him seriously, he commits suicide. As a result Elizabeth leaves the Emersons and returns home to her parents, feeling guilt and withdrawing further and further, not wanting anyone to rely on her for fear that she will cause more pain. Thus she increasingly separates herself from others.

Over a period of years Elizabeth changes, eventually consenting to return and nurse Mrs. Emerson after she has a stroke. Finally, by marrying Matthew Emerson, she is absorbed into the Emerson family. She explains to Mrs. Emerson how she lost her need for detachment. While watching a parade one day, she noticed the many parents and children in the crowd. Struck by how parents spend years trying to teach their children how to fit into the world, she mused:

> "What am I doing up here, anyway? Up in this shop where I'm bored stiff? And never moving on into something else, for fear of some harm I might cause? You'd think I was some kind of special case . . . but I'm not! I'm like all the people I'm sitting here gawking at, and I might just as well stumble on out and join them!"

When she is first seen in the novel, she expresses a dislike of children because she fears the harm she can do them; at the end she is surrounded by her own children. The sense of separation she cherished throughout much of the novel reflected fear of involvement; by its close she is absorbed in the Emerson family, providing it a much needed stability.

But one must wonder if she has too much neglected distance in favor of involvement. Tyler seems to think so, since she has commented, "I think Elizabeth does herself irreparable damage in not going farther than she does, but on the other hand what she does is the best and happiest thing for her. I think of it as a sad ending, and I've been surprised that not everybody does." Perhaps the sadness lies in Elizabeth's having lost her independence by accepting complete absorption in the family. The last chapter of the novel is told by Peter, the youngest and most alienated of the Emerson children. He and his new wife look figuratively from afar upon the supposedly happy domestic scene with skepticism, not seeing it as in any way ideal. Thus Tyler suggests a balancing view to what might seem a very happy ending.

Celestial Navigation, published two years after *The Clock Winder,* is similar in that this book covers many years and deals with the same problem, though this time from the point of view of the artist. While in the earlier novel a young woman wanted to retain her separateness, in this novel the woman embodies the family, and the artist-man is the character who tries to pull away. Anne Tyler has indicated that *Celestial Navigation* is her favorite novel because its central character, Jeremy Pauling, who lives life from a distance, is the closest she has come to writing about herself. Like her, Jeremy is an artist, but through him the author treats the *dangers* of living a detached life and indicates that engagement with others provides a necessary balance to the distance the artist must maintain. At the beginning of the novel, Jeremy, in his forties, and so disoriented that he will not leave his block in Baltimore, is so helpless that he must be cared for by the women who always hover around him. His life is all inward and is fragmented, as suggested by the form his art takes—collage. The title of the novel refers to him: he lives by "celestial navigation," a term perhaps evoking a higher vision but one also suggesting an inability to live on this earth.

At the opposite extreme from Jeremy is Mary Tell, an only child of middle-aged parents, who left home at age sixteen to marry and who has left her husband as the novel opens. She expresses another side of Anne Tyler, the side that is impatient at being able to live only one life and wants to live many. Unlike Jeremy she seeks involvement, not separation, coming to feel that "motherhood is what I was made for, and pregnancy is my natural state." Thus she embodies the same forces as the Emerson clan in *The Clock Winder.* She and Jeremy begin living together (they cannot marry because her husband will not grant her a divorce), and ultimately they produce six children.

Their relationship does modify Jeremy's behavior somewhat. He becomes more involved in the world and capable of acting for himself, though Mary still cares for him and handles practical matters. His art also deepens, its form becoming complex three-dimensional sculpture. Yet the tragedy of the novel results from Jeremy's continual attempts to pull back from involvement. He never understands, in fact often resents his children. The story's crisis occurs when Mary's husband finally divorces her and she and Jeremy can marry. Rather than doing so, he retreats to his studio to construct a sculpture of a man fleeing all entanglements. After Mary and the children leave, his life is empty, though while they were there he could never allow himself any real contact with them.

Thus in *Celestial Navigation* the extremes of detachment and involvement never meet as they do in *The Clock Winder*. No balance is found, and the characters are left lonely and isolated at the end. At one point Jeremy sees that the distance from which he has lived his life has limited his art. While walking down the street, he "thought of his sculptures, in which people like these so often appeared—standard representatives of what Brian called simple humanity, but anytime Jeremy went out he was forced to see that humanity was far more complex and untidy and depressing than it ever was in his pieces." Just as his art oversimplifies messy humanity, so, by living a life of detachment, he has oversimplified his life to the extent of denying human contact. While distance may be necessary for the artist (or any other person, for that matter), an extreme avoidance of involvement with others is debilitating. Perhaps through Jeremy, Anne Tyler attempts to exorcize a personal tendency toward excessive detachment. Certainly her art, unlike Jeremy's, includes humanity in all its complexity and untidiness.

Some years later, as if she felt she had not done justice to the potential joys of the life of the artist, Anne Tyler returns to him in *Morgan's Passing* (1980), one of her most unruly and untidy novels. Morgan Gower is reminiscent of Jeremy in several ways: he is middle-aged, is in his own way an artist, and has an uncertain relationship with his large family of seven daughters, wife, mother, and sister. At the same time he is unhappy that his daughters are grown and no longer need him, he resists being absorbed into the female family kingdom. His wife, Bonny, like Mary Tell, is endlessly adaptable and practical, and Morgan feels he must flee his family to find meaning in his life. Approaching middle age, he is haunted by the memory of his father, who committed suicide for no discernible reason. The only explanation Morgan can imagine is that his father, simply out of boredom, found no reason to live. For his part Morgan is determined that life be interesting and joyful. Devoted to wearing disguises and playing roles, he, like Anne Tyler herself, wants to live more than one life and like her can only do so by maintaining distance from others. An artist of sorts, though much more at ease in the world than Jeremy, he can play and be accepted in his roles because he lives in Baltimore, a large city where the contact between individuals tends to be fleeting and a role can be sustained for the short period of time necessary. So while Morgan is a joyful, attractive man, impatient with human limitations, like Jeremy he drifts through a fragmented life, avoiding close contact with people. As his wife says of him, " 'He likes to think he's going through life as a stranger.' "

Celestial Navigation ends with the breakup of the relationship of Jeremy and Mary, but *Morgan's Passing* goes a step beyond the earlier novel by developing Morgan's relationships with people outside his own family. Early in the novel he meets Leon and Emily Meredith while posing as a doctor and being forced to deliver their baby. Gradually he becomes involved in their lives, and as they grow apart he takes Leon's place. His sense of detachment thus begins to erode. In a gently ironic way Tyler suggests that neither Emily nor Morgan sees the truth about the other, but each does give the other a sense of completion. Emily is essentially shy, quiet, and passive, but Morgan feels and causes her to feel that her life as itinerant puppeteer is full of romance and excitement. On the other hand, she gives him a sense of stability. Their union is a union of opposites, as the marriages in Tyler's novels often are.

When Morgan learns that Emily is pregnant, he first experiences the sinking sensation that he will be trapped in another restrictive family situation. Yet he comes to view Emily and their child as a responsibility he must accept, and later, more expansively, life with them as a new existence full of possibility. The reader, however, should at least question his assessment. By the end of the novel he is a puppeteer rather than manager of a hardware store (he has taken both Leon's job and his name). He and Emily are associated with the Holy World Entertainment Troupe, so their lives will combine both movement and rootedness. Most important, perhaps, is the novel's conclusion. Morgan is still playing roles, this time as a mailman. The last words of the novel are: "Everything he [Morgan] looked at seemed luminous and beautiful, and rich with possibilities." He continues to seek distance and possibilities, but he is also rushing toward Emily and their child. Involvement with them, even if it will bring him frustration, will also provide a necessary balance to his life. In his spontaneous embrace of life, he thus is more fulfilled than Jeremy, though not so productive as an artist.

While a fine book, *Morgan's Passing* occasionally runs the risk of going out of control, as does its protagonist. Tyler's most successful novels, and the ones which treat the theme of distance and sympathy with the most complexity and penetration, are *Searching for Caleb* (1976) and *Dinner at the Homesick Restaurant* (1982). (*Earthly Possessions*, a runaway housewife novel, appeared in 1977 between these two but adds nothing substantial to the theme I am exploring.) They are the high points of Tyler's accomplishment thus far in her career. Through their circling structure, they comprehend virtually the entirety of their protagonists' lives, so she can explore all the ramifications of her concerns. In *Searching for Caleb* Tyler treats the familiar conflict between a family and those who rebel against it. The family is not the arena of engagement or involvement, as it has been in Tyler's previous works, however; rather the Peck family is detached from the world. In its uniformity, clannishness, and devotion to routine and habit, it attempts to construct a moat between itself and everyone else and keep the world at a distance. The rebels are the characters impatient with such a way of life.

Duncan and Justine Peck, first cousins who have married, live very rootlessly, in flight from the routine lives of the other Pecks. Duncan takes a new job every year and, just when he is becoming successful at it, packs up and leaves, fearing success will trap him. But at the same time that he flees what his family represents, he resembles the other Pecks in resisting engagement with the world and people outside his own immediate family. In fact his constant movement is a way of separating himself from others. Justine, perhaps the most engaging character in all Tyler's novels, attempts to bridge the world of her husband and the world of the Pecks. While committed to change and movement, she does not reject the Peck family as Duncan does. She appreciates their kindness and gentleness and especially sympathizes with her grandfather Peck in his search for his lost brother, Caleb. She is thus not as detached from others as is her husband; in fact she thrives on contact with a variety of other people. Through the course of the novel Justine becomes more and more dissatisfied with her life with Duncan, particularly after their daughter marries and her grandfather dies. She had felt that Caleb, the rebel who ran away from the family in 1912, could take her grandfather's place, but is frustrated when he does not even seem to be a Peck. Caleb, the ultimate rebel, finally flees again, leaving her lonelier than ever. Dissatisfied, she senses that, in her and Duncan's headlong pursuit of change and adventure, they have lost their selves, their very identities. Finally she decides she wants to live with the Peck family in Baltimore, an idea which Duncan hates but agrees to for her sake. Only in this way does Justine feel that she can overcome the sense of separation which has crept upon her. But her mind is changed again by receiving a thank-you note from Caleb. The note, which all Pecks were taught by their mothers to write after any visit, releases Justine from her frustration. In essence she realizes that one's family is not something to be either accepted or rejected. One carries its presence and influence wherever one goes. So it is not necessary to return to Baltimore to live with them in detachment from the world; she can feel their presence wherever she is. The job which she chooses for Duncan at the end of the novel illustrates her perception: he is to become a mechanic for a carnival. Their situation is like Morgan's and Emily's at the end of *Morgan's Passing.* Duncan and Justine will travel, will keep moving, but at the same time they will have a home where the carnival is permanently based. They will thus be able to combine change and movement with roots and stability, distance with engagement. Justine achieves a strong, integrative vision unique in Tyler's fiction. A joyful, spontaneous woman, she loves freedom but is mature enough to recognize that ties and responsibilities are a necessary aspect of life. Of all the characters that Anne Tyler has created, Justine is best able to combine the dichotomies which are her subject.

Her latest novel, *Dinner at the Homesick Restaurant,* while greeted enthusiastically by both critics and the general public, evinces little of the jaunty mood of the earlier novels and lacks a character with the breadth of vision and the understanding of Justine. It is a somber and powerful study of family determinism, focusing on the Tull family over a period of forty years and the effects of the desertion of Beck Tull on his wife Pearl and their three children.

Because she must be both father and mother to her children, Pearl is often frantic and on edge, feeling too burdened by family responsibilities. Frequently cruel, she resents and lashes out at her children even as she tries to make the family sufficient unto itself by isolating it from the outside world.

The effect of their father's desertion and their mother's actions on the children is, in various ways and for different reasons, to isolate them. Cody, the oldest, is tortured by guilt over his father's leaving, wondering if he caused it, and has a rage to dominate others, especially his brother Ezra. His competitive instinct is so active that he steals Ezra's fiancée from him, simply to prevent Ezra's marriage. Cody becomes an efficiency expert, perhaps to compensate for the inefficiency of his early family life. A transient, he never stays in one location long enough to find a place in a community and in fact does not really want one. Though determined not to desert his family as his father did him, he distances himself even from his wife and son, poisoning their lives with his resentment.

His sister Jenny also is condemned to a life detached from others. She marries three times, but only with her third husband does she find any kind of fulfillment. It comes about, however, primarily by her keeping other people at arm's length. Her earlier problems were caused by her closeness to others and involvement in their lives, so she determines to learn "how to make it through life on a slant. She was trying to lose her intensity." In her detachment she is especially reminiscent of Elizabeth Abbott of *The Clock Winder;* in addition to losing her intensity, however, she has also avoided involvement. When her stepson Slevin indicates he needs psychological help, all she can do is joke with him. In essence she protects herself by denying intimacy with others.

Ezra might seem the one Tull child who has retained his connection with others, since he is home oriented and a nurturer. He runs the Homesick Restaurant where he serves what he calls "consoling" food for which he feels people are homesick: " 'what you long for when you're sad and everyone's been wearing you down.' " Yet while he tries to provide affection and a homelike atmosphere, he senses a failure in his personal life, especially since he lost his fiancée. He comments to his mother that he too lives life in isolation:

> "I'm worried I don't know how to get in touch with people. . . . I'm worried if I come too close, they'll say I'm overstepping. They'll say I'm pushy, or . . . emotional, you know. But if I back off, they might think I don't care. I really, honestly believe I missed some rule that everyone else takes for granted."

So when he thinks he might have cancer, he actually greets the prospect of death with relief.

In spite of the fact that this novel is perhaps her grimmest since *Celestial Navigation,* Tyler does not allow it to conclude without a counterbalance to these instances of isolation. It occurs after Pearl's funeral, to which she had asked that her husband be invited. Throughout the novel Ezra has tried to have family dinners at the Homesick Restaurant, always to see them break up in argument. The funeral dinner seems no different, especially after Cody expresses his lifelong resentment of both his father and mother. Hurt, Beck Tull leaves, but everyone goes in search of him, absorbing both him and Cody back into the family group. Thus the two men who have been most estranged from the family are at least temporarily drawn back to it by the force of affection and need.

Almost every Anne Tyler novel includes a scene like the one of family unity at the end of *Dinner at the Homesick Restaurant*, scenes which can occur only when her characters overcome their detachment and disengagement to make the effort to reach out to others. Readers may feel that the characters' success in these scenes may be tenuous, but such events are the most joyous in her fiction and indicate the importance to her of the interconnectedness of human beings through sympathy. The people Tyler writes about are often peculiar, eccentric, almost grotesque, and while viewing *all* her characters with sympathy, she also regards them from the distance which allows them to be just what they most delightfully are. Delighting in human diversity, she feels that an appreciation of humanity involves leaving individuals alone. Tyler has described her fictional heroes in these words:

> I'm very interested in day-to-day endurance. And I'm very interested in space around people. The real heroes to me in my books are first the ones who manage to endure and second the ones who somehow are able to grant other people the privacy of the space around them and yet still produce some warmth.

Her heroes, then, resemble her in their ability to give others the distance to be themselves and also to relate to others with genuine sympathy. The most successful of them, especially Justine Peck, balance distance and sympathy, a combination toward which they all struggle, and a combination which alone leads to a meaningful life and human fulfillment.

Anne Tyler:
Medusa Points and Contact Points

MARY F. ROBERTSON

John Updike, a fan of Anne Tyler's work, remarked in a review that "Tyler, whose humane and populous novels have attracted (if my antennae are tuned right) less approval in the literary ether than the sparer offerings of Ann Beattie and Joan Didion, is sometimes charged with the basic literary sin of implausibility."[1] Indeed, Tyler's novels do not seem a promising hunting ground for critics, who seek advances in the experimental surface of fiction. Her most palpable narrative virtues are by and large traditional ones: memorable characters, seductive plots, imaginative and hawk-eyed descriptions. Tyler is adept with the simile, acute as a psychologist, and quite good at the meditative pause in dramatization, although the reflections usually come as ruminations of a character rather than as autonomous philosophical sorties like George Eliot's.

On first opening Tyler's novels—and perhaps until having read several—a reader is apprehensive that he or she has only encountered still more domestic dramas, seemingly oblivious of the public dimension of the life of men and women in society. A social critic might feel that Tyler's very limitation of subject matter confirms an ideology of the private family to the detriment of political awareness, and a feminist reader might think that only female actions having more public importance than Tyler's seem to have can help the cause of women. In this essay, however, I shall argue that Tyler's unusual use of narrative patterns accomplishes much that should interest the feminist and the social critic alike. To see how, perhaps Updike's word *implausibility* should be examined. This trait in Tyler's work might be a sticking point for some serious readers because of prejudices about what is realistic in the plots of novels about families. Words such as *zany* and *magical* that appear regularly on her book jackets amount to labels that are likely to encourage such prejudices, to invite readers to resist the uncomfortable psychological and political seriousness of Tyler's vision, and to settle for a "good read" instead. Such prejudices, however, are ultimately thwarted by Tyler's fiction; in fact, thwarted prejudices are

From Catherine Rainwater and William J. Scheick, eds., *Contemporary American Women Writers: Narrative Strategies* (Lexington: University Press of Kentucky, 1985), 119–42. Copyright © 1985 by the University Press of Kentucky. Reproduced by permission of the publishers.

exactly the point. Tyler's implausible narrative form is a door through which the reader passes to a deeper sense of realism.

Families are, of course, a traditional subject of fiction. Novels about families can be divided into two groups: those that explore the interior psychology of a family—*Mansfield Park, Sons and Lovers,* and *To the Lighthouse* are diverse examples—and those that use family sagas to represent larger historical changes—works ranging from *Absalom, Absalom* to *Giant* and *The Thorn Birds.* In either case, the genre depends traditionally on features that produce certain narrative expectations in the reader. Foremost, perhaps, is a clear conception of the boundary between the insiders of a family and its outsiders. The typical family novel reserves its emotional center for the insiders. No matter how many forays or entanglements the members of the family have with outsiders, such a novel gains its power from a clear definition of the traits of both the individual members and the family as a whole. One narrative consequence of this conventional boundary that a reader, accustomed to it, might not notice is that dialogues or interchanges among members of a family are usually more portentous for the themes and outcomes of the book than those between members of the family and outsiders. Even if family problems are not solved thematically in such moments, these moments are the points in the narrative at which the significance of the story accrues. There is a centripetal impetus in such interchanges in the traditional family novel that the narrative design does nothing to question.

This conventional attachment of weight to family interchanges produces a preference for formal purity in the narrative shape of the novel as a whole. The strategy of maintaining the boundary between insiders and outsiders is reflected in the reader's awareness of what is plot—action concerning the family history—and what is subplot—contingent action concerning outsiders who function thematically and narratively to push a character to some momentous choice as he or she develops the family's destiny but who then either recede or are absorbed into the family, for example, through marriage. Such peripheral matters as affairs or business dealings function, if anything, to make clear by contrast the central skein of reciprocal effects of members of the family on one another. Often, too, the chapters of such novels are organized according to the points of view of insiders to reflect the central significance of the family.

Independent of the particular thematic content of individual family novels, such generically conventional narrative patterns constitute a second-order system of signs. They imply a certain ideological relationship among family, identity, and history. The family is shown or implied to be the principal determinant of adult identity and the primary social unit. In conventional family novels a kind of binary thinking rules the narrative. The characters can either submit to or reject the family's ways and values; the family as a whole can either triumph or be destroyed. In either instance the concept of the private, inward-turning family remains coherent and ideologically definitive. Something about families, happy or not, makes them one of the very names of narrative order. If they "break down" in divorce, miscommunication, betrayal, or catastrophe, the reader is as uneasy as if people spoke to him or her in disrupted, nonsensical syntax. If families survive in even some good measure, the reader feels that something has been set right with the universe. In addition, even when the family is historically representative of general cultural movements, such an emphasis on the power of the family projects a certain idea of history. History is implicitly reduced to a narrative about families of unquestioned centrality. Families are perhaps the human race's oldest mode of plotting history, and long after more primitive family chronicles have been outgrown as the dominant mode of recording history, the family survives metaphorically in political histories of monarchies and nation-states.

Anne Tyler's narrative strategies disrupt the conventional expectations of the family novels, and thus the disruptions themselves also constitute a second-order system of signs that helps to dislodge the ideology of the enclosed family and the notion that the family is the main forum for making history.[2] These disruptions are undoubtedly responsible for the feeling of implausibility in Tyler's fiction; Tyler does not respect the usual patterns of the genre. The first "itch" caused by her narratives comes at what I shall call Medusa points. These are points at which a certain pattern obtains in the dialogues and interchanges among members of the family. The second itch arises from Tyler's unwillingness to manage the narrative so as to form a clear line of demarcation between insiders and outsiders. The outsiders assume roles that are more than contingent yet not quite surrogates for family roles. The points at which this ambiguity occurs I shall call contact points.[3] The third itch, the result of the first two, is that the pure narrative shape of the family novel is upset. Because the boundary between insiders and outsiders is continually transgressed, the progress of Tyler's novels is felt more as an expansion of narrative disorder than as a movement toward resolution and clarification. This larger narrative movement of disorder usually includes both negative and positive moments. A member of the family typically both sheds—somehow becomes unencumbered from his other family relations—and incorporates—forms significant new relationships with outsiders. If the reader is alert to the meaning of the disruptions of usual expectations of the genre, it becomes clear that Tyler's most pervasive structural preoccupation is with the family as a sign of order or disorder in personality and society.

This structural obsession with the family as a contender for the signs of identity manifests itself especially in Tyler's three most recent novels. In *Earthly Possessions* a middle-aged housewife named Charlotte, who has been thinking of leaving her preacher-husband, Saul, and her two children, goes to the bank to withdraw money for that purpose and is taken hostage by a bank robber, Jake Simms.[4] Until the end of the book she is held captive in this stranger's peripatetic stolen car, which he has chained shut on the passenger's side, and is allowed out only under close surveillance. This sudden traumatic intimacy, symbolized by the closed space of the car, is a parody of the very familial claustrophobia Charlotte had planned to throw off. Yet it proves to be an important opportunity for revelations about otherness and helps her to arrive at some mature distinctions she had not been in the habit of making. Since Tyler interweaves flashbacks to Charlotte's childhood and married life throughout the book, the implications of her eventual choice to risk at gunpoint leaving the robber and returning to her family can be appreciated fully.

In *Morgan's Passing* the overall tone is more lighthearted, but the structural pattern is similar.[5] The two chief characters are Gower Morgan [*sic*], an eccentric—who cannot resist impersonating others—with seven children and an unflappable wife, and Emily Meredith, a young married woman. The story opens with Morgan's delivering Leon and Emily Meredith's baby in a car after telling them untruthfully that he is a doctor. At first Morgan haunts the Merediths in a creepy way by trailing them; finally he is let into their lives as a valued friend. After a few years he reciprocates by allowing them into the life of his family. Later yet, he and Emily fall in love, have an affair, leave their marriages for each other, and produce a new child. This account does not begin to do justice to the disorder to be found in either of Morgan's households, nor to the ambiguous way his presence confounds the distinction between insider and outsider, no matter where he resides; but for the moment it is enough to show that, once again, a stranger disrupts a family's ordered life and alters its self-definition irrevocably.

In *Dinner at the Homesick Restaurant* the action takes us from the time when Pearl Tull, the self-sufficient mother, is dying, back through the history of her marriage and her children's adulthood, full circle to her funeral, when her long-lost husband, Beck, shows up for the day.[6] This book might be read only as a dramatization of what one therapist calls the family crucible; Tyler is very good at showing how neurotic traits ricochet off one another in a family and are passed on to the next generation. If that were all, however, the novel would be nothing special. Its particular virtue lies in the way it places the family's children, Jenny, Ezra, and Cody, in various exogenous relationships that prove as formative and valuable to them as do their family ties.

On numerous occasions in these novels there is a pattern of misconnection—what I call a Medusa point in the narrative—such as this one between Ezra Tull and his mother:

"I'm worried if I come too close, they'll say I'm overstepping. They'll say I'm pushy, or . . . emotional, you know. But if I back off, they might think I don't care. I really, honestly believe I missed some rule that everyone else takes for granted: I must have been absent from school that day. There's this narrow little dividing line I somehow never located." "Nonsense: I don't know what you're talking about," said his mother, and then she held up an egg. "Will you look at this? Out of one dozen eggs, four are cracked." [HR, 127]

Here is a similar interaction between Morgan and his wife, Bonny, who tries to assume the role of bride's mother for her engaged daughter:

> "Morgan, in this day and age, do you believe the bride's mother would still give the bride a little talk?" "Hmm?" "What I want to know is, am I expected to give Amy a talk about sex or am I not?" "Bonny, do you have to call it sex?" "What else would I call it?" "Well . . . " "I mean, sex is what it is, isn't it?" "Yes, but, I don't know . . . " "I mean, what would *you* say? Is it sex, or isn't it?" "Bonny, will you just stop *hammering* at me?" [MP, 110]

In *Earthly Possessions* the pattern is not dramatized but revealed through Charlotte's memories. A stubborn separateness at the center of the relationship of Charlotte with each member of her family—mother, father, husband—is emphasized. Though Charlotte's father adores her in one way, he makes her feel she can never please him. She cares all her life for her grotesquely obese mother, but never breaks through to her candidly about her fears and feelings. She is separated most from her husband, whom she plans to leave almost from the beginning and did not even really make an active decision to marry. Here is the way they become engaged:

> In May he bought me an engagement ring. He took it out of his pocket one night when the three of us were eating supper—a little diamond. I hadn't known anything about it. I just stared at him when he slipped it on my finger. "I thought it was time," he told me. "I'm sorry, Mrs. Ames," he said, "I can't wait any longer, I want to marry her." Mama said, "But I—" "It won't be right away," he said. "I'm not taking her off tomorrow. I don't even know what my work will be yet. We'll stay here as long as you need us, believe me. I promise you." "But—" Mama said. That was all, though. I should have refused. I wasn't helpless, after all. I should have said, "I'm sorry, I can't fit you in . . . But I didn't." [EP, 76–77]

None of these characters tries maliciously to damage his or her family interlocutors; in general, they try to help each other in the mundane ways of life. But in their minds and hearts they feel cut off, paradoxically because each feels suffocated by the other. After exposure to several Tyler novels a reader learns to bypass themes of the individual novels and understands that such nonsequiturs as occur in the conversation between Morgan and Bonny and such failures of communication as Charlotte's are best not read as individuals' character problems but as a narrative pattern drawn by Tyler to make a point about family relations in general. These points in the narrative assume a significance that stands apart from their particular content.

Through them Tyler shows that situations calling for responses considered proper in certain spousal and filial roles petrify people in both senses of the word: the constant intimate gaze threatens to turn people to stone and also scares them into stratagems to evade the threat, just as Perseus could not look at the Medusa directly but mediated the slaying with the mirror. Thus the phrase "Medusa points" seems useful for such moments in Tyler's narratives when a character refuses or is unable to respond to a family member in the way that member desperately needs or desires. These Medusa points are registered, if not in the reader's petrification, at least in exasperation, because what is "supposed to happen" in a family novel—that is, connection between intimates or at least a definitive antagonism—does not happen. Thus the narrative pattern is mirrored in the reading process as resistance.

The Perseus-Medusa image is appropriate for *Dinner at the Homesick Restaurant* in an even more special way. Tyler seems deliberately to invoke Eudora Welty's *The Golden Apples,* in which this myth is quite important.[7] The connection becomes becomes explicit when Beck Tull, who leaves his wife and children early in the book, just as King McLain does in *The Golden Apples,* returns to Pearl's funeral—King returns to Katie Rainey's funeral; Tyler writes: "King-like, he sat alone" (*HR,* 297). *The Golden Apples* is itself a mysterious and complex book, far more dreamlike and mythical than *Homesick,* but the two books dwell on the same two problems: people's existence in time and the profound ambivalence of human beings about identification with others. People suffer from their separateness and are especially drawn to merging with strangers who are exotic to them; yet, no sooner have they done so than they feel the petrification begin to set in and they fantasize evasion, abandonment, wandering. At the end of *The Golden Apples,* Virgie Rainey remembers the picture that hung on her piano teacher's wall of Perseus holding the Medusa's head. She thinks:

> Cutting off the Medusa's head was the heroic act, perhaps that made visible a horror in life, that was at once the horror in love—the separateness. . . . Virgie saw things in their time, like hearing them—and perhaps because she must believe in the Medusa equally with Perseus—she saw the stroke of the sword in three moments, not one. In the three was the damnation . . . beyond the beauty and the sword's stroke and the terror lay their existence in time— far out and endless, a constellation which the heart could read over many a night. . . . In Virgie's reach of memory a melody softly lifted, lifted of itself. Every time Perseus struck off the Medusa's head there was the beat of time, and the melody. Endless the Medusa, and Perseus endless. [*GA,* 275–76]

Tyler shares with Welty the modified view of the heroic Perseus and Medusa reflected in this passage. The principal difference from the classical view lies in Virgie's recognition that the struggle is never finished. Likewise the Medusa is never really killed in Tyler's novels. Indeed, in Tyler's fiction the Medusa points signify primarily by their irony because they are the points in the narrative at which the occurrence of climactic movements, connections, and definitive severances is expected but never witnessed. Thus in and of themselves these Medusa points signify Tyler's refusal to regard the family as the most significant agent of character development and social representation. A crucial stylistic difference between Tyler and Welty aids this narrative message. Welty's poeticizing style, uplifted and abstract, creates a transcendent aura somewhat at odds with the content of Virgie's insight about time. The style itself has a way of lifting and resolving what is unresolved in the subject. In contrast, Tyler's more ordinary prose stylistically places the Medusa syndrome in real historical time. Her prose enacts stylistically the full force of the "fall into time" of those potential Perseuses—characters or readers—who would finish off forever the Medusa of a too complete family communication or would be totally vanquished by it.

In each of the Tyler novels mentioned certain characters are identified most strongly with the Medusa influence. In *Homesick,* Pearl Tull, after being left with three young children and forced to become the breadwinner, defensively develops a rigid, claustrophobic family style. She has no friends, does not visit with the customers at the store where she works, does not encourage her children to bring friends home. For years, in her stubborn pride, she refuses to admit to her children that their father had left them—the abandonment was simply never mentioned as such during all the time they were growing up. Besides this steely silence, Pearl encourages an unhealthy self-sufficiency and iron discipline. When the young Ezra, who is the most sensitive of the three children and the one who takes on the role of family nurturer, asks Pearl whether she would let him stay home from school one day if on that day alone money grew on trees, she answers with a severe "No," and in response to further pleading erupts, "Ezra, will you let it be? Must you keep at me this way? Why are you so obstinate?" (*HR,* 18). A thousand such exchanges in the life of the family produce personalities inclined to give up on real candor and expression of feelings in the family arena. We see this when Cody, the oldest son, is about to leave for college. Pearl has finally brought herself to mention the most pervasive fact in each of their lives— their father's absence:

> "Children, there's something I want to discuss with you." Cody was talking about a job. He had to find one in order to help with the tuition fees. "I could work in the cafeteria," he was saying, "or maybe off-campus. I don't know which." Then he heard his mother and looked over at her. "It's about your father," Pearl said. Jenny said, "I'd choose the cafeteria." "You know, my darlings," Pearl told them, "how I always say your father's away on business." "But off-campus they might pay more," said Cody, "and every penny counts." "At the cafeteria you'd be with your classmates, though," Ezra said. "Yes, I thought of that." "All those coeds," Jenny said. "Cheerleaders. Girls in their

little white bobby sox." "Sweater girls," Cody said. "There's something I want to explain about your father," Pearl told them. "Choose the cafeteria," Ezra said. "Children?" "The cafeteria," they said. And all three gazed at her coolly, out of gray, unblinking, level eyes exactly like her own. [*HR*, 30]

In time Tyler's reader learns that the trick at such moments in the narrative is not to read them conventionally as the portrayal of psychological cripples and tragic family failures. The Medusa points are semantically complex because, while they depict the characters as stony to others in the family, they show at the same time (in the children's oblique comments just quoted, for example) the healthy partial escape from total petrification. Such points show characters who have learned to turn their eyes away from the monster of family self-absorption and to seek their maturity and identity by means of other resources.

The second generic disruption in narrative form that develops an independent significance in Tyler's novels is the altered treatment of outsiders. Pushed, like the characters, to swerve from the inconclusiveness of the Medusa moments and denied the satisfaction of the partial closures usually provided in the family interchanges, the reader must look closer at the supposedly marginal characters of the novel to find a new pattern of significance. The reader then realizes that Tyler shapes an unusual nexus of characters that forces him or her to take seriously Morgan's remark that "our lives depend on total strangers. So much lacks logic, or a proper sequence" (*MP*, 225). If said in a certain tone, of course, this statement *could* suggest an alienation like that of Joan Didion's characters and might reflect anomic acceptance of provisional but meaningless encounters with strangers—even intimates who feel like strangers. But alienation is not the contract offered by Tyler through such a thought. The concept of alienation depends on a firm conceptual boundary between the strange and the familiar, inside and outside; Tyler's narrative disposition of characters trangresses this boundary without eradicating it. The outsiders take over some of the usual functions of family, but their ultimate difference from family is their most significant trait. Such characters are signs of permanent human strangeness, but Tyler's work presents this strangeness as the very resource by which to prevent alienation.

Throughout her life an alienated woman, Pearl Tull, on her deathbed, reflects on the foolishness of holding herself inviolate from disruption: "It was such a relief to drift, finally. Why had she spent so long learning how? . . . She kept mislaying her place in time, but it made no difference" (*HR*, 33). This drift is not a feckless passivity such as that which leads Jenny, Emily, and Charlotte into their first marriages, but an ability to open oneself to the disorder and uncertainty that strangers bring into one's life; it is the ability to be enriched by these strangers, even to be derailed by them, without trying to erase their radical difference from oneself. Narratively, this theme of disorder is registered in a tension produced by Tyler's blurring of the boundary between insiders and outsiders. In their surface organization, whether linear or flashback in manner, her novels give the impression that she is interested in tracing chronological developments of certain families; but the real movements—spiritual, emotional, even material—occur in the marginal relations of members of the family with outsiders. Eventually, the image of the family in each novel becomes an empty presence. The reader feels like a person in a canoe who, while being carried forward by the straight-running current, is also swept sideways by a strong crosswind. In the phenomenological movement of reading, the reader, like the characters, is forced to drift into supposedly contingent, incomplete relations that never-theless prove to be the most important sources of meaning—the "real story," as a Sherwood Anderson character would say. The reader must be willing to "mislay his or her place" in the ostensible generic order of the novel. The family shape remains in some form to the end of each of these three Tyler novels, but the significant spiritual, emotional, and material movements are produced by the crosswinds of strangeness.

Thus Tyler differs from many radical contemporary writers who give us fragmentary texts in order to challenge us to find the unity beneath them. Hers is an opposite vector. She gives us the semblance of order in the overall family design of the novels, but hollows out such order from within by means of the relations of the family with strangers, thereby suggesting the inability of the family to transcend time and disorder, and the provisionality of every-one's life. Rather than the mounting feeling of inevitability to which we are accustomed in family narratives, Tyler's plots impart the feeling almost of random branching. She seems to need a minimum of three generations in her books, not to represent larger historical movements or stronger family defini-tion, but to allow for the free play of interruption of a family's order by the unexpected people who embody the Perseus movement against the Medusa. Her plots reveal along the horizontal axis a continual questioning of the proper vertical boundary between family and not-family. The margin thus always threatens the center, even as it paradoxically also provides an escape valve that enables the family to persist, in a manner of speaking. Intrigu-ingly, then, while Tyler would seem to be the last candidate for the ranks of the postmodernists, who are usually perceived as stylistically radical, her assault on the notion of what is a proper family makes her close in spirit to other postmodernists who regularly engage in what might be called category assassination, questioning just about every conventional distinction between one concept and another that we use to order our lives and thought.

Dinner at the Homesick Restaurant exhibits the features and principles just discussed. Family chronology seems to be respected in the linear movement of the characters' lives contained within the circle of Pearl's expiring life. Most of each chapter is told from the viewpoint of one member of the family—the first and the penultimate from Pearl's point of view and the others from the points of view of her children and her grandchild. In the final chapter the three generations are assembled at a meal to which the abandoning father has returned. Superficially, therefore, the form might seem to imply that families triumph, that we need the order they provide, that all the suffering and disappointment merely contributes to the family's growth. But the real story in *Homesick* does not confirm the family's heroism or even its lasting identity; it shows, rather, how the children have changed the signification of the family identity almost beyond recognition. The maturity of the members of the family is allied with successful disorder, a genuinely scattering movement in time. When Beck Tull left her, Pearl patterned her life on a model she had noted in her youthful diary: "Bristlecone pines, in times of stress, hoard all their life in a single streak and allow the rest to die" (*HR,* 279). Pearl's child, Cody, also tries to adopt this posture, but his son, Luke, belies his success. Jenny and Ezra, in contrast, develop the capacity to drift—that is, to discard both Pearl's notions of daily order in their lives and the conceptual order of family definition. The significance of their lives develops through their turning away from agony over the Medusa points in family life toward the energizing and formative contact points with sundry persons outside the family. They allow the disorder—from the point of view of what is proper—to open new routes without necessarily abandoning the old routes entirely. They exhibit the truth of Morgan's rhetorical assertion: "Aren't we all sitting on stacks of past events? And not every level is neatly finished off, right? Sometimes a lower level bleeds into an upper level. Isn't that so?" (*MP,* 143).

In *Homesick,* Ezra is the character who most fully embodies the narrative paradox of maintaining the outline of family relations while forming a mature identity through contact points outside the family. He lives his whole life at home, caring for Pearl, yet the center of his life is outside that home in the restaurant, in which at first he works for Mrs. Scarlatti and which he then inherits from her. The long intimacy between Ezra and Mrs. Scarlatti does not fit any of the usual categories. He never addresses her except as Mrs. Scarlatti, yet he is her "significant other" in her final illness in the hospital. The nature of their interaction in the hospital shows that Tyler considers it important that peripheral but significant figures remain confirmed in their recalcitrant otherness. Ezra brings her some soup he has made, knowing that

> after he left someone would discard his soup. But this was his special gizzard soup that she had always loved. . . . He only brought the soup out of helplessness; he would have preferred to kneel by her bed and rest his head on her sheets, to take her hands in his and tell her, "Mrs. Scarlatti, come back." But she was such a no-nonsense woman; she would have looked shocked. All he could do was offer this soup. . . . He only sat, looking down at his pale, oversized hands, which lay loosely on his knees. [*HR,* 115]

Mrs. Scalatti, then, has her own rigidities, but they do not paralyze Ezra with guilt as his mother's did. In fact, even before she dies, he begins to alter her restaurant radically, changing the menu from fancy French to down-home cooking, tearing out walls, leaving the kitchen exposed to the dining room and so on. When she unexpectedly makes a sufficient temporary recovery to return home and finds what he had done, she cries:" 'Oh, my God,' . . . She looked up into his eyes. Her face seemed stripped. 'You might at least have waited till I died,' she said. 'Oh!' said Ezra. 'No, you don't understand; you don't know. It wasn't what you think. It was just . . . I can't explain, I went wild somehow!' " (HR, 130). Tyler shows here that a person's contact points with outsiders are still subject to betrayals and difficulties; differences are not erased in some blissful harmony with outsiders that cannot be attained with insiders. But the fact that relationships with outsiders occur makes the crucial difference in the characters' ability to grow and be themselves. Even though Mrs. Scarlatti is appalled at Ezra's changes, she does not revoke her decision to leave him the restaurant, and though he is grief-stricken, her death clearly releases new energies in him. He soon changes the name from "Scarlatti's" to "The Homesick Restaurant," and he thrives by arranging matters more in his own way.

Jenny, another character who, like Ezra, escapes the rigid patterns of her early life, makes her own disorderly way through three marriages. She becomes a pediatrician, exerting in her work the same strong will as her mother, but each of her marriages represents a move away from rigidity to disorder. Her final marriage is to Joe, a man whose wife has left him with six children. He says he married Jenny because he "could see she wasn't a skimpy woman. . . . Not rigid. Not constricted. Not that super-serious kind" (HR, 193). But of course she had been more so in her younger days when she was closer to Pearl's influence. It may be implausible to us that she could run a household of nine and still not stint on a demanding career, but that seems beside the point that Tyler wishes to make. Jenny is shown to have moved through the nervous-breakdown stage into an impressive equanimity gained from learning to drift through demands upon her. She is perhaps at risk for turning everything into a joke; nevertheless, she is a compelling example of a character's ability to outgrow a destructive background. And not only does she show greater tolerance for the literal physical disorder of her new household, but in her way she accomplishes in her final marriage what Ezra accomplishes in his relationship with Mrs. Scarlatti; with her third marriage she breaks the purity of the family line decisively by blurring the boundary between who is real family and who is not. By the end, most of her immediate family is not even her own, but consists of stepchildren she has accepted the responsibility of nurturing.

Ezra and Jenny's brother, Cody, in Homesick, does not manage to form a flexible and freely determined personality as his siblings do. He is the classic example of the child who unwittingly replicates the very childhood condition he tries to flee. He considers Ezra his oldest enemy because Ezra was always liked more than he, and he keeps a distance from his mother and siblings most of his adult life. Yet Cody's hate is just the outer skin that hides his eternal longing to be like Ezra. For much of the book the reader feels that Cody is a villain. The reader would like to roast him over hot coals when, a Cain to Ezra's Abel, in a calculated way he woos Ezra's fiancée, Ruth, away from his lovable brother. Ruth and Ezra had seemed destined only for each other, since they are both eccentric in the same way. The defection of Ruth to Cody is an interesting example of those implausible turns in Tyler's narrative design for which a higher logic must be sought than character psychology alone would provide. It is difficult to credit that Cody, the rich city slicker, would fall in love with this barefoot country girl and even more difficult to believe that she would go with him. True, the episode does teach us something profound about the dialectics of longing, but Tyler wishes above all to use the implausibility to make a narrative argument that people will often choose strangeness over similarity for their own self-preservation. Her narrative ethos, borne out in the other novels too, seems to say that such a choice is somehow right, as if Ezra and Ruth are too much alike for their own good. Tyler does not seem to allow relationships between like and like to flourish. While Cody and Ruth's marriage is not especially happy, it is loyal, and we do not, as we expect, hear Ruth complaining later that she should have married Ezra. She seems to have known she needed something different in life from living with her soul twin. And, through Ruth, Cody is able in part to incorporate that lost part of himself—the brother whom he so wished to be like. Thus, Cody too is a character affected beneficially by disorder and strangeness.

Cody's son, Luke, is the only third-generation member of the family to have a viewpoint chapter of his own. What emerges is the likeness, much to Cody's overt disgust, between Luke and Ezra. Cody rails at it and probably damages the boy somewhat by absurdly and jealously accusing Ruth of having had Ezra's son rather than his own. Cody feels that the resemblance is the vengeance of fate, but we see it as a kind of fortunate prevention of a too-pure family identity, for Cody has tried to seal off his own family just as Pearl had. Cody's rigidity is reflected in his profession, that of efficiency expert, doing time-and-motion studies for industry. He tells us: "Time is my favorite thing of all. . . . Time is my obsession: not to waste it, not to lose it. It's like . . . I don't know, an object to me; something you can almost take hold of. If I could just collect enough of it in one clump, I always think. If I could pass it back and forth and sideways, you know? If only Einstein were right and time were a place or river you could choose to step into at any place along the shore" (*HR*, 228). This insight is the opposite of Virgie's perception about time in *The Golden Apples* or Pearl's drift. Cody dreams of killing the Medusa in one final stroke, but he is forced through Luke and Ezra to submit to time, like everyone else, as the repetition of ceaseless conflict. Cody might fight disorder, but it is always there to exert a pressure on him to be more flexible than he might otherwise be.

Running through *Homesick* like a bolt through a door hinge is a series of six family dinners he has tried to make "just like home" that Ezra plans at the restaurant. The inability of the family ever to complete a meal eventually becomes comical in spite of our sympathy for Ezra's disappointments. Yet this unfinished-dinner pattern is the book's strongest narrative emblem for Tyler's complex vision of order, disorder, and the family. Ezra is the "feeder," unlike his mother, who, Cody reflects, was a "non-feeder if there ever was one . . . neediness: she disapproved of neediness in people. Whenever there was a family argument, she most often chose to start it over dinner" (*HR*, 162–63). Tyler never uses gender stereotypes; men can be nurturing as well as women, and women can exhibit patriarchal attitudes. Indeed, Pearl is at first the reason Ezra's dinners are never finished before someone walks out. In being stalled by someone's bitterness the dinners are emblems of the Medusa syndrome, but in going on anyhow, eventually by including more outsiders, they are also emblems of Perseus' slaying of the Medusa through the fruitful disorder of contact points. The first four breakdowns during meals occur because Pearl thinks that one character or another is insufficiently concerned about the family's integrity: Ezra's business partnership will dissolve the family; Jenny is too familiar with Ezra's eccentric friend, Josiah; Jenny does not heed her mother's opinion; Cody has "set up shop too far from home." The fifth breakdown occurs because Cody reacts jealously when his wife talks to Ezra; his jealousy often cuts his family off entirely from innocent interchanges with others. Through the failure of meals, which are usually the classic expression of family order, Tyler shows symbolically the family's inability to thrive when its ideals are hermetic.

Ezra occupies an ambiguous position in this narrative pattern, and eventually his actions prevent the total petrification of the family. No one wishes more than he that the family care about one another, and, he cries, "I wish just once we could eat a meal from start to finish" (*HR*, 111). Yet he is not annihilated when things fall apart; he does not give up but placidly and resiliently keeps the institution going, even in apparent defeat. Significantly, however, in keeping the tradition going, Ezra does not follow an orthodox plan for family meals. They occur in a public place, the restaurant, where the members of the family are always in marginal relation to others, such as Mrs. Scarlatti, the kitchen crew, the friend, Josiah (whom Pearl had made unwelcome in her house), and the other customers. That is, Ezra upholds the tradition of the family meal in one way, yet he revises it, loosens its joints, forces it to articulate with outsiders who remain outsiders. Though it is true that the family never stops arguing and never finishes the meals, even its minimal survival as a unit thus "depends on total strangers" in order to keep it from being turned into stone altogether.

With the last dinner, not only has Ezra's more public sphere replaced Pearl's tightly guarded kitchen as the family meeting place, but the composition of the family has become less pure. The direct descendents among the grandchildren, Cody's Luke and Jenny's Becky, are vastly outnumbered by Joe's gaggle of children, who are technically outsiders. Beck starts to swell with grandfatherly pride when he looks around the table, but Cody says, "It's not really that way at all. . . . Don't let them mislead you. It's not the way it appears. Why, not more than two or three of these kids are even related to you. The rest are Joe's by a previous wife" (*HR,* 300). Furthermore, Beck's unexpected presence conveys no sense of the missing piece that triumphantly closes the circle in an image of final reconciliation and unity. On the contrary, it is clear that he returns as a stranger and will always be a stranger, like a bird alighted on a branch, about to depart at any moment. When Joe's baby chokes on a mushroom, distracting everyone, Beck slips out before the meal is over. Ezra, beside himself at another unfinished dinner, organizes the whole party to run out in different directions to find Beck. Cody is the one to do so and brings him back after finally hearing his father's side of the story of the abandonment. There is a hint that Cody will be somewhat liberated from his constricting beliefs after receiving this information, but, if so, only because Beck makes real for Cody his father's separate existence, forces Cody to see him not as Cody's projection but as a person with his own needs and rights. Beck agrees to go back to the meal for "one last course," but says, "I warn you, I plan to leave before the dessert wine's poured." The reason he must leave is that he feels obliged to return to a woman he is dating and will marry now that Pearl is dead. The progenitor does not finally offer an image of reunion, wholeness; he too, in fact, moves in the direction of another connection peripheral to the original family. The meal is more nearly finished than any of the previous ones, but it is not finished with everyone who would symbolically confirm the intactness of the Tull family present. Thus "Homesick" in the name of the restaurant is a pun: people go there who yearn for the nurturing of home, but the restaurant stands equally as an alternative to the home which, if too much ingrown, or if conceived of as the place of a golden age, is sick. The Tull family is finally like this restaurant itself: the shell of the original still stands, but the interior has been demolished and refashioned through the beneficial agency of significant outsiders. The tones and meanings are now quite as different as Ezra's food is from French cuisine. Thus the overall narrative shape that might have signified that the family is a real sign of order and growth is so heavily qualified by the actual patterns of meaning and growth as to be voided as a narrative and thematic signifying system.

Space does not permit detailed documentation of the way *Morgan's Passing* and *Earthly Possessions* exhibit a similar narrative semiosis questioning the traditional family as a sign of order, but it is important to recognize that such narrative semiosis exists in each novel, in which plot and character patterns show meanings independent of their special content. The charming Morgan himself, a Hermes-like figure lurking at boundaries, provides a vehicle to show that energy comes from the disorderly transactions both within and between families. Just as Morgan is the character who shakes up the Merediths' lives for the better, so, in *Earthly Possessions,* Jake, the bank robber, pulls Charlotte roughly out of her trancelike life and forces her to recognize that the Medusa is not so much in her husband's domestic style as it is in her own inner, unspoken dream of perfect order for herself. She finally perceives that there is no need to unload those she had thought responsible for her unhappiness.

Tyler also has a suitably wry sense that the most disorderly characters themselves have a fascination with or craving for order. Morgan says comically as he shakes out Emily's purse,

> "Look at that! You're so orderly." Emily retrieved her belongings and put them back in her purse. Morgan watched, with his head cocked. "I too am orderly," he told her. "You are?" "Well, at least I have an interest in order. I mean order has always intrigued me. When I was a child, I thought order might come when my voice changed. Then I thought, no, maybe when I'm educated. At one point I thought I would be orderly if I could just once sleep with a woman." . . . Emily said, "Well?" "Well what?" "Did sleeping with a woman make you orderly?" "How can you ask?" he said. He sighed. [*MP,* 140]

Similarly, Jake the robber detests the irregularity of his life on the lam, and his conscience causes him to head the stolen car for the home of a girl he had made pregnant. This dangerous adventure thus soon bogs down in domestic problems such as the girl's nausea and the care of the cat she has brought with her.

In *Homesick,* the narrative pattern of family dinners is symbolic of disorderly movement within an apparently fixed figure; in *Morgan,* Tyler makes the same point, that nothing in our lives can or should stay rigid, through the symbolism of both Emily's puppets and the leotards she always wears. Leon Meredith explains in a condescending manner that, whereas he can improvise in his management of the puppet shows which are their livelihood, "Emily makes them according to a fixed pattern. *They're* not improvised." Emily thinks to herself, however, "This was true, in a way, and yet it wasn't. Emily did have a homemade brown-paper pattern for the puppets' outlines, but the outlines were the least of it. What was important was the faces, the dips and hills of their own expressions, which tended to develop unexpected twists of their own no matter how closely she guided the fabric through the sewing machine" (*MP,* 131–32).

Later, when Morgan has become her new husband and is characteristically chafing at the very disorder he brings with him, he complains,

> We don't have any chance to be alone. . . . Mother, Brindle, the baby . . . it's like a transplant. I transplanted all the mess from home. It's like some crazy practical joke." . . . "I don't mind it." Emily said. "I kind of enjoy it." "That's easy for you to say," he told her. "It's not your problem, really. You

stay unencumbered no matter what, like those people who can eat and eat and not gain weight. You're still in your same wrap skirt. Same leotard." Little did he know how many replacement leotards she had had to buy over the years. Evidently, he imagined they lasted forever. [*MP,* 307]

In *Earthly Possessions,* Charlotte's found trinket saying "Keep on truckin' " is the symbol equivalent to the dinners of *Homesick* and Emily's puppets and leotards in *Morgan.* When she finds it, Charlotte takes it as a sign that now is the time to leave Saul. After her abduction, however, she returns to Saul with a different sense of the phrase; now the phrase suggests endurance, and the novel finishes this way: "Maybe we ought to take a trip, he says. Didn't I use to want to? But I tell him no. I don't see the need, I say. We have been traveling for years, traveled all our lives, we are traveling still. We couldn't stay in one place if we tried. Go to sleep, I say. And he does" (*EP,* 222). Yet Tyler is no Hegelian of domesticity, portraying disorder merely as an antithetical way station to greater order, recapturing drift for the greater benefit of the concept of the private family. Charlotte does go back to Saul, but Jenny and Emily both rightly obtain divorces. Tyler designs narratives in which there is constant oscillation between shedding and incorporation without any suggestion of some final resting place, either totally within the family or totally outside it.

While freedom from suffocation of family life is a favorite theme of feminist writers, Tyler's prescription about means differs notably from those writers, such as Tillie Olsen, to whom *drift* is a red-flag word signaling loss of coherent identity and personal purpose. Olsen's Eva in "Tell Me a Riddle" is a famous example of a character who evinces this sense of loss. While raising her family, Eva had to abide by the idea that "empty things float," but the story represents such drift as a tragic forfeiture of her own identity, which she can only recover bitterly as she is dying. Ruth, in Marilynne Robinson's *Housekeeping*[,] might seem closer to Tyler, since she asserts the value of drift and sheds domestic encumbrances by choosing the equivalent of Huck Finn's "lighting out for the territory" and leaving with her eccentric Aunt Sylvie for a vagrant life on the railroad boxcars. Yet that pattern obviously perpetuates the old either-or dilemma for those stifled by family closeness. Sylvie and Ruth become pariahs. For Tyler, the negative freedom of merely shedding is undesirable. In her novels, drift signifies not only such emptiness of infinite potential, but also a movement toward a positive condition of greater fullness accomplished through commitments in exogeneous exchanges. For Tyler, drift must include the second phase of incorporation, taking into one's life, however temporarily, others who do not merge with oneself but remain different; otherwise one merely reproduces within oneself the Medusa influence of family life.

In Tyler's narratives that represent this oscillation between shedding and incorporation, metonymies of household effects are abundant. They might remind the reader of Kafka's *Metamorphosis,* but the difference from Kafka is instructive. In Kafka's story both the emptying and refilling of Gregor's room are symptoms of alienation. In *Homesick* Ezra's demolition of Scarlatti's restaurant is a sign of his rejection of Mrs. Scarlatti's dominance, a temporary alienation perhaps, but the demolition also allows for the constructive substitution of his own adult identity, which is being formed through his life outside his family. He does go nearly bankrupt at first, but when the restaurant fills up again, it does not parallel Gregor's trash-filled room, which is a sign that Gregor no longer matters. On the contrary, the crowded restaurant testfies to Ezra's significance. The same is true of the overstuffed households of Emily and Morgan and Charlotte and Saul. Both women realize there is no exit from the disorder of claims upon them by people who are technically outsiders to their own families, but it does not feel like hell to them because they have learned to respect true difference as nourishing. Tyler's stories might be seen as affirmative complements to Kafka's fable about the damaging effects on personality of a rigid family identity.

The bountiful environments portrayed in Tyler's conclusions suggest that Updike is right to contrast Tyler with Beattie and Didion, whose "spareness" is a result of their vision of alienation. A critic who believes that alienation is still the only authentic response to the world will not like Tyler. Her work makes room for the alienated moment, but it finally makes one wonder whether the alienated attitude does not rest on a secret, stingy resentment that the world and its many people are different from oneself.

Even Tyler's physical settings underscore her rejection of alienation and her theme that disorder is a remedy for excessive family order. In each novel a building structure symbolizes the paradox that one can best be oneself if one is connected in some significant way with those in the public who are different from oneself. Charlotte's house has a room with an outside door which serves as a photography studio that is open to the public. Ezra's "homesick" restaurant similarly connotes both the public and the private life. The Merediths' apartment, into which Morgan eventually moves with Emily, is located above a public crafts shop with a common hallway. Further suggesting connectedness of the private to the public scene, Tyler's novels are emphatically urban rather than suburban. Charlotte's neighborhood changes from strictly residential to partly commercial when Amoco buys the property next door for a filling station. Ezra's is a city restaurant in Baltimore, and Morgan's people reside in Baltimore too. Morgan says, "We're city people. . . . We have our city patterns, things to keep us busy" (*MP,* 164). The city is of course the place where one is maximally involved with the difference of other people in one's daily affairs.

Tyler's insistence on the public and urbane quality even of family life calls to mind the argument of an urban theorist, Richard Sennett, whose ideas seem remarkably apposite to Tyler's vision. In *The Uses of Disorder,*

Sennett argues that our contemporary society, with its preference for seques-tered surburban life or for the highly rationalized city of city planners, instantiates an adolescent mode of personality development in our public life.[8] According to Sennett, adolescence is marked by a rigid drive for a "purified identity," which enables the powerless youth to mediate his self-image and his image of the outside world (*UD,* 17–18). Beneficial as it is at that stage, this drive is "extremely dangerous if it remains fixed in a person's life, if it meets no challenge and becomes a permanent modality. . . . It can lead to a language that similarly does away with the 'factness' of new people or new experiences . . . and assumes that one has had the meanings of experience without the threat of actively experiencing" (*UD,* 22–25). Sub-urbs and rationalized cities, by restricting the number of contact points for citizens, lock our public life into such a defensive, closed-off mode that we never learn the essential lesson of adulthood, which the real city teaches us—how to live with the "unachieved situations" that the radical differences of others impose on us. Sennett says that this *"intense family life is the agent, the middleman for the infusion of adolescent fear into the social life of modern cities. . . .* It is exactly the character of intense families to diminish the diversity of contact points that have marked out a community life in the teeming cities at the turn of the century" (*UD,* 67).

Whatever we might feel about certain corollary arguments in Sennett's book, which, if followed, could produce municipal anarchy, his diagnosis seems cogent, and Tyler's novels echo it. They enact thematically the growth from adolescent notions of identity to the adult willingness to live with unachieved situations of involvement with people's otherness. In her quiet way, Tyler stakes out a position against the whole existentialist nausea over "otherness" and makes it seem puerile. Emily reflects toward the end of *Morgan's Passing,* "You could draw vitality from mere objects, evidently—from these seething souvenirs of dozens of lives raced through at full throttle. Morgan's mother and sister (both in their ways annoying, demanding, queru-lous women) troubled her not a bit, because they weren't hers. They were too foreign to be hers. Foreign: that was the word. . . . She drew in a deep breath, as if trying to taste the difference in the air. She was fascinated by her son, who did not seem really, truly her own, though she loved him immeasur-ably" (*MP,* 289). Tyler's typical narrative patterns mirror this theme by refusing the kind of unswerving focus on members of a family as the reposi-tory of meaning that we expect in a family novel and by spinning the plots off at tangents that are not just detours from which we return. Likewise, her endings are not merely inconclusive and ambiguous as so many modernist fictional endings are, but instead convey more aggressive images of continu-ing flux, of the unachieved situation, understood and welcomed as such, like that we saw in *Homesick*'s final dinner, or in Morgan and Emily's improvisa-tional spirit at the end of *Morgan,* or in Charlotte's thoughts as she returns to Saul in *Earthly Possessions.*

Tyler's emphasis on continuing flux, moreover, bears upon a serious problem with which feminist writers struggle: the difficulty of depicting feminist men and women using their knowledge in plausible ways in actual society. A careful reader can see that Tyler has to a great extent come to terms with that problem. A main ingredient, if not the essence, of the patriarchal attitude is a hypostatization of category differences—family/outsiders, for example—that makes it possible to transcend the disorderly flux of real relations among members of different classes. It might plausibly be argued that the whole notion of "proper" family is patriarchal; it was surely not the mothers who cared whether their children were bastards or whether blood relatives were treated better than outsiders. The nature of patriarchal thought, as of all ideologies, is Medusa-like in its reifications. The feminine personality has traditionally been allowed a dispensation from this way of thinking, but only at the price of being segregated from the world of significant action, which seems to require firm categories, and of being marked as amorphous—thus the fear of drift as regressive by many feminists. It seems difficult to dramatize people who are both taken seriously by society and consistently question prevailing conceptual boundaries, precisely for the reason that actual society does not take them seriously; indeed, they are marginalized as implausible, unrealistic, or irresponsible. Delightful or not, for example, Gower Morgan is probably perceived by many readers as little more than a humorous, self-indulgent stunt man and Ezra, Jenny, and Emily as memorable for their weirdness. If taken seriously as possible types of real people they threaten the system that depends on ideological purities of various sorts. A reader who indulges in Tyler's novels for their "zaniness," however, does himself or herself a disservice. Tyler is rare in her ability to portray practical and constructive ways in which impatience with the "drive for purification" can translate into concrete, constructive action. Here these boundary-doubters are actually seen acting in a recognizable world.[9] None of what might seem at first implausible in Tyler is really so unrealistic. It is not even so farfetched these days that one might be taken hostage, and a person who was might have gained from Earthly Possessions some realistic instruction, not only in the psychology of the outlaw, but in the real horizons of his or her ordinary life, which had conveniently gone unnoticed. Likewise, the implausible semifriendship that develops between Morgan's first wife and Emily, once Bonny's anger at Morgan's leaving has cooled, is not really so uncommon these days among divorced families. Time magazine and the U.S. Census tell us that the typical nuclear family is much in the minority now, but ideologically the model still has a grip on us. Thus Tyler's idea that a respect for the difference of "significant others" in such disorderly family structures can liberate us is valuable in a practical way.

Indeed, Tyler's narrative vision of family disorder seems to have been derived directly from her sense of her own life's problems and patterns. The fact that she is married to an Iranian is bound to have had some influence on Tyler's theme of difference. Her essay "Still Just Writing" shows that as a writer and mother her personal anxiety is with the problem of interruption of her work and, by extension, the threat of "disorderly" deviations from her path as a writer. She seems to have learned the coping mechanism of drift from her father rather than from her mother. She explains that whenever his schedule was interrupted, even to the extent of having to cancel a long-awaited foreign sojourn at the last minute, he just whistled Mozart and occupied himself with whatever was available to him at the time. She claims to have found that the threatening detours actually enrich her work. This equanimity, however, is not without recognition of the dangers. Clear-eyed she says, "What this takes, of course, is a sense of limitless time, but I'm getting that. My life is beginning to seem unusually long. And there's a danger to it: I could wind up as passive as a piece of wood on a wave. But I try to walk a middle line."[10] This sense of limitless time should not be read, I think, as the classic feminine suspension above a real-world sense of deadlines and irrevocable actions. It is more like Virgie Rainey's "beat of time." A musical beat is a concrete commitment, a movement from the virtual to the actual, just as the productive interruption in Tyler's novels is. Virgie's phrase is also a way of recognizing that our short-sighted desire for finalities is often blind to time's amplitude and to the way unexpected turns taken by the beat can make life more interesting and fulfilling.

Although she lacks his stylistic genius, Faulkner is in a way the American author to whom Tyler seems closest. He too depicted the way a "drive toward purification" could ruin personalities and the whole culture of the South. Just as he saw at the center of the ideal of white supremacy the taboo against miscegenation as the chief means of sapping the vital energy of the South, so Tyler shows that the desire for family purity leads to entropy. The social critic might respect Tyler's family novels about private existence as significant for public life. If, as Sennett says, the family is the "middleman" institution between our psychological fears and our public life, then a novelist who alters the narrative line of the family novel to open it up to the radical disorder of outside influences that are not merely contingent does her part to suggest a new possibility for our actual history. She also does her part in altering the very idea of history, which, in the guise of recording events in time, more often artificially kills time, the beat of time, through concepts, such as the family, that deny history's real randomness and disorder.*

*In an interview with me conducted by mail in August 1989, Anne Tyler indicated her lack of familiarity with Richard Sennett's study ("I've never heard of *The Uses of Disorder*") and disavowed any connection between Welty's *The Golden Apples* and *Dinner at the Homesick Restaurant:* "No specific elements have been borrowed from [Welty's] work to my knowledge, and certainly not Beck's sitting 'king-like.' " Even so, Sennett's ideas regarding disorder remain useful for understanding Tyler's world view, while Welty's example first inspired Tyler to pursue a career as a writer—Ed.

Notes

1. John Updike, review of *Dinner at the Homesick Restaurant, New Yorker* 58 (5 April 1982): 193–95.

2. Jane Marcus has called attention to the dissatisfaction with the Victorian patriarchal family among certain influential women of the modernist period. In "*The Years* as Greek Drama, Domestic Novel, and Götterdämmerung," *Bulletin of the New York Public Library,* Winter 1977, 277, she quotes the anthropologist Jane Harrison as saying, "Family life never attracted me. At its best it seems to me rather narrow and selfish; at its worst a private hell. . . . On the other hand, I have a natural gift for community life. . . . I think, as civilization advances, family life will become, if not extinct, at least much modified and curtailed." Marcus suggests, in this article and in "Pargeting 'The Pargeters,' " *Bulletin of the New York Public Library,* Spring 1977, 416–35, that in *The Years* Virginia Woolf experiments narratively with altering the traditional family novel by organizing it around relationships between sisters and aunts and nieces rather than around fathers and sons or fathers and daughters. Marcus reads *The Years* tragically, however, as an *Antigone* for the women and a *Götterdämmerung* for the patriarchs. As I shall argue, Tyler starts from a position well beyond the tragic view of the demise of the traditional family. Furthermore, it is doubtful that Woolf really meant to let go of the ideal of family unity; she wished rather to broaden or change the definition of such unity to include the important transmissions and transactions among the female members of a family.

3. The phrase is Richard Sennett's in *The Uses of Disorder* (New York: Vintage Books, 1970), which I shall discuss later.

4. Anne Tyler, *Earthly Possessions* (New York: Berkley Books, 1977); hereafter cited in the text as *EP.*

5. Anne Tyler, *Morgan's Passing* (New York: Berkley Books, 1980); hereafter cited in the text as *MP.*

6. Anne Tyler, *Dinner at the Homesick Restaurant* (New York: Berkley Books, 1982); hereafter cited in the text as *HR.*

7. Eudora Welty, *The Golden Apples* (New York: Harcourt, Brace and World, 1947); hereafter cited in the text as *GA.*

8. Sennett, *Uses of Disorder,* passim; hereafter cited in the text as *UD.*

9. An interesting contrast, for example, is with *The White Hotel* by D. M. Thomas, in which Lisa Erdman also has little time for ordinary family boundaries, but is depicted as even moderately victorious only in an imagined purgatorial place after her death.

10. "Still Just Writing," in *The Writer on Her Work,* ed. Janet Sternburg (New York: W. W. Norton, 1980), 11.

ORIGINAL ESSAYS

◆

Anne Tyler's Emersonian Balance

SANFORD E. MAROVITZ

The soul . . . is a light. . . . [W]e are nothing, but the light is all.
—Emerson, "The Over-Soul"

The whole world is a series of balanced antagonisms.
—Emerson, *Journals*, 4/5 1

Pieces of Emersons were lodged within Elizabeth like shrapnel.
—Tyler, *The Clock Winder*

In *Dinner at the Homesick Restaurant* (1982), Anne Tyler's ninth novel, Pearl Tull reads and rereads to her sick granddaughter, Becky, Virginia Lee Burton's enduring children's story, *The Little House,* originally published in 1942. Becky's mother, Jenny, now in her third marriage, listens to her own mother's voice and recalls how she herself as a child had urged Pearl to read repeatedly the same story to her every evening.[1] Tyler has attributed to a stage in her own early childhood this replicating of experience. In 1986 she acknowledged not only the effectiveness of Burton's rhythmic writing style but also the illumination of what she identified as "the real point" of the book for her as a child, which was to recognize the nature of time as a continuum, a succession of stages rather than a series of "sudden jolts."[2] In his recent study of Tyler's fiction, Joseph C. Voelker suggests that *The Little House* illustrates both the passing and the circularity of time in *Dinner at the Homesick Restaurant,* and he notes time's thematic importance to the novel as a whole.[3]

But if Tyler's consciousness of time and its manifold effects in her fiction can be attributed to *The Little House,* as the author herself believes, this responsiveness to time is not the only major advantage she gained from her early, intimate acquaintance with that book. Earlier still, and no less consequential, must have been the revelatory, liberating value of light in Burton's illustrated story. Indeed, her imaginative use of light in relation to color— she illustrated the book herself—provides a significant dimension for her

This essay was written specifically for this volume and is published here for the first time by permission of the author.

text that is crucial to a child's apprehension of the whole. Surely, the child sees as the mother reads and the pages turn. This observation is especially pertinent for Tyler, who would like to have been an artist and who, as late as 1980, "still entertain[ed] the fantasy that she might become a book illustrator."[4] The double-page illustrations beautifully complement the text with their emphasis on light, color, and circularity. The simple story tells of a small house in the country that is sold by its original owners and victimized, as it were, by an expanding, encroaching city. As years pass, the natural landscape of the house drastically changes; in place of sunny meadows, clusters of trees, and a nearby pond with a brook flowing from it are smoky factories, skyscrapers, elevated trains, and busy thoroughfares with overhead bridges. The horizontal gives way to the vertical; light and color succumb to sooty grays and muddy browns; the open curves of furrowed hills and a winding country road constrict to mechanized blight amid the prevailing shadows of urban domination. When the house seems doomed, children of the original owners purchase and move it to a new, but pondless, country site,[5] a sentimental if unrealistic restoration from their childhood past.

Important here is not the implausibility of Burton's little narrative but the way the light and openness of the illustrations complement her text and reinforce both a moral theme and the idea of generational continuity through a pattern of controlled circularity. I suggest that Tyler employs a similar but necessarily more sophisticated figurative approach in much of her own fiction through her graphic use of words alone. To be sure, where Burton emphasizes story, Tyler develops character, but for both authors a moral significance is implied through the dynamic positive employment of light and the negativity connoted by its absence. Where light exists in *The Little House* so also do cleanliness, happiness, color, and the suggestion of free, natural movement; in contrast, the absence of light suggests dirt, sadness, shadow, and restrictive mechanization. In Tyler's novels a moral imperative is rare if not altogether absent, but the connotative value of her light imagery is highly consistent with the implicit reference to good and bad, right and wrong, wise and unwise. Her application of light imagery in this manner corresponds to Emerson's basic observation on the underlying significance of pictorial language. In *Nature* and "The Poet" he elaborates on the symbolic value of language and all natural phenomena; for Tyler, as for him, light brings life, and life fully led predicates several of his major insights dealing with character, experience, wholeness (or unity), generational continuity, and significant art. These ideas, the relations among them, and the adverse effects generated when they are absent or insufficient are thematically central in Tyler's richest fiction, notably *The Clock Winder* (1972), *Celestial Navigation* (1974), and *Dinner at the Homesick Restaurant,* her most complex and probably best novel to date.

The Clock Winder is governed by light, and its manifold Emersonian implications are presented directly or represented indirectly by abundant patterns of circles and curves. The reader's first view of the Emerson home, with its wraparound veranda and shuttered windows, suggests the isolation and limited vitality of its owner. When Elizabeth Abbott arrives, she brings new life to the Emerson family, though she is an ambiguous figure because of her basic immaturity, lack of self-confidence, and fear of assuming the responsibility that normally comes with adulthood. Awakening in the room of the Emersons' daughter, Margaret, after assuming the role of Mrs. Emerson's "handyman," Elizabeth is "amazed . . . that she had finally become a grownup,"[6] but despite her 18 years and seeming independence she is emotionally passive, uncommitted; she goes wherever she is invited with whomever asks her first, does whatever her job requires (apart from killing a turkey, which, as a life-bringer, she cannot do), allows circumstances to determine her behavior. So unfocused a life inevitably leads to problems between Elizabeth and the Emersons, who find her unpredictable and contrary, as when she invites one of the Emersons' sons, Matthew, home to meet her family when she is apparently keeping steady company with the other son, Timothy. To the Emersons, her behavior seems irresponsible.

Paradoxically, however, she has the innate capacity to transcend the complexities of system, which she abhors,[7] and achieve the effects to which they lead. She does not understand machines, but she is a capable driver; she whittles "barely recognizable figures" (33), suggestive of her own inner formlessness, but she uses an electric drill; although she is "a born fumbler," she possesses "miraculous repairing powers" (79). "Genius organizes or it is lost," Emerson wrote.[8] "Why don't you get *organized?*," Timothy asks Elizabeth, and she replies, "What for?" (69). Her response strengthens the impression conveyed of her apparently whimsical nature, but below the level of consciousness Elizabeth's unstudied sense of order enables her to accomplish what the more self-conscious members of the Emerson family cannot. She can synchronize the Emerson clocks, for example; she can stun the more calculating Timothy in a chess game with a surprising—and presumably successful—move; and she can nurse the stroke-suffering Mrs. Emerson back to reasonably good health.

Elizabeth's intrinsic capacity to discipline herself and thereby assume the responsibilities of adulthood is suggested at first with images of light. When Timothy comes to pick her up, for instance, the house lights throw a regular pattern of "long yellow squares across the white lawn" (52); later, as she tends the senile Mr. Cunningham, Elizabeth rolls up the shade, and "Sunlight pour[s] into the room," whitening everything (165, 189). Other light imagery subtly accentuates her gradually developing character. She speaks with Timothy, "with the firelight turning her face pink and soft" (57). Driving her employer, Elizabeth changes lanes in long arcs, while "Buttery sunlight warm[s] her lap" (79). Much later, as she helps Mrs. Emerson overcome the severe effects of a stroke, the older woman smiles at her "with the pale yellow sunlight softening for face" (269). By then, the ailing and confused Mrs. Emerson has inadvertently renamed her Gillespie, a cognomen that Elizabeth retains and that therefore implies a drastic change in character. But Elizabeth has matured, not radically transformed, and the stages of her maturation are indirectly revealed through complementary associations with light, especially sunlight, which reinforces her life-giving capacity. Near the end of the novel her development is complete when Tyler describes her nursing her baby "like a broad golden madonna" (309). "A man is a golden impossibility," Emerson wrote, and "The line he must walk is a hair's breadth."[9] Elizabeth gains maturity but not at the cost of her youthful sense of pleasure in the moment—also an Emersonian quality. Soon after being characterized maternally, she places her foot across the path of a locust crawling across the kitchen floor, "and when she grinned at George she looked like another child" (311). Elizabeth has learned to walk the line.

"[T]he soul . . . is not an organ . . . [or] a faculty, but a light," Emerson says; "we are nothing, but the light is all." When the soul "breathes through [the] intellect, it is genius; when it breathes through [the] will, it is virtue; when it flows through [the] affection, it is love."[10] His tripartite delineation of this soul-light provides an excellent gloss on Elizabeth's emotional and psychological growth. It accounts for the apparent contrasts in her abilities and behavior, disclosing how she can synchronize the Emersons' clocks with recourse not to calculation ("Nature hates calculators," Emerson says)[11] but to genius; how she is drawn back by virtue to nurse Mrs. Emerson after refusing absolutely to return; and how she can adapt perfectly through love to a maternal role despite her initial efforts to remain detached from children. Emerson often conceptualized in patterns of threes, sometimes hierarchically, sometimes not. With respect to his distinguishing these three functions of the soul, he appears to have been thinking equilaterally rather then progressively as of three facets of the same spiritual source, the same inner light. In *The Clock Winder,* however, Tyler does suggest stages of Elizabeth's development through the light imagery that accompanies her actions and infuses them with moral significance.

What a contrast exists between the light images associated with Elizabeth and those related, for example, to Timothy Emerson. Timothy is a static figure who leaves home and returns without new advantage. His life is limited and fixed; escape through wine is a device, a "trick," as Emerson calls it in "The Poet,"[12] a temporary and illusory evasion. For Emerson, to remain static is to die: "*Becoming somewhat else* is the whole game of nature, & death the penalty of standing still. 'Tis not less in thought. . . . Liberty means the power to flow. To continue is to flow. Life is unceasing parturition."[13] Whereas Elizabeth brings life, Timothy takes it, first the holiday turkey's, then his own. Tyler complements the restrictive sphere of his self-consciousness by describing the lamps in the pullman kitchen of his small apartment as throwing "soft, closed circles on the table-tops" (94). In reference to Timothy, the circle is not a dynamic continuity, an endless flow, as for Emerson and Elizabeth, but an enclosure of artificial and limited light, not only an image but a symbol of his futile attempts to grow, as is evident through Tyler's tautological application of "closed" to describe the circle. In Emersonian terms, Timothy suffers "the penalty of standing still"; Elizabeth maternally represents life through "unceasing parturition" beyond her in future generations. Literally and figuratively by the end of the novel, "Pieces of Emersons were lodged within Elizabeth like shrapnel" (150), and emanations from Emerson himself seem to have affected Tyler as her fourth novel developed.

Oddly enough, the author considered the ending of *The Clock Winder* to be a sad one because Elizabeth is apparently trapped for life among the Emersons. Voelker sensibly observes, however, that if she is trapped at the end, her plight is a happier one than her noncommittal, detached existence as a borderline vagabond when the novel opens. [14] Radiant as the sun in the form of a "broad golden madonna," Elizabeth virtually reflects the "buttery," life-giving sunshine that frequently attends her. Emerson would have assessed her situation favorably; he would have seen Elizabeth as confronting her destiny and accepting it, not as the iron bars of Fate, but as "the Beautiful Necessity," [15] for she has recognized her limits, learned to work within them, and begun a fruitful life accordingly.

In contrast to Elizabeth's golden future at the end of *The Clock Winder* is the bleak state of Jeremy Pauling at the close of *Celestial Navigation,* published two year later. Voelker proposes that Jeremy is the author's persona in that his art "directly reflects" Tyler's own. [16] This view may be Tyler's as well, for only a few years after writing it, she held *Celestial Navigation* as her favorite novel to date (1977), possibly, Marguerite Michaels believes, because Jeremy "is the closest Anne Tyler had come to writing about herself." [17] However she may have felt about Jeremy then or may consider him now, on reflection, nearly two decades later, the resemblance between the author and her character is superficial at best. Whereas he fears life, she, as Emerson advises, represents it. Jeremy transforms the clippings and trivia of his surroundings into surrealistic sculptures revealing his inner world; Tyler, in contrast, employs an image-laden popular vernacular to dramatize and otherwise intensify the eccentricities and antagonisms she recognizes from her background and her Baltimore environs. Like Jeremy, she works with details, but she far surpasses him as an artist by perceiving "the whole of things," a capability Jeremy lacks from the outset and never acquires. [18] The poet "stands among partial men for the complete man," Emerson writes in "The Poet," "and apprises us not of his wealth, but of the commonwealth." [19] Detached even from the members of his own household, the achievement of such a composite vision is impossible for Jeremy. He has a home full of children he has fathered, but he has never wed the woman who bore them, Mary Tell, not because of some rebellious philosophical stance or conscious desire for noncommitment, but simply because he cannot act responsibly. He forgets, he overlooks, he allows the opportunity to pass, with the result that she, with her brood of loving offspring, leaves him alone with his sculpture and an equally alienated resident of his boarding house, Miss Vinton.

Jeremy is highly conscious of sensation and his own thoughts, but "Nothing outside touches him" (215). Unfazed by experience, lacking "what they call 'personality' " (215), and void of the inner hardness that enables people to cope with the contingencies of life and progress—not merely pass—through it, he is a nebulous figure altogether without character. Thus detached from externality and preoccupied with his inner world, Jeremy is helplessly withdrawn, and his apprehension of Mary is more imaginative than real. For him, Mary is a romanticized figure, not the flesh-and-blood woman with whom he lives: "In his mind she glided; in real life she stepped squarely on her heels" (99). Mary's apparent effect on his art is an increased density of texture, but there is no corresponding enrichment of his character. Essentially, then, he is unaffected by her as well as by other people and current affairs, global or provincial.

Uncomprehending and fearful of the outside world, Jeremy sees life not as a sequence of connected events but in correspondence to his marginality, as a series of unrelated flashes separated by long periods of darkness (43). In this respect, what Emerson suggests of us all in his *Journal* is particularly germane when applied to Jeremy: "we want . . . consecutiveness. 'Tis with us a flash of light, & then a long darkness, & then a flash again. This separation of our days by a sleep almost destroys identity."[20] Jeremy has not matured to the extent of acquiring an identity; as Voelker suggests, his invisibility is central in the novel.[21] His flashes of inspiration lead to the externalization of his inner world in the form of popularly received sculptures, but they do not help him develop as a whole person; he is subject to experience not as an enrichment but only as an unconnected series of frantic conceptualizations. "Dream delivers us to dream," Emerson writes, "and there is no end to illusion."[22] In fact, Jeremy longs for identity, but however intense his desire for "just one heroic undertaking" to which he can commit himself (252), he is too firmly bound by his intensively protective agoraphobia, and his longing is futile.[23] His final position is identical to that of his art dealer Brian's boat in the penultimate chapter: securely moored and turning in wide circles, fixed and closed.

Mary Tell, on the other hand, learns from her experience. After putatively marrying Jeremy and perceiving that he will not change from his peculiar habits, "she grew quieter, older, stronger" (145). In her life, experience *tells*. Mary deals with the daily contingencies; her life is given to Jeremy, their children, her diurnal routine; in her existence, there is no preoccupation with self. When her husband, Guy, grows detached from her, she begins to establish her independence; when the wife of her lover, John, returns to live in his house, Mary realizes how deceptive he has been and leaves him. If Jeremy represents Anne Tyler as artist, Mary represents her as wife, mother, and responsible adult. "Our life looks trivial and we shun to record it,"[24]

Emerson notes, but like Tyler, Mary tells by doing. Observes Emerson, "Life is not intellectual or critical, but sturdy. Its chief good is for well-mixed people who can enjoy what they find, without question."[25] Whereas Jeremy longs for heroic commitment, Mary knows that "There are no heroes in real life" and believes, in an overstatement that surely goes far beyond Tyler's own view, that "All events, except childbirth, can be reduced to a heap of trivia in the end" (223).

Nonetheless, while Jeremy's past has taught him nothing, Mary's past tells all in the progressive enrichment of her character, the widening circles of her growth. Notes Emerson, "The life of man is a self-evolving circle, which, from a ring imperceptibly small, rushes on all sides outwards to new and larger circles, and that without end."[26] Emerson's conceptualization is directly applicable to Mary, whose unified character is nourished organically by her past, her surroundings, and her sustained inner light, whereas the frustrated Jeremy exists within the confines of circular fixity. What Tyler allegedly learned from *The Little House* about the sequential nature of time she represents through Mary, while Jeremy still regards time disjunctively, like a child, as a sporadic series of flashes in a long darkness. More than a "perpetually pregnant, long-suffering," dominated housekeeper, Mary continues in the role of the "strong, independent" woman that Alice Hall Petry recognizes in Tyler's first novel, *If Morning Ever Comes* (1964).[27]

If Ezra Tull manifests aspects of Jeremy in *Dinner at the Homesick Restaurant,* his sister Jenny embodies a more complex and definitive version of character development along the lines of Mary Tell. Jenny, in fact, almost perfectly represents Emerson's vision of character achieved through organic wholeness and ever-widening spheres of understanding. Among other things, *Dinner at the Homesick Restaurant* exposes the layering of experience from one generation to the next. Although Jenny is but one of three siblings who, with their mother, are central in the novel, she more than the others grasps how readily she has allowed herself to be guided, manipulated, and even driven by the past and how necessary it has thus become to determine her own course. Like her mother, she initially blames herself for her two failed marriages; as her daughter Becky ages, Jenny becomes irritated with her over minor if not illusory infractions and slaps the little girl "hard over the mouth," thus reenacting the way she recalls having often as a child been beaten by Pearl (209).[28] After repeating this violence toward Becky, Jenny realizes how traumatically she had been affected by Pearl's outbreaks and determines to rid herself of this dire influence. By that time, she had already begun "learning how to make it through life on a slant. She was trying to lose her intensity" (212). " 'You've changed,' her mother said (all intensity herself). 'You've grown so different, Jenny. I can't quite put my finger on what's wrong, but *something* is' " (212).

For high-strung Pearl, the loss of intensity is wrong, but not so for Jenny. Her gradual success is later made apparent when she shows her husband Slevin, Joe's oldest child, several of Ezra's old family photographs; after she identifies herself at 13 in one of them, Slevin shrilly refuses to believe it is she: "It isn't! Look at it! Why, it's like a . . . concentration camp person, a victim. Anne Frank! It's terrible! It's so sad! . . . It's somebody else. . . . Not you; you're always laughing and having fun. It's not you" (203). An outstanding student in high school, Jenny had already commenced to change during her first year away at college, when "her looks lost a little of their primness" (82).

Nevertheless, she remains a maze of contradictions until long after completing medical school. She marries Harley, more intense, systematic, and dictatorial even than Pearl—who considers him a perfect match for Jenny (101)—but almost immediately after leaving him to visit her mother, she finds herself drawn toward Ezra's eccentric friend, Josiah: "It seemed he had never once left her mind. Even Harley, she saw, was just a reverse kind of Josiah, a Josiah turned inside out: equally alien, black-and-white, incomprehensible to anyone but Jenny" (105). Gradually she breaks free of Pearl's maternal domination, free of circumstantial control, toward an ever-increasing self-reliance. The extent of her new self-confidence is evident in her interview with Slevin's teacher, who attributes the boy's scholastic apathy to problems in his home life: "I don't see the need to blame adjustment, broken homes, bad parents, that sort of thing," Jenny explains to the teacher, insisting, "We make our own luck, right? You have to overcome your setbacks" (196). Jenny understands that "[t]he whole world is a series of balanced antagonisms," as Emerson depicts it,[29] but because she, like Elizabeth Abbott and Mary Tell, maintains the balance after experience discloses the folly of acting in accord with romantic dreams (such as marrying Harley, "the mighty leap into space with someone she hardly knew"; 89), her life is fulfilled. Even so, a residue from her romanticizing continues to glimmer in the back of her mind; when seated beside Joe at the dining table she suddenly has "an unsettling thought: it occurred to her that this would have to be her permanent situation." Having married Joe, assumed responsibility for his six children, and gained their trust, "she could not in good conscience let them down. Here she was, forever. 'It's lucky we get along,' she said to Joe. 'It's extremely lucky,' he said, and he patted her hand and asked for the mustard" (194).

The crucial difference between Jenny's being moored "forever" and Jeremy's at the close of *Celestial Navigation* is that Jenny's boat, as it were, floats in steadily expanding circles as she confronts external realities without becoming detached from the stabilizing permanent center, whereas Jeremy's rotation is fixed, limiting both his vision and his function. "I affirm the divinity of man," Emerson entered in his *Journal* in 1850, but "I know well how much is my debt to bread, & coffee, & flannel, & heated room. . . . I cannot reconcile that absolute with this conditional."[30] Intellectually, perhaps, he could not, but pragmatically he could, which he proved by the example of his own career as family man, citizen, and Transcendentalist. In Jenny's life and probably Anne Tyler's as well, the division is not so extreme, to be sure, but the difference is one of degree, not quality.

No one else in *Dinner at the Homesick Restaurant* can compare with Jenny in terms of balanced character development. Though her brothers attempt to slough off Pearl's channeling maternal influence in their own ways—Cody by becoming an efficiency expert in a linear mode with a fixation on time; Ezra, by serving meals with love in a cyclical mode at the Homesick Restaurant—their motives have been directly or indirectly determined by their childhood experience with their mother, who has reared them alone following the desertion of her husband, Beck. Her experience as the only support of her family and her defensive pride in not revealing the desertion generate inside her an inverted, twisted sense of self-reliance that brings tension and violence to her home.

As Pearl tells Cody, she perceives within her an alternate, more objective self than the compulsive, emotionally charged, deserted mother of three. "I know when I'm being unreasonable," she says. "Sometimes I stand outside my body and just watch it all, totally separate" (140). But she acknowledges as well that she is helplessly driven by her compulsion to do or say the wrong thing. Cody, guilt-laden over blaming himself for Beck's desertion and envious of Ezra's passive attraction to women, is similarly divided. He has the capacity to withdraw into himself and appear perfectly level, balanced, and blank, "like a plaster clothing model. Meanwhile, his ragged, dirty, unloved younger self . . . clenched his fists and howled" (131). Ezra's duality becomes apparent when he is discharged from the army for sleepwalking, "eyes wide open but flat as windows" (81), suggesting both his limited breadth of vision and his inadequacy to deal with external reality from a holistic perspective. Inevitably his attempts to achieve a unified family dinner at the Homesick Restaurant are destined to fail as long as the Tull mother and siblings are divided by internal and internecine conflicts. Not Pearl, or Beck, or either of their two sons can balance the self-conflicts with Jenny's effectiveness.

Pearl's attempt to keep the family together is a projection of her desire to integrate the conflicting sides of her own consciousness. The children give her life meaning; effectively, they are the light of her narrow existence, a light that dimmed as they matured and left home, "as if they took some radiance with them as they moved away" (21). Pearl envisioned her childbearing in terms of light, she tells Cody. When the children were small, she says, "it seemed I was full of light; it was light and plans that filled me. . . . I was the center of your worlds! I was everything to you! . . . [N]ow I'm old and I walk along unnoticed" (21, 141–42). Ironically, Pearl at times seems prepared to closet herself away from light, as when she observes Ezra taping cardboard squares to the broken windowpanes in Cody's farmhouse and realizes that soon "they'll be working in the dark. It's as if they're sealing themselves in, windowpane by windowpane"(170). Pearl does not want the dark, but she can no more avoid closing herself off from the light than she can resist speaking when she knows she should remain silent. Her objective self inevitably succumbs to her compulsion toward isolation and darkness. "[T]he soul . . . is . . . a light," Emerson wrote; "we are nothing, but the light is all."[31] Whereas Emerson speaks here of a spiritual light, Pearl is thinking of herself as a life-giving solar center around which her children orbit by her essential attraction; whereas Emerson's light emanates permanently, Pearl's is self-generated, centripetal, and necessarily temporary. The one anticipates wholeness, as it does with reference to Elizabeth in *The Clock Winder;* the other, fragmentation and entropy.

Emerson's concept of wholeness is, of course, based on integration, not the narrow channeling and fixation that characterize the lives of Pearl, Beck, and Cody. Pearl has never had friends of her own and knows of the outside world only what her children tell her. Cody cannot verge from his obsession with time (and his son Luke appears to be headed in the same direction). He seems to have inherited this limiting feature from Beck, who says that he left Pearl and the family because, among other reasons, he became upset with the "grayness of things; half-right-and-half-wrongness of things. Everything tangled, mingled, not perfect any more. I couldn't take that. Your mother could," he tells Cody, "but not me" (301). This inability to balance, to straddle between the "perfect" and the mundane, makes it impossible for Beck to attain the unity his daughter achieves.

In a sense, however, the three other central members of the Tull family—Pearl, Cody, and Ezra—find wholeness in their lives, though it is only momentary. Pearl's moment occurred one day while she was weeding by the stable. As she lies on her deathbed, Ezra reads the record of that moment from the description in her diary written years before: "*a bottle fly was buzzing in the grass, and I saw that I was kneeling on such a beautiful green little planet. I don't care what else might come about, I have had this moment. It belongs to me*" (277). The oral reading, of course, strongly affects Ezra; he "felt he was being tugged back through layers of generations" (264). After finishing, he walks Pearl to lunch and suddenly undergoes an epiphany in which all the emotionally charged entries of her diary are in his mind simultaneously with Pearl and himself, the two of them "traversing the curve of the earth, small and steadfast, surrounded by companions"—family, friends, and many others—and all are connected "as mysteriously as Ezra himself was connected to this woman beside him" (278). Cody's moment comes at the end of the novel when he prepares to return with Beck to Ezra's restaurant for dinner with the remaining Tull clan after Pearl's death: "Overhead, seagulls drifted through a sky so clear and blue that it brought back all the outings of his boyhood" (303), including the instant suspended in time just before his mother was accidentally struck by an arrow from his bow.

Although the moment for each of them is transitory, according to Emerson its perfection endures. "Our faith comes in moments. . . . Yet there is a depth in those brief moments which constrains us to ascribe more reality to them than to all other experiences," he wrote in "The Over-Soul."[32] In his *Journal* nearly 20 years later, he again wrote of experiencing the joy that thrills and elevates, the same kind of mystical perception that comes to Pearl, Ezra, and Cody: "For a moment, the eyes of my eyes were opened, the affirmative experience remains, & consoles through all suffering."[33] The intensity of their momentary experiences brings permanent enlightenment through a transcendent apprehension of unity. If it does not bring to their lives the organic balance that Jenny enjoys through a harmony of self-confidence, responsibility, and love, at least it gives them the advantage of a new holistic perspective from which to consider their own diversified lives and affairs: "We live in succession, in division, in parts, in particles," Emerson observed; "[m]eantime within man is the soul of the whole; . . . the universal beauty, to which every part and particle is equally related; the eternal ONE."[34] In contrast to the light of self-projection that Pearl envisioned among her children, the light of Emerson's moment of illumination patently corresponds to the unifying glimpses of truth beheld at different times by Pearl herself and her two sons.

This truth may be experienced and characterized through imagery, but it cannot be accurately expressed in finite terms. When Beck tells Pearl that he is leaving her and does not plan to visit the children, she thinks: "There ought to be a whole separate language . . . for words that are truer than other words—for perfect, absolute truth" (10). But words, as "finite organs of the infinite mind," Emerson says, "cannot cover the dimensions of what is in truth. They break, chop, and impoverish it."[35] For Emerson, thought unifies; all thought flows from the inner source and therefore relates directly to it. Words, on the other hand, originate with human beings and nature; hence they may be suggestive, symbolic, indicative of things in the world of time and place, a means of linking individuals into families and communities, but they are essentially fragmentary. Thinking about her imminent death, Pearl realizes that she has no final answers to eternal questions that she can express to her children, the result of some dramatic "turning point" in her life, "a flash of light in which she'd suddenly find out the secret" (30). Perhaps her perfect moment, weeding by the stable wall, could have conveyed that secret had she been more receptive to it as an absorptive instant of moral awareness as well as a state of earthly perfection for the self in a circumstantial world.

Like Emerson, Anne Tyler writes of what he called in "Experience" "the lords of life": "Illusion, Temperament, Succession, Surface, Surprise, Reality, Subjectiveness,—these are threads on the loom of time, these are the lords of life."[36] But, Emerson continues, beneath these facets of the phenomenal world exists the deeper cause that becomes visible "in flashes of light" that reveal "a new and excellent region of life . . . as if the clouds that covered it parted at intervals."[37] Emerson's "threads on the loom of time" also color and shape the lives of Tyler's inhabitants of Baltimore, though it is not likely she had his conception specifically in mind as she developed her novels and the characters who come to life among them. Nor do I propose that she had Emerson consciously in view when she created her family of Emersons involved in *The Clock Winder,* though the possibility is not remote. After all, Tyler was reared in an "experimental Quaker community" under, as Anne R. Zahlan phrases it, the "Emersonian ideal" to which her parents subscribed.[38] Under these circumstances she was likely to have been affected by Emerson's use of language as well as his transcendental ideas precisely as she was influenced by the illustrations as well as the story in Burton's *The Little House.* Hence the significance of light, the patterns of circles and curves, the relation of character to the kind of holistic unity Emerson advocated—all these may well be attributable in part to strong incidental influences from Tyler's family background as a child.

Be that as it may, the correspondences are there. The philosophical and psychological elements of Tyler's novels have often been addressed. The clear associations with Emerson's thought imply that the moral content is worthy of more attention as well. Neither allegorist nor preceptor, Tyler promotes no special moral imperative, but she exposes a variety of alternatives, and her Emersonian correspondences complement what appear to be her own preferred positions. "There are no fixtures in nature," Emerson says,[39] and no contemporary American author illustrates his point with more grace than Anne Tyler. With one eye on realism and the other on celestial navigation, she has melded the aesthetic and moral virtues of a childhood favorite, *The Little House,* with the creative genius of Emerson into the Baltimorean world of her own imagination.

Notes

1. Anne Tyler, *Dinner at the Homesick Restaurant* (New York: Knopf, 1982), 210–11; hereafter cited in the text.

2. Anne Tyler, "Why I Still Treasure 'The Little House,' " *New York Times Book Review,* 9 November 1986, 56.

3. Joseph C. Voelker, *Art and the Accidental in Anne Tyler* (Columbia: University of Missouri Press, 1989), 136.

4. Mary Ellen Brooks, "Anne Tyler," *Dictionary of Literary Biography,* ed. James E. Kibler, Jr. (Detroit: Gale Research/Bruccoli Clark, 1980), 6:337.

5. Tyler emphasizes the absence of a pond in the new location, questioning whether or not it is intentional ("Why I Still Treasure 'The Little House,' " 56).

6. Anne Tyler, *The Clock Winder* (New York: Knopf, 1972), 38; hereafter cited in the text.

7. For example, Elizabeth hates the complex design of Mrs. Emerson's numerous Oriental rugs (29).

8. *Journal,* 24(?) April 1841; from Ralph Waldo Emerson, *Selected Writings,* ed. William

H. Gilman (New York: Signet, 1965), 101; hereafter this collection will be cited as Emerson, followed by the date of his journal entry or the title of his essay and the relevant page number.

9. Emerson, "Experience," 338.

10. Emerson, "The Over-Soul," 282.

11. Emerson, "Experience," 339.

12. Emerson, "The Poet," 319.

13. Emerson, *Journal*, 1855, 164.

14. Tyler's mixed assessment of Elizabeth betrays her own ambivalence toward the character. She says, "I think Elizabeth does herself irreparable damage in not going farther than she does, but on the other hand *what she does is the best and the happiest thing for her.* I think of it as a sad ending, and I've been surprised that not everybody does"; quoted (with my emphasis) from Clifford A. Ridley, "Anne Tyler: A Sense of Reticence Balanced by 'Oh, Well, Why Not?,' " *National Observer*, 22 July 1972, 23. See also Volker, 65.

15. Emerson, "Fate," 402.

16. Voelker, 70.

17. Marguerite Michaels, "Anne Tyler, Writer 8:05 to 3:30," interview with Anne Tyler, *New York Times Book Review*, 8 May 1977, 42.

18. Anne Tyler, *Celestial Navigation* (New York: Knopf, 1974), 45; hereafter cited in the text.

19. Emerson, "The Poet," 308.

20. Emerson, *Journal*, March (?) 1864, 175.

21. Voelker, 86.

22. Emerson, "Experience," 330.

23. Voelker treats this topic at length in his discussions of *The Clock Winder* and *Celestial Navigation*.

24. Emerson, "Experience," 328.

25. Emerson, "Experience," 334.

26. Emerson, "Circles," 297.

27. Alice Hall Petry, "Anne Tyler and the Fate of Feminism," paper presented at the American Literature Association conference, San Diego, 31 May 1990, 9–10. I am grateful to Professor Petry for making a copy of her paper available to me and for her many helpful editorial suggestions that led to the improvement of this essay. Here I might also add that I find Mary Ellen Brooks's view of Mary a little difficult to understand, because she describes Mary as completely "independent and self-sufficient" yet waiting at the end for "another man [who] will eventually provide for her and her children when her resources run out" (Brooks, 341–42). This characterization appears to me self-contradictory. Moreover, I believe that by being self-reliant on the one hand and willing to commit herself to husband and family on the other, Mary is representative of the Emersonian position on strength of character that I have defined throughout my essay.

28. A dialogue between Ezra and Cody near the end of the novel casts some doubt on the frequency of Pearl's beatings. Cody recalls that she was "A raving, shrieking, unpredictable witch" because as children they "never knew from one day to the next, was she all right? Was she not? The tiniest thing could set her off." But Ezra replies, "It wasn't like that. . . . [S]he wasn't *always* angry. Really was angry very seldom, only a few times, widely spaced, that happened to stick in your mind." Hearing this, "Cody felt drained" and could not eat his dinner (294–95).

If this passage generates ambiguity with respect to Pearl's rage and beatings, it does no more than that. Ezra may have forgotten what Cody and Jenny remembered, or Pearl may have treated each of her children differently. Pearl blames herself and fate "that her family has failed"; she acknowledges having made many mistakes, but what could she have done, she asks herself, "when one son is consistently good and the other consistently bad?" (184–85). This perception and assessment, accurate or not, may well have led to Cody's being beaten more often and more violently than Ezra. Moreover, Jenny—as an intern progressing toward a career in child psychiatry—believes she has been "damaged, . . . injured" by Pearl's violent outbreaks (210). It is impossible to determine which of the childhood memories is more accurate, but in effect, it does not matter, for the minds and behavioral patterns of all three siblings have been largely determined by their perceptions of Pearl as they were maturing and afterward.

29. Emerson, *Journal,* March 1851, 151.

30. Emerson, *Journal,* January 1850, 146.

31. Emerson, "The Over-Soul," 282.

32. Emerson, "The Over-Soul," 280.

33. Emerson, *Journal,* August 1859, 170.

34. Emerson, "The Over-Soul," 281.

35. Emerson, *Nature,* 207.

36. Emerson, "Experience," 346.

37. Emerson, "Experience," 340.

38. Anne Tyler, "Still Just Writing," in *The Writer on Her Work: Contemporary Women Writers Reflect on Their Art and Situation,* ed. Janet Sternburg (New York: Norton, 1980), 11; Anne R. Zahlan, "Anne Tyler," in *Fifty Southern Writers after 1900: A Bio-Bibliographical Sourcebook,* ed. Joseph M. Flora and Robert Bain (Westport, Conn.: Greenwood, 1987), 491; and Voelker, 1–3.

39. Emerson, "Circles," 296.

Killing off the Mother: Failed Matricide in *Celestial Navigation*

GRACE FARRELL

> For man and for woman the loss of the mother is a biological and psychic
> necessity, the first step on the way to becoming autonomous. Matricide is our
> vital necessity.
>
> —Julia Kristeva, *Black Sun: Depression and Melancholia*

Jacques Lacan discusses the formation of the function of the "I" as occurring
only when the child discovers his or her separation from the mother and
experiences the gap between self and Other.[1] Without the loss of absolute
unity with the mother, we could not conceive of ourselves, could not give
birth to ourselves, as separate entities. But loss creates a gap, "a hole in the
real," Lacan calls it,[2] which one nostalgically longs to fill with the lost
object. Nostalgia for the lost primal unity is countered in the healthily
developing individual by an impulse toward separation: one is attracted to
the security of the womb but is repulsed by the death of self implicit in it. If
one resists the pain of separation, the birth pangs of the individual coming to
be, then one participates in the death of one's own self. Thus, observes
Kristeva, "matricide is our vital necessity, the sine-qua-non condition of our
individuation,"[3] but everywhere, as Freud pointed out, recurs the *"impossible
mourning for the maternal object."*[4]

Anne Tyler's *Celestial Navigation* is about that "impossible mourning,"
about the necessity of navigating the seas of life alone—autonomous,
motherless—and the inability of most of us to accomplish this task. To
navigate celestially, that is, without mechanical aids, one must find a fixed
point in the heavens and orient oneself in relation to it. In *Celestial Navigation,* loss is that necessary fixed point which must be clearly sighted if one is
to make an authentic journey through life. The novel is a collage of voices,
each in various stages of blocked bereavement, unable to accept loss and
unable to embrace autonomy. The form the novel takes mirrors the art of its

This essay was written specifically for this volume and is published here for the first time by permission of
the author.

central character, Jeremy Pauling, an agoraphobic artist who lives in a board-inghouse with Mary Tell and their several children and who gathers up domestic trash to form collages. The voices and perspectives of Jeremy and Mary, whose relationship dramatizes the central issues of loss and autonomy, are framed by a chorus of marginalized voices, the voices of Amanda Pauling, Miss Vinton, and Olivia, women responding to loss by denying their pain, blocking their grief, or acting out in self-destructive ways the heartbreak of their abandonment.

The first of these voices is that of Amanda Pauling, who disappears from the novel after making her one plaintive and complaining appearance. By the time the novel is over, first-time readers have often forgotten that Amanda was even in it, yet her voice is key to an understanding of the novel, for she introduces the essential matter of the text—loss of the mother and the inability to sufficiently mourn that loss.

The novel begins with a death in the family. Jeremy Pauling's mother dies, and his sisters, Amanda and Laura, return to the family home, now a boardinghouse, for the funeral. The first voice we hear is Amanda's, giving us an unsentimentalized and sardonically humorous view of her dead mother: "You hear people say, at funerals, 'How natural she looks! As though she were asleep!' And most of the time they are telling a falsehood, but in Mother's case it was absolutely true. Of *course* she looked natural; why not, when she went through life looking dead?"[5] Tremendous anger continually seeps through Amanda's brittle humor, giving energy to her sharp-tongued wit, a wit and an anger directed repeatedly toward her dead mother. We are told that Mrs. Pauling, in her youth, had painted forget-me-nots on china plates, but how, Amanda asks, could anyone know that "she would stay frozen in china-painting position for the rest of her life" (30)?

Amanda's anger is symptomatic of her profound, unexpressed pain over her mother's death. Death is, for the survivor, the final abandonment, and anger is an appropriate response to such an abandonment. Amanda's rage over her mother's death, however, is never directly expressed but is instead continually displaced onto her response to an earlier abandonment, one that occurred when she felt her mother had emotionally deserted her for the younger children: "[S]he did love him more. And next to him, Laura. The pretty one, who in those days was only slightly plump and had hair that was really and truly golden. Me last of all. Well, I couldn't care less about that *now*, of course. I never even think about it" (31). But it is all she thinks about. It is the central emotional fact of her life.

One way of dealing with such pain is to deny that one feels it. The cost is very high, for tremendous emotional energy is expended in repressing a pain that, like Amanda's, continually resurfaces. Her anger and jealousy are expressed as a child might express them: "Do you think mother would have let Laura or me get away with that? Never for a minute. . . . Does that seem fair?" (19). And like a child she, at age 46, still resents the loss of "her room," rented out to a boarder: "The only time we ever saw our own room was at Christmas and Easter, when Mrs. Jarrett went off to visit her married daughter. . . . Oh, this house had closed over our leavetaking like water; not a trace of us remained" (29). Amanda adds, characteristically, "I had never been bothered by it before" (29).

Her mother, too, had been abandoned. Mr. Pauling went out for a breath of air one day and never came back. He sent a postcard two weeks later:

> "I *said* I needed air, didn't I?" "Yes, he said that as he left, I remember he did," said Mother, dim-witted as ever. She . . . never to my knowledge shed a tear, not even a year and a half after that when he was killed in an auto accident and the insurance company notified her by mail. And look on her nightstand! There he was, big and dashing in an old-fashioned collar and a villain's pencil-line mustache. Handsome, I suppose some might say. (As a small girl I admired my father quite a bit, though not, or course, after he deserted.) (30)

Mrs. Pauling, too, responds to abandonment with the denial of blocked grief. In effect, she denies that her husband ever left, keeping his brushes on the bureau, his shaving mug in the bathroom, his photograph on the nightstand. Her father's desertion adds both a second tier of abandonment to Amanda's history and yet another element to her rage against her mother, a mother who could not even keep an adored father from leaving home. Amanda's characteristic denial of pain is confined within parentheses, highlighting both the depth of that pain and the effort at denial: "(As a small girl I admired my father quite a bit, though not, of course, after he deserted.)"

So desperate is Amanda to control her own feelings that she tries to control everybody else's, too, becoming a stiff-spined disciplinarian, intent on making everybody over in her own image. "Pull yourself together" (15), she tells the benumbed Jeremy, who blinks up at her with "lashless, puffy eyes" (15). Unable to tolerate his agoraphobia, she drags him out into the street, where he crumples up on the sidewalk, "shapeless and boneless," and Amanda is left to cry out, "I don't understand. . . . I don't see" (39), statements she often repeats. Her pain seems too great to risk any revelation, and so she remains blind to those around her and to herself.

Only once does Amanda falter in her determination not to face her feelings. The loss of her suitcase, stolen from the boardinghouse porch while she and Laura are at the funeral home, leads her to list all she has lost in life:

> I know what I am, I'm not blind. I have never had a marriage proposal or a love affair or an adventure, never any experience more interesting than patrolling the aisles of my Latin class looking for crib sheets and ponies—an old-maid schoolteacher. There are a thousand jokes about the likes of me. None of them are funny. . . . I suspected all along that I would never get what comes to others so easily. I have been bypassed, something has been held back from me. And the worst part is that I know it.

Here are the other belongings I had in that suitcase: my brown wool suit that was appropriate for any occasion, my blouse with the Irish lace at the collar, the lingerie set Laura gave me for my birthday. . . . You couldn't replace things like that. You couldn't replace the suitcase itself, which our mother chose entirely on her own and lugged all the way to my graduation ceremony on a very warm spring day a quarter of a century ago. It had brass-buckled straps and a double lock; it was built to last. The handle was padded for ease of carrying. Oh, the thought of that suitcase made me ache all over. I felt as hurt as if Mother had asked for it back again. How would I ever find another one so fine?

I was tired, that was all. Just tired and chilled. The next morning I rose as bright as a penny and I handled all the arrangements, every detail. But that one night I must have been at a low point and I lay on my back in the dark, long after Laura was asleep, going over all the objects I had ever lost while some hard bleak pain settled on my chest and weighed me down. (41–42)

The hard, bleak pain, of course, is the loss of her mother and, with that loss, the termination of all hope of her mother's love. But although Amanda's late-night litany brings her to the edge of self-revelation, she does not permit herself to make the precarious move beyond the edge. She displaces all the hurt over her mother's death onto the lost items in the suitcase and finally onto the suitcase itself, her mother's gift to her. She holds back from her very self, while acknowledging that something has been held back from her. She remains blind, while denying her blindness. Instead she rises "bright as a penny," diminishing the depth of her anguish to the level of cliché—a "low point" to be controlled as efficiently as all the other "arrangements" in life are "handled."

Whereas in the face of death Amanda remains blind, acknowledging her loss but denying the emotions engendered by it, Miss Vinton's eyes are wide open but her grief is absent. A longtime boarder at the Paulings', Miss Vinton, after years of caring for her own mother, and listening to her labored breathing, is awakened by the silence of her death: "*Solitude* shocked my eyes open. I was alone" (139). Miss Vinton freezes her life at that moment of solitude. She remains "fully composed" (139) during her mother's funeral but sequesters herself for the remainder of her life at the Paulings' and convinces herself that privacy is of paramount importance to her: "If you want my opinion," she says diffidently, not wanting to impose even an opinion on those around her, "our whole society would be better off living in boarding houses. I mean even families, even married couples. Everyone should have his single room with a door that locks, and then a larger room downstairs where people can mingle or not as they please" (141).

As if to subvert this opinion, Miss Vinton's section of the book is filled with the expression of her love for the ever-enlarging Pauling family and of the enormous effort she must make to hold back that love lest it encroach on her solitude. She watches Jeremy: "He wore no coat or jacket, nothing but

own nest" (172), and he is left to wonder if she ever wished "that she too had a man who would carry her up castle stairs or defend her with his sword or even, perhaps, frighten her a little with his dark, mysterious gaze" (175).

Mary has read those "sleazy romance novels, beautiful heroines in anguish. I loved them. I close my eyes and see myself on the plastic sofa with a book on my stomach, Gloria beside me snapping her gum, great swells of organ music rising from the television" (72–73). It is not surprising that Mary associates romance novels with the comfort of Gloria's presence, for the pattern of the anguished and helpless heroine awaiting rescue by a hero is an analogue of the pattern of the aggrieved child awaiting reunion with the all-embracing mother. Both are patterns of behavior that refuse to acknowledge the primal loss, to give up dependency, and to accept autonomy.

For all her capable motherliness, Mary Tell is not an autonomous adult. She has always dreamed of rescue. Her pattern is one of leaving but of never going anywhere. She transplants rather than transforms herself, re-creating in new contexts what she has just escaped. She escapes her parents by marrying Guy; Guy, by leaving with John. John is soon replaced by Jeremy, and if Jeremy cannot come to the rescue, then Brian, his art dealer, waits in the wings. As precaution against a real escape, Mary leaves a note for Jeremy specifying her destination, before she "sails away" in Brian's "ridiculous baby-blue car" (195), as if she were one of her own babies, carried away "wrapped in powder blue" (150).

With the ever-hopeful longing of the true damsel in distress, Mary believes that if only Jeremy would say "a single word to keep me with him, I would gladly stay forever. I didn't *want* to go" (194). She sends "messages" to him "through the dark: Come and get us" (202), and not until she has spent months sequestered with her six children in Brian's dilapidated beach shack does it dawn on her that she is not going to be rescued. This insight comes to her only when she realizes that the last of her children is ready to wean herself:

> All my children lost interest in nursing once they could walk. They took off out the door one day to join the others, leaving me babyless, and for a few months I would feel a little lost until I found out I was pregnant again. Only now, it wasn't going to be that way. I hadn't considered that before. I stood staring at Rachel, my very last baby, while she fought off all those grubby little hands that were trying to reseat her. "Look, Rachel," they said, "we just want you to show Mom. Sit a minute, Rachel."
> For the first time, then, I knew that Jeremy was not going to ask us back. (211–12)

Mary has made herself into Mother in order to keep at bay her feelings of loss and of being lost. Now she realizes that this source of comfort, always temporary but until now repeatable, is coming to an end. This realization is linked with, because it is analogous to, her acknowledgment that her hero will not be coming to rescue her. Neither being Mother nor being damsel in distress can keep her safe forever from the loss she has never fully faced.

Jeremy actually does come to the beach house, making a mock-heroic journey all the way across town. He comes out of a prolonged creative haze to remember Mary's voice asking "How's your supply of socks?" (251) and his mother's voice "weaving its way through a tangle of other people's words" (251), and he tries to imagine "just one heroic undertaking the he could aim his life toward" (252). On foot and by bus this agoraphobic Odysseus finally reaches his Penelope, whose loom takes the comic, domestic form of strings of diapers hanging up and down the length of the inside of the house.

The painful last encounter between Jeremy and Mary reveals that the delicate balance of their mutual dependency has been irrevocably upset. At first, when he was so childlike and she in such distress, they could each be to the other what they fantasized being, and they could each give to the other what each needed. She could mother him and touch his need for mothering, and he could be her hero and touch her need for being rescued. But as her mothering grew and with it the recognition not only of his vulnerabilities but also of his inadequacy as any kind of a rescuer, his heroic fantasies were undermined. As Mary acknowledges, "I depended on his dependency" (214). Now, seeking to impress Mary with his manly "efficiency and authority" (268), Jeremy performs mock-heroic domestic chores around the beach shack, unwittingly assaulting her need to be rescued and carried off rather than be prepared for a lonely winter on her own. When his heroic undertakings involve taking five of the children out in a dinghy, the mother in her reasserts itself and in so doing destroys the pretence on which so much of their relationship has come to depend:

> "Wait! they heard. Jeremy turned and saw Mary flying down the slope toward them with the baby bouncing on her hip and her face pale and her eyes dark and wide, almost without whites to them. He thought something terrible must have happened. He had never seen her look so frightened. When she came up beside him she was breathless. "Mary?" he said. "What is it?"
> "Jeremy, I—please don't take the children."
> He felt as if she had hit him in the stomach. While she gasped for breath he did too, clenching his end of the rope. (272)

None of Mary's excuses can placate Jeremy. He sees clearly that she sees him clearly. The game is up.

Alone, Jeremy, slowly and with heroic effort, lets go of that umbilical rope he has been clenching and moves from the dinghy to Brian's ketch in order to unfurl and dry the sails. Wind fills the sails, and the moored boat takes Jeremy on the final loop of his mock-heroic journey—around and around its own mooring "in wider and faster circles" (274). Jeremy remains securely anchored to yet another umbilical mooring, and, with a turn of the page, the novel too circles back: "This house is back to its beginnings now. Lonely boarders thumb through magazines" (275), and now it is Miss Vinton who takes Jeremy out for an occasional walk to the grocery store. Jeremy never frees himself from the mooring or the mothering. Like every character whose voice we hear, Jeremy too is unable to kill off the Mother, to complete the matricide, to become autonomous.

The reader is left with a feeling of great loss. The novel has assumed the shape Jeremy describes as that of his life, which he sees as "eye-shaped—the tight pinched corners of childhood widening in middle age to encompass Mary and the children, narrowing back now to this single lonely room" (250). When that eye is at its widest, the boardinghouse is filled with a family feeling: boarders bustling about in the kitchen, delivery men bringing in one oversize appliance after another, the spilling forth of "shouts and laughter and scoldings" (176). There are clutter and tumult and, inevitably, great risk, for, as Miss Vinton knows, to partake of the joy of this eccentric family is to put oneself at risk. With its dissolution comes the pain of loss. With great power, Anne Tyler engages the reader in this family and, in so doing, positions us as each of the characters in the novel is positioned: facing the inevitability of loss, loss that, in one form or another, ultimately violates all domestic units, leaving abandoned survivors. As Jeremy says to Olivia, "My mother died and so did both my sisters. . . . Also my father. . . . Then her. Everybody left me" (243).

Jeremy's final piece of art, which, like all his work, is about domesticity—his collages piecing together fragments of children's toys, snippets from the hems of Mary's dresses—expresses the sudden violation of death. Olivia describes it:

> Imagine a wooden soft drink crate, only bigger, standing on end. A set of compartments, and in each compartment a different collection of objects. Like an advertisement showing a cross-section of a busy household. . . . Only in Jeremy's piece, there were no people. Only the *feeling* of people—of full lives suddenly interrupted, belongings still bearing the imprint of their vanished owners. Dark squares upstairs full of toys, paper scraps, a plastic doll bed lying on its side as if some burst of exuberance had flung it there and then passed on, leaving such a vacancy it could make you cry. (246)

There is no protection against such loss. Neither Amanda's bitterness nor Miss Vinton's retreat, neither Olivia's cry nor Mary's immersion in the details of domestic life can keep one forever safe from its inevitability. That "vacancy," that "hole in the real," is what each of *Celestial Navigation*'s voices struggles against. Jeremy, the most obviously dependent, is the one who, through his art, expresses that loss most clearly. The others, equally but more obliquely mother-bound, seek to avoid it. Their failure to kill off the mother—to acknowledge, mourn, and let go of the primal loss—is a refusal to acknowledge the fearsome truth of one's vulnerability in the world, separate and alone. It is a failure to live without illusion in the face of death.

Adam Phillips writes that "Freud began to believe that lives were about achieving loss, eventually one's own loss, so to speak, in death; and that art could be in some way integral to this process, a culturally sophisticated form of bereavement. A work of art was a work of mourning—and mourning itself was an art."[7] Anne Tyler's *Celestial Navigation* is itself a work of mourning, a novel that shows us how extraordinarily difficult achieving loss is.

Notes

1. Jacques Lacan, "The Mirror-Phase as formative of the Function of the I," trans. Jean Roussel, *New Left Review* No. 51 (September/October 1968): 71–77.

2. Jacques Lacan, "Desire and the Interpretation of Desire in *Hamlet*," in *Literature and Psychoanalysis: The Question of Reading Otherwise,* ed. Shoshana Felman (Baltimore: Johns Hopkins University Press, 1982), 37ff.

3. Julia Kristeva, *Black Sun: Depression and Melancholia,* trans. Leon S. Roudiez (New York: Columbia University Press, 1989), 27–28.

4. Kristeva, 9. For studies of bereavement, see Sigmund Freud, "Mourning and Melancholia," in *Collected Papers,* vol. 4, ed. Ernest Jones (New York: Basic Books, 1959), and John Bowlby, *Loss* (New York: Basic Books, 1980).

5. Anne Tyler, *Celestial Navigation* (New York: Alfred A. Knopf, 1974), 8; hereafter cited in the text.

6. Lacan, "Desire," 39.

7. Adam Phillips, "What Is There to Lose?" *London Review of Books,* 24 May 1990, 6. My thanks to Robert Sullivan for bringing this essay to my attention.

"Mere Reviews": Anne Tyler as Book Reviewer

Elizabeth Evans

In 1897 when W. B. Yeats was preparing a review of Robert Bridges's plays, Bridges wrote Yeats a letter—a letter from an author to his reviewer that expresses at once anxiety and indifference:

> I am very sorry indeed that you are engaged in such a dull task—and I am afraid that you may not be in a particularly good humour with me when you come [for a visit]—But let me reassure you on one point, i.e. that you need not be afraid of hurting my feelings, and are, as far as I am concerned, at full liberty to say anything that you wish. I lack that distinctive mark of the poet, the touchiness, which resents criticism. Honestly I am indifferent to these things: (and I don't mind if anyone shd say that I am vain of being proud—) . . . Nero Pt. II, which completed my volume of 8 plays, was sent to 44 papers and reviews, and so far as I know it had *no* notice whatever except in the Times.[1]

Bridges perhaps protests too much. If he were immune to the stings of criticism, he was stung—as are most writers—when reviews failed to appear.

Anne Tyler as novelist is subjected to the assessment of reviewers and she herself is—from the large number she has produced—an important reviewer of books. In that role she demonstrates her prodigious reading as well as her capacity to hit the mark when she praises and when she criticizes. Although Tyler primarily reviews fiction, she ranges wide—from Walker Percy's semiotic-based essays, *The Message in the Bottle,* to *Remembering America: A Sampler of the WPA American Guide.* When she reviews, Tyler places the title within the context of the author's work, showing how the book at hand surpasses (or fails to meet) the achievement of earlier work. Tyler, like all serious reviewers, seems to have read everything the author has written. While she can bluntly point out weaknesses, Tyler never trashes a book even if that exercise is merited. (Indeed, Tyler takes issue with Barbara Grizzuti Harrison because she attacks Joan Didion in *Off Center,* Harrison's collection of essays. Tyler's position is that when a writer is in conflict with another

This essay was written specifically for this volume and is published here for the first time by permission of the author.

writer—either because of the issue or because of the position—one should probably decline to review the book at hand.)

As reviewer, Tyler can give unqualified praise. For example, she ends her review of Bobbie Ann Mason's *Shiloh and Other Stories* with great enthusiasm, urging readers to resist being satisfied with a borrowed copy and being content only with buying a copy. Tyler's frequent advice to readers is that they should enjoy what they read, and her own pleasure in reading shimmers throughout these reviews. As a body of work, Anne Tyler's book reviews go beyond the bounds of discussing the text at hand to comment on the short story and the novel as narrative forms. They also indicate Tyler's views on certain social and political matters, particularly feminism. And admirers of Anne Tyler are pleased to find fairly frequent biographical information—details of her own reading and work habits as well as anecdotes from her family life.

As reader and reviewer, Tyler expects fiction writers to assume a reasonable narrative obligation; when they do not, the book falls short. D. M. Thomas's 1983 novel *Ararat* is a case in point. The plot, Tyler says, is the problem. To follow it, you have to diagram it, and she does so in two separate schemes because Thomas often breaks the narrative sweep and bewilders the reader. Tyler explains:

> It's not really necessary, of course, for a reviewer to make the plot entirely clear to prospective readers. But in *Ararat,* the whole point is the plot—its devilish cleverness, or its maddening obscurity, however you choose to view it. In any case, it's not an honest plot. If a contract exists between writer and reader that the writer will do his best to draw the reader in and the reader will do his best to follow, D. M. Thomas has reneged on his part of the deal.[2]

Tyler's sense of narrative obligation should not be construed as opposition to the results of postmodernism. Even though her own novels are not experimental (and some reviewers have chided Tyler for not taking more narrative risks), she is responsive to writers who engage in bold and unconventional directions. In 1972 Donald Bartheleme published *Sadness* (a short story collection), which Tyler reviewed in the *National Observer.* The experimental exercises that Bartheleme displayed impressed Tyler, although she found some stories baffling. Still, it is interesting that the most traditional story in the collection, "The Sandman," was so straightforward that Tyler found it boring. Her sensitivity to the leaps of imagination in style that other writers bring off suggests that although she herself prefers to avoid the experimental, she is by no means insensitive to its power and success. But extreme narrative risks can limit the fiction's effect. Three years later, when Tyler reviewed Barthelme's *The Dead Father,* she suggested that he was now imitating himself—a dead end, of course, if continued, and a direction that probably demands yet another new narrative device.

To Anne Tyler, fiction is not something merely to divert or entertain readers; fiction should engage readers, make them react to and connect with what they read. In reviewing Rachael Billington's *A Woman's Age,* Tyler complains about prose that sounds as if the researcher lifted it whole cloth from the research sheet; even the entertaining lives the characters lead cannot compensate for prose that is too stiff. Generally, such writing leaves the reader untouched. Nevertheless, the means by which readers are affected vary and can occur even in bad writing. Tyler reviewed Cynthia Ozick's *The Messiah of Stockholm* for the *New Republic,* describing the author as "intelligent, skilled, and consummately serious" and the plot as "provocative." The writing style, however, suffers because "great clots of turgid phrases pour forth; long sentences knot upon themselves and swallow their own tails." The point, Tyler argues, is not whether Ozick is a good or a bad writer but whether "you expect from your reading a visceral experience or an intellectual exercise. I vote for the visceral experience myself."[3] And Ozick had provided just that in spite of turgid prose.

Fiction can thus survive lapses of bad prose, but for Anne Tyler it does not work unless the reader finds some aspect to like in the characters. Tyler avoids the trite phrase "redeeming quality," but that is, I think, precisely what she means. She makes this point about several quite different novels. Tyler reviewed Margaret Atwood's *Life Before Man* for the *Detroit News,* summarizing the pattern of marriages, breakups, affairs, and so on that the characters live through. Even though the episodes and the events of these characters' lives interest the reader, Tyler's point is that these characters never become people that draw the reader into a state where he or she *likes* the characters. Such a state, Tyler suggests, puts the reader at arm's length. When Tyler reviewed Alice McDermott's *A Bigamist's Daughter,* she emphasized that the book was spared the tell-tale marks of a first novel; however, Tyler noted that at times its flaws nearly spoiled its virtues, especially in the central characters whose manners failed to make the reader wonder what happened to them. In her review of Shelby Hearon's *A Prince of a Fellow,* Tyler comments on the heroine whose voice seems to echo popular magazines rather than life's real experiences, a veneer that keeps the reader from caring. You can, Tyler suggests, center your novel around an unappealing character, but he or she had better ring true and manifest some kind of worth, or the reader will most likely turn side. Tyler's insistence that characters merit the reader's interest and concern relates to the quality of the writing as well as to the actions of the characters and their sense of themselves.

Other flaws bother Tyler. If a writer's style is florid or unduly obscure (William Lavender's *Flight of the Seabird*), or is obscure to the point of insulting the reader (Jamaica Kincaid's *At the Bottom of the River*), or is downright longwinded (John Irving's *The World According to Garp*), or is just too clever in catching the reader's eye (Evelyn Wilde Mayerson's *If Birds Are Free*) or contains sentences that a fourth-grade teacher might give to his or her class for corrections in punctuation (Herbert Gold's *Waiting for Cordelia*), then Tyler does not hesitate to call foul and to remind writer and reader that the text deserves their best effort. What probably irritates Tyler most is the kind of lapse (or worse, a conscious intent) in which dialogue, loaded with exposition, appears in half-page chunks. In *Poppa John* Larry Woiwode has sentences that "cover a third of a page or more, often beginning in mid-phrase. They twist and drone and meander so that we have to blink, shake off our confusion, sit up straighter and go back to the beginning."[4]

Tyler knows it is hard for writers to use brand names and elements from popular culture successfully. As Tyler points out, such uses succeed when those details lend credibility as they do in Bobbie Ann Mason's *Shiloh and Other Stories*. (In "Still Life with Watermelon," for example, Louise throws a Corning Ware Petit Pan at Tom and cuts his ear. Her irresponsible friend, Peggy, reads Harlequin romances while she watches TV but will sit up to pay attention when the minister of "The 700 Club" comes on the screen to give advice on budgets.) However, such particularity fails, Tyler maintains, if it keeps readers outside the world the characters inhabit and makes them feel that they have no place at all in that world, a condition that exists in Herbert Gold's *Waiting for Cordelia*. A writer can, Tyler insists, use details such as brand names, popular TV shows, and the latest fashion hints. When writers observe these details in the daily lives of their characters, they can accurately portray a way of life that is all too recognizable in America. However, if writers themselves indulge in these details rather than assigning them to characters, the dependence on the contemporary world of advertising and pop culture limits the fiction. Tyler finds Judith Rossner's *Looking for Mr. Goodbar* so dependent on contemporary detail that in years to come, she says, readers will need footnotes in order to understand the life presented in the novel.

One of Tyler's most favorable reviews is of Shirley Hazzard's *The Transit of Venus,* in which she cites Hazzard's particular strengths in plot, language, and detail. Of the plot Tyler says, "Every line is beautifully considered. The most minor character has his role, and there isn't a single occurrence that fails to tie in, intricately, economically, with the flow of the central plot." Tyler indicates the value of the well-constructed plot and the necessity to keep every other aspect of the book in tune with it. Loose ends, like red herrings, distract. Hazzard's language gives power to every word, Tyler says. The ironies and ambiguities in her language cause it to become almost "a character in its own right." The figurative language is equally effective: "the perfect simile, the exactly right metaphor, is arrived at by so breathtaking a leap that it stops us in our tracks, causes us to pause and consider it privately before we applaud and move on." Yet another narrative skill Tyler praises is Hazzard's use of details: they resonate because "the physical detail here implies the mental detail, or is it the other way around?"[5]

In her essay, "The Nature and Aim of Fiction," Flannery O'Connor cites a sentence from *Madame Bovary* to illustrate how much exact detail counts.

From the Flaubert sentence which begins with Emma striking a chord on the piano and stops at the other end of the village with the bailiff's clerk in his list slippers and the paper in hand, O'Connor concludes: "It's always necessary to remember that the fiction writer is much less *immediately* concerned with grand ideas and bristling emotions than he is with putting list slippers on clerks."[6] Tyler is also mindful of carefully used detail. In Nadine Gordimer's *July's People,* for example, the profusion of details never incumbers the story line but instead imbues the plot with energy and life. This, to Tyler, is the point of details in fiction. Tyler qualifies her reservations over Maxine Hong Kingston's *Tripmaster Monkey: His Fake Book* (she found the book at times exhausting—much as if a "23-year-old [novelist] had taken up residence in our living room, staying way too long") because Kingston succeeds with details. The virtue that keeps the reader moving through this 400+-page book are "the tiny, meticulously catalogued details that fill his quieter moments." Details in and of themselves *are* interesting, but their real service in fiction can "remind us how infinitely entertaining everyday life can be when it's observed with a fresh eye."[7] Kingston does this well.

On occasion, details can rescue potentially sentimental scenes by rendering moments with specific accuracy. Attention to detail is a hallmark of Tyler's own fiction. In *Celestial Navigation,* for example, when Jeremy, the protagonist, begins his one heroic undertaking, he assembles his provisions (two cheese sandwiches, a thermos of coffee, an apple, a flashlight, and all the rent money from the cookie jar), an exercise that in a lesser writer's hand could well lapse into sentimentality. He then packs these essentials in a "pink nylon backpack" belonging to his daughter Abbie.[8] One needs to know the novel and the character to appreciate the inevitable rightness of each detail.

Tyler also values novels in which certain moments in the plot are so vividly rendered that (as in *July's People*) she expects to see some scenes "clearly, in full color, ten or twenty years from now just by glimpsing the title on a shelf."[9] Such memorable episodes, like exact details and characters who invite our vested interest, suggest that writer and reader have met and found the experience worthwhile.

Tyler has reviewed books by authors whose names are literary household words—Joan Didion, Walker Percy, Vladimir Nabokov, Gabriel García Marquez, Margaret Drabble, Margaret Atwood, Bruno Bettleheim, Gail Godwin—and she also reviews less familiar authors, often with such enthusiasm that her review accomplishes its ultimate aim: the reader of the review becomes the reader of the book reviewed. For example, Edward Swift's *Splendora* received such praise from Anne Tyler that even the most hesitant reader would be persuaded to read his book: "Edward Swift has a particular gift for capturing the continuous low musical murmur of small-town gossip: the ladies on their telephones, comparing opinions, telling secrets, sorting out the substance of other people's lives. He knows how stories seem to grow on their own, drifting almost unnoticeably toward the mythical."[10] (One looks twice here to be sure these words aren't being said about Eudora Welty's work instead of Swift's.) The British author James Hanley also impresses Tyler. He is "a most remarkable writer—a creator of small but extraordinarily immediate, dense, sharply defined worlds." But just try to find his books—they "are hard to come by. You inquire in vain at the local bookstores, trudge off to various branch libraries, send search slips downtown to Central."[11] Tyler, of course, persists, finds Hanley's books, and through her review introduces him to readers.

Biographical material interweaves itself through these reviews, providing at times relatively trivial-seeming information (in reviewing Philip O'Connor's *Stealing Home,* Tyler reveals that she is a closet baseball fan, for instance), and at times providing deep insights into Tyler as person and writer. When Eudora Welty's *Collected Stories* appeared in 1980, Tyler published pieces about it in both the *New York Times Book Review* and in the *Washington Star.* Strong links exist between Welty and Reynolds Price and between Tyler and Price (whose class she took as a freshman at Duke University and who early recognized her talent), and it is useful to note these writers' various connections. Tyler shares with Welty a southern childhood, with a northern edge. Welty, of course, was born (and has always lived) in Jackson, Mississippi, but her father had been raised on an Ohio farm, her mother in the West Virginia mountains. In the *Washington Star* piece, Tyler (born in Minneapolis) describes herself at a distance from the South, a distance she senses in Eudora Welty.

> For me as a girl—a Northerner growing up in the South, longingly gazing over the fence at the rich, tangled lives of the Southern neighbors—Eudora Welty was a window upon the world. If I wondered what went on in the country churches and "Colored Only" cafes, her writing showed me, as clearly as if I'd been invited inside.
>
> But what seems obvious only now, with the sum total of these collected stories, is that Eudora Welty herself must once have felt the need for such a window.[12]

On the more mundane level of daily life, Tyler discovers that Welty "shares my fear of merging into freeway traffic." Welty speaks of that driving hazard as "entering a round of hot-pepper in a jump-rope game: 'Oh, well,' you think, 'maybe the next time it comes by. . . .' (I always did know freeways reminded me of something; I just couldn't decide what is was").[13] There is something genuine about two writers sharing intellectual *and* ordinary experiences.

Anne Tyler the writer has emerged from Anne Tyler the reader. Three illustrations drawn from her book reviews (or from short pieces about books) give a chronological sweep and allow one to trace her steady, insightful love affair with books. A piece entitled "Why I Still Treasure *The Little House,*" fondly recalls this children's classic, a book Tyler received as a gift on her fourth birthday. Even though someone had to read the book to her on that first occasion, the impact was profound and, more importantly, an experience she remembers vividly years later.

> I had a sudden spell of . . . wisdom, I guess you could say. It seemed I'd been presented with a snapshot that showed me how the world worked: how the years flowed by and people altered and nothing could ever stay the same. Then the snapshot was taken away. Everything there is to know about time was revealed in that snapshot, and I can almost name it. I very nearly have it in my grasp . . . but it's gone again and all that's left is a ragged green book with the binding falling apart.[14]

Has the sudden insight into time's reality ever been more precisely rendered?

This early experience reveals a gifted listener; the book reviews of her adult years show what a gifted and sensitive and wide-ranging reader Anne Tyler is. In 1975 she reviewed *The Collected Stories of Hortense Calisher,* a task that evoked memories of Tyler's reading during college years. Tyler remembers reading a story by Calisher when she was a student at Duke University and, despite the intervening years, remembered it virtually word for word. More importantly, Tyler is pleased to now confirm her good judgment as a student reader. The story holds up and further suggests that Tyler's precocious insight was not limited to her early experience with *The Little House.*

In a piece recommending favorite books of 1978, Tyler shows that even close kin can't be forgiven if they fail to see the glory of a particular title. "A fews years back," Tyler writes, ". . . I handed a brother of mine the novel I love best of all (*One Hundred Years of Solitude*) and sat myself at his feet to watch for the enraptured expression that would surely come over his face as he read it. He managed two pages, yawned, checked the cover and said, 'Didn't I start this in an airport once?' Start it? He could start it and not finish it? And then forget the whole experience?"[15] Reading for Anne Tyler is always a visceral and memorable experience, not a casual false start.

These biographical glimpses are especially important since from early on Tyler has been labeled a recluse. That term is unfair. It is true that Tyler has not been tempted nor obligated to join the writers' circuit of readings and workshops on college and university campuses. And if she does choose to skip ceremonies where she is numbered among the award winners, that action hardly makes her a recluse. Indeed, evidence to the contrary is strong, especially in her prompt and helpful responses to the serious inquiries of scholars.

Because she is married to an Iranian who also writes novels, details in the reviews about her domestic life are of obvious interest. Tyler met her husband, Taghi Modarressi, at Duke University, where he took his residency in psychiatry. Her marriage to an Iranian brought a cultural adjustment far deeper than the one required of a northern-born girl being raised in the South. Thus far, Tyler has not used the Iranian experience in her novels; however, this material appears in some of her short stories and with special effectiveness in "Your Place Is Empty."[16] And in the *New York Times Book Review,* Tyler published a piece she called "Please Don't Call It Persia"; here she recalls with nostalgia her first visit to Iran in 1964 when she journeyed there to meet her husband's family. At that time, she muses, you *could* call that rich country Persia—"muezzins calling the faithful to prayers, bazaars of gold and silver, and peddlers singing in the street." The lavish, comfortable routine of her husband's family showed the world he had enjoyed, a world she enters briefly. Naps follow the midday banquet, and then the long family discussions of "marriages and births and deaths, little scandals, feuds that had lasted 20 years and would probably continue for another 20." But then word began to come of people vanishing in the night, of some returning with "horrible unexplained scars," of some not returning at all. "Please Don't Call It Persia" appeared in 1979. In that year Tyler watched events from Iran on television, wondering if anyone could at all maintain the image of Persia, "of minarets and indolent veiled women."[17] This piece calls up the exotic and mysterious Middle East, lost totally now in the turmoil of hostage crises, oil cartels, and endless hostility that daily disturbs the world. Although "Please Don't Call It Persia" reviewed four books—*The Caspian Circle,* by Donné Raffat; *Foreigners,* by Nahid Rachlin; *Identity Card,* by E. M. Esfandiary; and *An Anthology of Modern Persian Poetry,* by Ahmad Karimi-Hakkak—its primary value lies in the biographical information it provides.

Although Tyler's book reviews provide rich biographical information, they primarily show an active reader at work. A Tyler book review does not sound as though it had been tossed off to meet a deadline. Instead, her reviews reflect her insight as reader, her skill as writer. When Tyler reviewed Elizabeth Hardwick's *Bartleby in Manhattan,* she questioned the wisdom of Hardwick including some of the book reviews she had written. They are, after all, Tyler says, "mere reviews"; regardless of how fine they are in themselves they are limited by the fact of temporality.[18] Hardwick thought otherwise. And so did Eudora Welty when she published *The Eye of the Story: Selected Essays and Reviews.* Section 3 consists of book reviews by Welty—from *The Western Journals of Washington Irving* to *Charlotte's Web* by E. B. White. Anne Tyler readers should, of course, put her fiction first. But as a book reviewer she has given us far more than "mere reviews."

Notes

1. Richard J. Finneran, ed., *The Correspondence of Robert Bridges and W. B. Yeats* (London: Macmillan Company, 1977), 9.

2. "Stories Within Stories," review of *Ararat,* by D. M. Thomas, *New Republic,* 4 April 1983, 30.

3. "The Mission," review of *The Messiah of Stockholm*, by Cynthia Ozick, *New Republic*, 6 April 1987, pp. 40, 41.

4. "The Fall of a Star," review of *Poppa John*, by Larry Woiwode, *New Republic*, 9 Dec. 1981, 37.

5. Review of *The Transit of Venus*, by Shirley Hazzard, *New Republic*, 26 January 1980, 30.

6. Flannery O'Connor, *Mystery and Manners. Occasional Prose*, selected and edited by Sally and Robert Fitzgerald (New York: Farrar, Straus & Giroux, 1969) 70.

7. "Manic Monologue," review of *Tripmaster Monkey: His Fake Book*, by Maxine Hong Kingston, *New Republic*, 17 April 1989, 46.

8. Anne Tyler, *Celestial Navigation* (New York: Knopf, 1974) 252.

9. "South Africa After the Revolution," review of *July's People*, by Nadine Gordimer, *New York Times Book Review*, 7 June 1981, 26.

10. "Pretty Boy," review of *Splendora*, by Edward Swift, *New York Times Book Review*, 6 Aug. 1978, 27.

11. "Life in the Ingrown Household," review of *Against the Grain*, by James Hanley, *New York Times Book Review*, 17 Jan. 1982, 7.

12. "The Fine, Full World of Welty," review of *The Collected Stories of Eudora Welty*, *Washington Star*, 26 Oct. 1980, D, 7–8.

13. "A Visit with Eudora Welty," *New York Times Book Review*, 2 Nov. 1980, 33–34.

14. Anne Tyler, "Why I Still Treasure *The Little House*," *New York Times Book Review*, 9 Nov. 1986, 56.

15. ["The Books of Christmas One"], *Washington Post*, 3 Dec. 1978, E1, 4.

16. Anne Tyler, "Your Place Is Empty," *New Yorker*, 22 Nov. 1976, 45–54.

17. "Please Don't Call It Persia," review of *The Caspian Circle*, by Donné Raffat; *Foreigners*, by Nahid Rachlin; *Identity Card*, by E. M. Esfandiary; *An Anthology of Modern Persian Poetry*, by Ahmad Karimi-Hakkak, *New York Times Book Review*, 18 Feb. 1979, 34.

18. "A Civilized Sensibility," review of *Bartleby in Manhattan*, by Elizabeth Hardwick, *New Republic*, 20 June 1983, 32–33.

Works Cited: Book Reviews and Occasional Pieces by Anne Tyler

"For Barthelme, 'Words Are What Matter,' " review of *Sadness*, by Donald Barthelme, *National Observer*, 4 Nov. 1972, 21.

"When the Novel Turns Participant, the Reader Switches Off," review of *Looking for Mr. Goodbar*, by Judith Rossner, *National Observer*, 14 June 1975, 19.

"Tales of an Apocalypse Served Up in a Tureen," review of *The Collected Stories of Hortense Calisher*, *National Observer*, 22 Nov. 1975, 21.

"Barthelme's Joyless Victory," review of *The Dead Father*, by Donald Barthelme, *National Observer*, 27 Dec. 1975, 17.

"Herbert Gold, Two Bags, $20, and California. What?", review of *Waiting for Cordelia*, by Herbert Gold, *National Observer*, 6 June 1977, 19.

"Meg and Hannah and Elaine," review of *Flight of the Seabird*, by William Lavender; *The Goat, the Wolf, and the Crab*, by Gillian Martin; *Landfill*, by Julius Horowitz, *New York Times Book Review*, 31 July 1977, 14.

"Lady of the Lone Star State," review of *A Prince of a Fellow*, by Shelby Hearon, *Washington Post Book World*, 2 April 1978, 4.

"Pretty Boy," review of *Splendora*, by Edward Swift, *New York Time Book Review*, 6 Aug. 1978, 14, 27.

["The Books of Christmas One"], *Washington Post*, 3 Dec. 1978, E1, 4.

"Please Don't Call It Persia," review of *The Caspian Circle*, by Donné Raffet; *Foreign-*

ers, by Nahid Rachlin; *Identity Card,* by E. M. Esfandiary; *An Anthology of Persian Poetry,* by Ahmad Karimi-Hakkak, *New York Times Book Review,* 18 Feb. 1979, 3, 34.

Review of *The Transit of Venus,* by Shirley Hazzard, *New Republic,* 26 Jan. 1980, 29–30.

"Woman Coping," review of *A Woman's Age,* by Rachael Billington, *New York Times Book Review,* 10 Feb. 1980, 15, 37.

"Pale People, but Rich Cosmic Dreams," review of *Life before Man,* by Margaret Atwood, *Detroit News,* 17 Feb. 1980, C2.

"Everyday Events," review of *A Matter of Feeling,* by Janice Boissard, translated by Elizabeth Walter, *New York Times Book Review,* 9 Mar. 1980, 10.

Review of *Three by Irving,* by John Irving, *New Republic,* 26 Apr. 1980, 32–33.

Review of *Off Center,* by Barbara Grizzuti Harrison, *New Republic,* 7 June 1980, 31–32.

"The Fine, Full World of Welty," review of *The Collected Stories of Eudora Welty, Washington Star,* 26 Oct. 1980, D 1, 7–8.

"A Visit with Eudora Welty," *New York Times Book Review,* 2 Nov. 1980, 33–34.

"Portrait of a Bag Lady," review of *If Birds Are Free,* by Evelyn Wilde Mayerson, *Washington Post Book World,* 23 Nov. 1980, 10.

"South Africa after Revolution," review of *July's People,* by Nadine Gordimer, *New York Times Book Review,* 7 June 1981, 1, 26.

"The Fall of a Star," review of *Poppa John,* by Larry Woiwode, *New Republic,* 9 Dec. 1981, 36–38.

"Life in the Ingrown Household," review of *Against the Grain,* by James Hanley, *New York Times Book Review,* 17 Jan. 1982, 7.

Review of *A Bigamist's Daughter,* by Alice McDermott, *New York Times Book Review,* 21 Feb. 1982, 1, 28.

"Kentucky Cameos," review of *Shiloh and Other Stories,* by Bobbie Ann Mason, *New Republic,* 1 Nov. 1982, 36, 38.

"Stories within Stories," review of *Ararat,* by D. M. Thomas, *New Republic,* 4 April 1983, 30–32.

"A Civilized Sensibility," review of *Bartleby in Manhattan and Other Essays,* by Elizabeth Hardwick, *New Republic,* 20 June 1982, 32–33.

"Mothers and Mysteries," review of *At the Bottom of the River,* by Jamaica Kincaid, *New Republic,* 31 Dec. 1983, 32–33.

"Why I Still Treasure *The Little House,*" *New York Times Book Review,* 9 Nov. 1986, 56.

"The Mission," review of *The Messiah of Stockholm,* by Cynthia Ozick, *New Republic,* 6 Apr. 1987, 39–41.

"Manic Monologue," review of *Tripmaster Monkey: His Fake Book,* by Maxine Hong Kingston, *New Republic,* 17 April 1989, 44–46.

Review of *Stealing Home,* by Philip O'Connor, *Washington Post Book World,* 18 March 1979, E1, 6.

Notes on Contributors of
Original Materials

◆

Elizabeth Evans earned her Ph.D. at the University of North Carolina, Chapel Hill, and taught English for 26 years at the Georgia Institute of Technology. She has written on Thomas Wolfe, Eudora Welty, and May Sarton and is currently completing a volume on Anne Tyler for Twayne's United States Authors Series. At present she is a visiting professor at Western Carolina University.

Grace Farrell is Rebecca Clifton Reade Professor of English at Butler University, Indianapolis. She is the author of *From Exile to Redemption: The Fiction of Isaac Bashevis Singer* (Southern Illinois University Press), as well as numerous essays on nineteenth- and twentieth-century fiction. Currently she is recovering the fiction of nineteenth-century American writer and suffragist Lillie Blake.

Sanford E. Marovitz is professor and chair of English at Kent State University, where he has taught since 1967. He earned his B.A. with honors at Lake Forest College and his M.A. and Ph.D. at Duke University. He has been a Woodrow Wilson fellow (1960–61), a Fulbright scholar at the University of Athens, Greece (1965–67), and a visiting professor of English at Shimane University, Japan (1976–77). In 1985 he received the Distinguished Teaching Award at Kent State. Coeditor of *Artful Thunder: Versions of the Romantic Tradition in American Literature in Honor of Howard P. Vincent* (Kent State University Press) and cocompiler of *Bibliographical Guide to the Study of the Literature of the U.S.A.*, 5th ed. (Duke University Press), Professor Marovitz has published widely in critical collections and professional journals, primarily on nineteenth- and twentieth-century American literature.

Alice Hall Petry, associate professor of English at the Rhode Island School of Design, is a former Fulbright scholar in Brazil, USIA lecturer in Japan, and visiting professor at the University of Colorado, Boulder. Her books include *Understanding Anne Tyler* (University of South Carolina Press), *A Genius in His Way: The Art of Cable's "Old Creole Days"* (Fairleigh Dickinson University Press), and *Fitzgerald's Craft of Short Fiction: The Collected Stories, 1920–1935* (UMI Research Press; paperback, University of Alabama Press).

Index

♦